without a cause
shall be in danger of the judgment;
and whoever shall say to his brother,
'Raca!' [You good-for-nothing]
shall be in danger of the council;
and whoever shall say,
'You fool!'
shall be in danger of the fire of Gehenna."

5:21-22

"If therefore you are offering your gift at the altar,
and there remember
that your brother has anything against you,
leave your gift there before the altar,
and go your way.
First be reconciled to your brother,
and then come and offer your gift.
Agree with your adversary quickly,
while you are with him on the way;
lest perhaps the prosecutor deliver you to the judge,
and the judge deliver you to the officer,
and you be cast into prison.
Most certainly I tell you,
you shall by no means get out of there,
until you have paid
the last penny."

5:23-26

"You have heard that it was said,
'You shall not commit adultery',
but I tell you
that everyone who gazes at a woman
to lust after her
has committed adultery with her already
in his heart.
If your right eye
causes you to stumble,
pluck it out
and throw it away from you.
For it is more profitable for you
that one of your members should perish,
than for your whole body
to be cast into Gehenna.

If your right hand
causes you to stumble,
cut it off,
and throw it away from you.
For it is more profitable for you
that one of your members should perish,
than for your whole body
to be cast into Gehenna."                              5:27-30

"It was also said,
'Whoever shall put away his wife,
let him give her a writing of divorce'
but I tell you
that whoever puts away his wife,
except for the cause of sexual immorality,
makes her an adulteress;
and whoever marries her
when she is put away
commits adultery."                                      5:31-32

"Again
you have heard
that it was said
to them of old time,
'You shall not make false vows,
but shall perform to the Lord your vows,'
but I tell you,
don't swear at all:
neither by heaven,
for it is the throne of God;
nor by the earth,
for it is the footstool of his feet;
nor by Jerusalem,
for it is the city of the great King.
Neither shall you swear by your head,
for you can't make one hair white or black.
But let your 'Yes' be 'Yes'
and your 'No' be 'No.'
Whatever
is more than these
is of the evil one."                                    5:33-37

"You have heard that it was said,
'An eye for an eye, and
a tooth for a tooth.'
But I tell you,
don't resist him
who is evil;
but whoever strikes you on your right cheek,
turn to him the other also.
If anyone sues you
to take away your coat,
let him have your cloak also.
Whoever compels you to go one mile,
go with him two.
Give
to him
who asks you,
and don't turn away
him who
desires to borrow
from you."                                                                    5:38-42

"You have heard that it was said,
'You shall love your neighbor
and hate your enemy.'
But I tell you,
love your enemies,
bless those who curse you,
do good to those who hate you,
and pray for those
who mistreat you and persecute you,
that you may be
children of your Father
who is in heaven.
For he makes his sun to rise
on the evil
and the good,
and sends rain
on the just
and the unjust.
For if you love those who love you,
what reward do you have?"

Don't even the tax collectors do the same?
If you only greet
your friends,
what more do you do than others?
Don't even the tax collectors do the same?
Therefore you shall be perfect,
just as
your
Father in heaven
is
perfect."

5:43-48

---

MATTHEW 6

---

**"Be careful**
that you don't do your charitable giving
before men,
to be seen by them,
or else
you have no reward
from your Father who is in heaven.
Therefore
when you do merciful deeds,
don't sound a trumpet before yourself,
as the hypocrites do in the synagogues
and in the streets,
that they may get glory
from men.
Most certainly
I tell you,
they have received their reward.
But when you do merciful deeds,
don't let your left hand know
what your right hand does,
so that your merciful deeds
may be in secret,
then your Father
who sees
in secret
will reward you openly."

6:1-4

"When you pray,
you shall not be as the hypocrites,
for they love to stand
and pray in the synagogues and in the corners of the streets,
that they may be seen by men.
Most certainly,
I tell you,
they have received their reward.
But you,
when you pray,
enter into your inner room,
and having shut your door,
pray to your Father
who is in secret,
and your Father who sees
in secret
will reward you openly.
In praying,
don't use vain repetitions,
as the Gentiles do;
for they think that they will be heard
for their much speaking.
Therefore don't be like them,
for your Father knows what things you need,
before you ask him.
Pray like this:
'Our Father in heaven,
may your name be kept holy.
Let your Kingdom come.
Let your will be done,
as in heaven, so on earth.
Give us today our daily bread.
Forgive us our debts,
as we also forgive our debtors.
Bring us not into temptation,
but deliver us from the evil one.
For yours is the Kingdom,
the power,
and the glory forever. Amen.'"

6:5-13

"For if you forgive men
their trespasses,
your heavenly Father will also forgive you.

But if you don't forgive men their trespasses,
neither will your Father forgive your trespasses."                6:14-15

"Moreover when you fast,
don't be like the hypocrites,
with sad faces.
For they disfigure their faces,                    .
that they may be seen by men to be fasting.
Most certainly
I tell you,
they have received their reward.
But you,
when you fast,
anoint your head, and wash your face;
so that you are not seen by men to be fasting,
but by your Father
who is in secret,
and your Father,
who sees
in secret,
will reward you."                                                6:16-18

"Don't lay up treasures for yourselves on the earth,
where moth and rust consume,
and where thieves break through and steal;
but lay up for yourselves treasures in heaven,
where neither moth nor rust consume,
and where thieves don't break through and steal;
for where your treasure is,
there your heart will be also."                                  6:19-21

"The lamp of the body
is the eye.
If therefore your eye is sound,
your whole body will be full of light.
But if your eye is evil,
your whole body will be full of darkness.
If therefore the light that is in you is darkness,
how great is the darkness!"                                      6:22-23

"No one can serve two masters,
for either he will hate the one

and love the other;
or else he will be devoted to one
and despise the other.
You can't serve both God and Mammon.
Therefore, I tell you,
don't be anxious for your life:
what you will eat,
or what you will drink;
nor yet for your body,
what you will wear.
Isn't life more than food,
and the body
more than clothing?
See the birds of the sky,
that they don't sow,
neither do they reap,
nor gather into barns.
Your heavenly Father feeds them.
Aren't you of much more value than they?"                6:24-26

"Which of you,
by being anxious,
can add one moment to his lifespan?
Why are you anxious about clothing?
Consider the lilies of the field,
how they grow.
They don't toil,
neither do they spin,
yet I tell you
that even Solomon in all his glory
was not dressed like one of these.
But if God so clothes the grass of the field,
which today exists,
and tomorrow is thrown into the oven,
won't he much more clothe you,
you of little faith?"                                        6:27-30

"Therefore don't be anxious,
saying, 'What will we eat?',
'What will we drink?' or,
'With what will we be clothed?'
For the Gentiles seek after all these things;

for your heavenly Father knows that you need all these things.
But seek first God's Kingdom,
and his righteousness;
and all these things will be given to you as well.
Therefore don't be anxious
for tomorrow,
for tomorrow
will be anxious for itself.
Each day's own evil is sufficient."                        6:31-34

- - - - - - - - - - - - - - - - - - - - - - - - - - - - - - - - - - - - - - - - - - - - - - - - - - - - - - - - - - - - - - - - - - - - - - -

MATTHEW 7

- - - - - - - - - - - - - - - - - - - - - - - - - - - - - - - - - - - - - - - - - - - - - - - - - - - - - - - - - - - - - - - - - - - - - - -

**"Don't judge,**
so that you won't be judged.
For with whatever judgment
you judge,
you will be judged;
and with whatever measure
you measure,
it will be measured to you.
Why do you see
the speck
that is in your brother's eye,
but don't consider
the beam
that is in your own eye?
Or how will you tell your brother,
'Let me remove the speck from your eye;'
and behold, the beam is in your own eye?
You hypocrite!
First remove the beam out of your own eye,
and then
you can see clearly
to remove the speck out of your brother's eye."        7:1-5

"Don't give that which is holy to the dogs,
neither throw your pearls before the pigs,
lest perhaps they trample them under their feet,
and turn and tear you to pieces."                          7:6

"Ask,
and it will be given you.

Seek,
and you will find.
Knock,
and it will be opened for you.
For everyone who asks
receives.
He who seeks
finds.
To him who knocks
it will be opened.
Or who is there among you, who,
if his son asks him for bread,
will give him a stone?
Or if he asks for a fish,
who will give him a serpent?
If you then,
being evil,
know how to give good gifts to your children,
how much more
will your Father who is in heaven
give good things
to those who ask him!
Therefore whatever you desire
for men to do to you,
you shall also do to them;
for this is the law and the Prophets."                    7:7-12

"Enter in
by the narrow gate;
for wide is the gate
and broad is the way
that leads to destruction,
and many are those who enter in by it.
How narrow is the gate,
and restricted is the way
that leads to life!
Few are those
who find it."                                              7:13-14

"Beware of false prophets,
who come to you in sheep's clothing,
but inwardly are ravening wolves.

By their fruits
you will know them.
Do you gather grapes from thorns,
or figs from thistles?
Even so, every good tree
produces good fruit;
but the corrupt tree
produces evil fruit.
A good tree
can't produce evil fruit,
neither can a corrupt tree
produce good fruit.
Every tree that doesn't grow good fruit
is cut down, and thrown into the fire.
Therefore,
by their fruits
you will know them.
Not everyone who says to me,
'Lord, Lord,'
will enter into the Kingdom of Heaven;
but he who does the will
of my Father who is in heaven.
Many will tell me
in that day,
'Lord, Lord,
didn't we prophesy in your name,
in your name
cast out demons,
and in your name
do many mighty works?'
Then I will tell them,
'I never knew you.
Depart from me,
you who work iniquity.'"

7:15-23

"Everyone therefore who hears these words of mine,
and does them,
I will liken him to a wise man,
who built his house on a rock.
The rain came down, the floods came,
and the winds blew,
and beat on that house;
and it didn't fall,

for it was founded on the rock.
Everyone who hears these words of mine,
and doesn't do them
will be like a foolish man,
who built his house on the sand.
The rain came down,
the floods came,
and the winds blew,
and beat on that house;
and it fell
— and great was its fall."                                           7:24-27

---

MATTHEW 8

---

**"I want to.**
Be made clean."                                                      8:3

"See that you tell nobody,
but go,
show yourself to the priest,
and offer the gift that Moses commanded,
as a testimony to them."                                             8:4

"I will come and heal him."                                          8:7

"Most certainly
I tell you,
I haven't found
so great a faith,
not even in Israel.
I tell you
that many will come from the east and the west,
and will sit down with Abraham, Isaac, and Jacob
in the Kingdom of Heaven,
but the children of the Kingdom
will be thrown out
into the outer darkness.
There will be weeping and gnashing of teeth."                        8:10-12

"Go your way.
Let it be done for you
as you have believed."                                               8:13

"The foxes have holes,
and the birds of the sky have nests,
but the Son of Man
has nowhere
to lay his head."                                                                    8:20

"Follow me,
and leave the dead
to bury their own dead."                                                             8:22

"Why are you fearful,
O you of little faith?"                                                              8:26

"Go!"                                                                                8:32

- - - - - - - - - - - - - - - - - - - - - - - - - - - - - - - - - - - - - - - - - - - - -

MATTHEW 9

- - - - - - - - - - - - - - - - - - - - - - - - - - - - - - - - - - - - - - - - - - - - -

**"Son,**
cheer up!
Your sins are forgiven you."                                                         9:2

"Why do you think evil in your hearts?
For which is easier,
to say,
'Your sins are forgiven;'
or to say,
'Get up, and walk?'"                                                                 9:4-5

"But that you may know that
the Son of Man has
authority
on earth to forgive sins"...
"Get up,
and take up your mat,
and go
up to your house."                                                                  9:6

"Follow me."                                                                         9:9

"Those who are healthy have no need for a physician,
but those who are sick do.

But you go and learn what this means:
'I desire mercy, and not sacrifice,'
for I came not to call the righteous,
but sinners to repentance."                                            9:12-13

"Can the friends of the bridegroom mourn,
as long as the bridegroom is with them?
But the days will come
when the bridegroom will be taken away from them,
and then they will fast.
No one puts a piece of unshrunk cloth on an old garment;
for the patch would tear away from the garment,
and a worse hole is made.
Neither do people put new wine into old wineskins,
or else the skins would burst,
and the wine be spilled,
and the skins ruined.
No, they put new wine
into fresh wineskins,
and both are preserved."                                               9:15-17

"Daughter,
cheer up!
Your faith has made you well."                                         9:22

"Make room,
because the girl isn't dead,
but sleeping."                                                         9:24

"Do you believe that I am able to do this?"                            9:28

"According to your faith
be it done to you."                                                    9:29

"See that no one knows about this."                                    9:30

"The harvest indeed is plentiful,
but the laborers are few.
Pray therefore
that the Lord of the harvest
will send out laborers into his harvest."                              9:37-38

## "Don't go among the Gentiles,

and don't enter into any city of the Samaritans.
Rather, go to the lost sheep of the house of Israel.
As you go, preach, saying,
'The Kingdom of Heaven is at hand!'
Heal the sick,
cleanse the lepers,
and cast out demons.
Freely you received,
so freely give.
Don't take any gold, nor silver,
nor brass in your money belts.
Take no bag for your journey,
neither two coats, nor shoes, nor staff:
for the laborer is worthy of his food.
Into whatever city or village you enter,
find out who in it is worthy;
and stay there until you go on.
As you enter into the household,
greet it.
If the household is worthy,
let your peace come on it,
but if it isn't worthy,
let your peace return to you.
Whoever doesn't receive you,
nor hear your words,
as you go out of that house or that city,
shake off the dust from your feet.
Most certainly
I tell you,
it will be more tolerable
for the land of Sodom and Gomorrah
in the day of judgment
than for that city."                                                      10:5-15

"Behold,
I send you out as sheep in the midst of wolves.
Therefore be wise as serpents,
and harmless as doves.

But beware of men:
for they will deliver you up to councils,
and in their synagogues they will scourge you.
Yes, and you will be brought before governors and kings
for my sake,
for a testimony to them and to the nations.
But when they deliver you up,
don't be anxious
how or what you will say,
for it will be given you
in that hour what you will say.
For it is not you who speak,
but the Spirit of your Father
who speaks in you."                                                         10:16-20

"Brother will deliver up brother to death,
and the father his child.
Children will rise up against parents,
and cause them to be put to death.
You will be hated by all men
for my name's sake,
but he who endures to the end will be saved.
But when they persecute you in this city,
flee into the next,
for most certainly
I tell you,
you will not have gone through the cities of Israel,
until the Son of Man has come."                                             10:21-23

"A disciple is not above his teacher,
nor a servant above his lord.
It is enough for the disciple that he be like his teacher,
and the servant like his lord.
If they have called the master of the house Beelzebul,
how much more those of his household!
Therefore don't be afraid of them,
for there is nothing covered
that will not be revealed;
and hidden
that will not be known.
What I tell you in the darkness,

speak in the light;
and what you hear whispered in the ear,
proclaim on the housetops.
Don't be afraid of those who kill the body,
but are not able to kill the soul.
Rather, fear him
who is able to destroy
both soul and body in Gehenna."                                                10:24-28

"Aren't two sparrows sold for an assarion coin?
Not one of them falls on the ground
apart from your Father's will,
but the very hairs of your head are all numbered.
Therefore don't be afraid.
You are of more value than many sparrows.
Everyone therefore who confesses me before men,
him I will also confess before my Father who is in heaven.
But whoever denies me before men,
him I will also deny before my Father who is in heaven."                        10:29-33

"Don't think that I came to send peace on the earth.
I didn't come to send peace,
but a sword.
For I came to set
a man at odds against his father,
and a daughter against her mother,
and a daughter-in-law against her mother-in-law.
A man's foes will be those of his own household.
He who loves father or mother
more than me
is not worthy of me;
and he who loves son or daughter
more than me
isn't worthy of me.
He who doesn't take his cross
and follow after me,
isn't worthy of me.
He who seeks his life
will lose it;
and he who loses his life
for my sake
will find it.

He who receives you
receives me,
and he who receives me
receives him who sent me.
He who receives a prophet
in the name of a prophet
will receive a prophet's reward.
He who receives a righteous man
in the name of a righteous man
will receive a righteous man's reward.
Whoever gives one of these little ones
just a cup of cold water
to drink in the name of a disciple,
most certainly
I tell you
he will in no way lose his reward."                              10:34-42

---

MATTHEW 11

---

**"Go**
and tell John
the things which you hear and see:
the blind receive their sight,
the lame walk,
the lepers are cleansed,
the deaf hear,
the dead are raised up,
and the poor have good news preached to them.
Blessed is he who finds no occasion
for stumbling in me."                                             11:4-6

"What did you go out into the wilderness to see?
A reed shaken by the wind?
But what did you go out to see?
A man in soft clothing?
Behold,
those who wear soft clothing are in king's houses.
But why did you go out?
To see a prophet?
Yes, I tell you, and much more than a prophet.
For this is he, of whom it is written,

'Behold,
I send my messenger before your face,
who will prepare your way before you.'
Most certainly
I tell you,
among those who are born of women
there has not arisen anyone greater than
John the Baptizer;
yet he who is least in the Kingdom of Heaven
is greater than he.
From the days of John the Baptizer until now,
the Kingdom of Heaven suffers violence,
and the violent take it by force.
For all the prophets and the law prophesied until John.
If you are willing
to receive it,
this is Elijah,
who is to come.
He who has ears to hear,
let him hear."                                                                11:7-15

"But to what shall I compare this generation?
It is like children
sitting in the marketplaces,
who call to their companions
and say, 'We played the flute for you, and you didn't dance.
We mourned for you, and you didn't lament.'
For John came neither eating nor drinking,
and they say, 'He has a demon.'
The Son of Man came eating and drinking,
and they say, 'Behold, a gluttonous man and a drunkard,
a friend of tax collectors and sinners!'
But wisdom is justified by her children."                                     11:16-19

"Woe to you, Chorazin! Woe to you, Bethsaida!
For if the mighty works had been done in Tyre and Sidon
which were done in you,
they would have repented long ago in sackcloth and ashes.
But I tell you,
it will be

more tolerable
for Tyre and Sidon
on the day of judgment
than for you.
You, Capernaum, who are exalted to heaven,
you will go down to Hades.
For if the mighty works had been done in Sodom
which were done in you,
it would have remained until this day.
But I tell you
that it will be
more tolerable
for the land of Sodom,
on the day of judgment,
than for you."                                          11:21-24

"I thank you,
Father,
Lord of heaven and earth,
that you hid these things
from the wise and understanding,
and revealed them to infants.
Yes,
Father,
for so it was well-pleasing in your sight.
All things have been delivered to me
by my Father.
No one knows the Son,
except the Father;
neither does anyone know the Father,
except the Son,
and he
to whom the Son desires to reveal him."                 11:25-27

"Come to me,
all you who labor
and are heavily burdened,
and I will give you rest.
Take my yoke upon you,

and learn from me,
for I am gentle
and lowly in heart;
and you will find rest for your souls.
For my yoke is easy,
and my burden is light."                                          11:28-30

---

---

**"Haven't you read**
what David did,
when he was hungry,
and those who were with him;
how he entered into God's house,
and ate the show bread,
which was not lawful for him to eat,
neither for those who were with him,
but only for the priests?
Or have you not read in the law,
that on the Sabbath day,
the priests in the temple profane the Sabbath,
and are guiltless?
But I tell you
that one greater than the temple is here.
But if you had known
what this means,
'I desire mercy, and not sacrifice,'
you would not have condemned the guiltless.
For the Son of Man is Lord of the Sabbath."                       12:3-8

"What man is there among you,
who has one sheep,
and if this one falls into a pit on the Sabbath day,
won't he grab on to it, and lift it out?
Of how much more value then is a man than a sheep!
Therefore it is lawful to do good on the Sabbath day."            12:11-12

"Stretch out your hand."                                          12:13

"Every kingdom divided against itself
is brought to desolation,
and every city or house divided against itself

will not stand.
If Satan casts out Satan,
he is divided against himself.
How then will his kingdom stand?
If I by Beelzebul cast out demons,
by whom do your children cast them out?
Therefore they will be your judges.
But if I by the Spirit of God cast out demons,
then the Kingdom of God has come upon you.
Or how can one enter into the house of the strong man,
and plunder his goods,
unless he first bind the strong man?
Then he will plunder his house."

12:25-29

"He who is not with me
is against me,
and he who doesn't gather with me,
scatters.
Therefore I tell you,
every sin and blasphemy will be forgiven men,
but the blasphemy against the Spirit
will not be forgiven men.
Whoever speaks a word against the Son of Man,
it will be forgiven him;
but whoever speaks against the Holy Spirit,
it will not be forgiven him,
neither in this age,
nor in that which is to come."

12:30-32

"Either make the tree good, and its fruit good,
or make the tree corrupt, and its fruit corrupt;
for the tree is known by its fruit.
You offspring of vipers,
how can you, being evil, speak good things?
For out of the abundance of the heart,
the mouth speaks.
The good man out of his good treasure
brings out good things,
and the evil man out of his evil treasure
brings out evil things.
I tell you
that every idle word

that men speak,
they will give account of it
in the day of judgment.
For by your words
you will be justified,
and by your words
you will be condemned."

12:33-37

"An evil and adulterous generation
seeks after a sign,
but no sign will be given it
but the sign of Jonah the prophet.
For as Jonah was three days and three nights
in the belly of the whale,
so will the Son of Man be three days and three nights
in the heart of the earth.
The men of Nineveh will stand up in the judgment
with this generation, and will condemn it,
for they repented at the preaching of Jonah;
and behold,
someone greater than Jonah is here.
The queen of the south will rise up in the judgment
with this generation, and will condemn it,
for she came from the ends of the earth
to hear the wisdom of Solomon;
and behold,
someone greater than Solomon is here.
But the unclean spirit,
when he is gone out of the man,
passes through waterless places,
seeking rest,
and doesn't find it.
Then he says,
'I will return into my house from which I came out,'
and when he has come back,
he finds it empty,
swept,
and put in order.
Then he goes,
and takes with himself seven other spirits more evil than he is,
and they enter in and dwell there.

The last state
of that man
becomes worse than the first.
Even so will it be
also to this evil generation."

12:39-45

"Who is my mother?
Who are my brothers?"

12:48

"Behold,
my mother and my brothers!
For whoever does the will of my Father
who is in heaven,
he is my brother,
and sister,
and mother."

12:49-50

---

MATTHEW 13

---

**"Behold,**
a farmer went out to sow.
As he sowed,
some seeds fell by the roadside,
and the birds came and devoured them.
Others fell on rocky ground,
where they didn't have much soil,
and immediately they sprang up,
because they had no depth of earth.
When the sun had risen,
they were scorched.
Because they had no root,
they withered away.
Others fell among thorns.
The thorns grew up and choked them.
Others fell on good soil,
and yielded fruit:
some one hundred times as much,
some sixty,
and some thirty.
He who has ears to hear,
let him hear."

13:3-9

"To you it is given
to know the mysteries
of the Kingdom of Heaven,
but it is not given to them.
For whoever has,
to him will be given,
and he will have abundance,
but whoever doesn't have,
from him will be taken away even that which he has.
Therefore I speak to them in parables,
because seeing
they don't see,
and hearing,
they don't hear,
neither do they understand.
In them the prophecy of Isaiah is fulfilled, which says,
'By hearing you will hear,
and will in no way understand;
Seeing you will see,
and will in no way perceive:
for this people's heart has grown callous,
their ears are dull of hearing,
they have closed their eyes;
or else perhaps they might perceive with their eyes,
hear with their ears,
understand with their heart,
and should turn again;
and I would heal them.'"                                                                13:11-15

"But blessed are your eyes,
for they see;
and your ears,
for they hear.
For most certainly
I tell you
that many prophets and righteous men
desired to see the things which you see,
and didn't see them;
and to hear the things which you hear,
and didn't hear them."                                                                  13:16-17

"Hear, then,
the parable of the farmer.
When anyone hears the word of the Kingdom,
and doesn't understand it,
the evil one comes,
and snatches away that which has been sown in his heart.
This is what was sown by the roadside.
What was sown on the rocky places,
this is he who hears the word,
and immediately with joy receives it;
yet he has no root in himself,
but endures for a while.
When oppression or persecution arises
because of the word,
immediately he stumbles.
What was sown among the thorns,
this is he who hears the word,
but the cares of this age
and the deceitfulness of riches
choke the word,
and he becomes unfruitful.
What was sown on the good ground,
this is he who hears the word,
and understands it,
who most certainly bears fruit,
and brings forth,
some one hundred times as much,
some sixty,
and some thirty."

13:18-23

"The Kingdom of Heaven is like a man
who sowed good seed in his field,
but while people slept,
his enemy came and
sowed darnel weeds also among the wheat,
and went away.
But when the blade sprang up
and brought forth fruit,
then the darnel weeds appeared also.
The servants of the householder came and said to him,
'Sir, didn't you sow good seed in your field?
Where did this darnel come from?'"

13:24-27

"He said to them, 'An enemy has done this.'
"The servants asked him,
'Do you want us to go and gather them up?'"                    13:28

"But he said, 'No,
lest perhaps while you gather up the darnel weeds,
you root up the wheat with them.
Let both grow together
until the harvest,
and in the harvest time I will tell the reapers,
"First, gather up the darnel weeds,
and bind them in bundles to burn them;
but gather the wheat into my barn."'"                         13:29-30

"The Kingdom of Heaven is like a grain of mustard seed,
which a man took,
and sowed in his field;
which indeed is smaller than all seeds.
But when it is grown,
it is greater than the herbs,
and becomes a tree,
so that the birds of the air come
and lodge in its branches."                                   13:31-32

"The Kingdom of Heaven is like yeast,
which a woman took,
and hid in three measures of meal,
until it was all leavened."                                    13:33

"He who sows the good seed is the Son of Man,
the field is the world;
and the good seed,
these are the children of the Kingdom;
and the darnel weeds are the children of the evil one.
The enemy who sowed them is the devil.
The harvest is the end of the age,
and the reapers are angels.
As therefore the darnel weeds are gathered up
and burned with fire;
so will it be at the end of this age.
The Son of Man will send out his angels,

and they will gather out of his Kingdom
all things that cause stumbling,
and those who do iniquity,
and will cast them into the furnace of fire.
There will be weeping and the gnashing of teeth.
Then the righteous will shine forth
like the sun in the Kingdom of their Father.
He who has ears to hear,
let him hear."                                                                13:37-43

"Again, the Kingdom of Heaven is like
a treasure hidden in the field,
which a man found,
and hid.
In his joy,
he goes and sells all that he has,
and buys that field."                                                         13:44

"Again, the Kingdom of Heaven is like
a man who is a merchant seeking fine pearls,
who having found
one pearl of great price,
he went and sold
all that he had,
and bought it."                                                               13:45-46

"Again, the Kingdom of Heaven is like
a dragnet, that was cast into the sea,
and gathered some fish of every kind,
which, when it was filled,
they drew up on the beach.
They sat down,
and gathered the good into containers,
but the bad they threw away.
So will it be in the end of the world.
The angels will come forth,
and separate the wicked from among the righteous,
and will cast them into the furnace of fire.
There will be the weeping and the gnashing of teeth."                         13:47-50

"Have you understood all these things?"                                        13:51

"Therefore, every scribe
who has been made a disciple
in the Kingdom of Heaven
is like a man who is a householder,
who brings out of his treasure
new and old things."

13:52

"A prophet is not without honor,
except in his own country,
and in his own house."

13:57

## MATTHEW 14

**"They don't need to go away.**
You give them something to eat."

14:16

"Bring them here to me."

14:18

"Cheer up!
It is I!
Don't be afraid."

14:27

"Come!"

14:29

"You of little faith,
why did you doubt?"

14:31

## MATTHEW 15

**"Why do you also disobey the commandment of God**
because of your tradition?
For God commanded,
'Honor your father and your mother,'
and, 'He who speaks evil of father or mother,
let him be put to death.'
But you say,
'Whoever may tell his father or his mother,
"Whatever help you might otherwise have gotten from me
is a gift devoted to God,"
he shall not honor his father or mother.'
You have made the commandment of God void because of your tradition.

You hypocrites!
Well did Isaiah prophesy of you, saying,
'These people draw near to me with their mouth,
and honor me with their lips;
but their heart is far from me.
And in vain do they worship me,
teaching as doctrine rules made by men.'"

15:3-9

"Hear, and understand.
That which enters into the mouth
doesn't defile the man;
but that which proceeds out of the mouth,
this defiles the man."

15:10-11

"Every plant which my heavenly Father didn't plant
will be uprooted.
Leave them alone.
They are blind guides of the blind.
If the blind guide the blind,
both will fall into a pit."

15:13-14

"Do you also still not understand?
Don't you understand
that whatever goes into the mouth
passes into the belly,
and then out of the body?
But the things which proceed out of the mouth
come out of the heart,
and they defile the man.
For out of the heart
come forth evil thoughts, murders,
adulteries, sexual sins, thefts,
false testimony, and blasphemies.
These are the things which defile the man;
but to eat with unwashed hands
doesn't defile the man."

15:16-20

"I wasn't sent to anyone
but the lost sheep of the house of Israel."

15:24

"It is not appropriate to take the children's bread
and throw it to the dogs."

15:26

"Woman, great is your faith!
Be it done to you even as you desire."

15:28

"I have compassion on the multitude,
because they continue with me now three days
and have nothing to eat.
I don't want to send them away fasting,
or they might faint on the way."

15:32

"How many loaves do you have?"

15:34

---

MATTHEW 16

---

**"When it is evening, you say,**
'It will be fair weather,
for the sky is red.'
In the morning,
'It will be foul weather today,
for the sky is red and threatening.'
Hypocrites!
You know how to discern the appearance of the sky,
but you can't discern the signs of the times!
An evil and adulterous generation seeks after a sign,
and there will be no sign given to it,
except the sign of the prophet Jonah."

16:2-4

"Take heed
and beware
of the yeast of the Pharisees and Sadducees."

16:6

"Why do you reason among yourselves,
you of little faith,
'because you have brought no bread?'
Don't you yet perceive,
neither remember the five loaves for the five thousand,
and how many baskets you took up?
Nor the seven loaves for the four thousand,
and how many baskets you took up?
How is it that you don't perceive
that I didn't speak to you concerning bread?
But beware
of the yeast of the Pharisees and Sadducees."

16:8-11

"Who do men say that I, the Son of Man, am?"                              16:13

"But who do you say that I am?"                                           16:15

"Blessed are you,
Simon Bar Jonah,
for flesh and blood has not revealed this to you,
but my Father who is in heaven.
I also tell you that you are Peter,
and on this rock I will build my assembly,
and the gates of Hades will not prevail against it.
I will give to you the keys of the Kingdom of Heaven,
and whatever you bind on earth
will have been bound in heaven;
and whatever you release on earth
will have been released in heaven."                                      16:17-19

"Get behind me, Satan!
You are a stumbling block to me,
for you are not setting your mind on the things of God,
but on the things of men."                                               16:23

"If anyone desires to come after me,
let him deny himself,
and take up his cross,
and follow me.
For whoever desires to save his life
will lose it,
and whoever will lose his life
for my sake
will find it.
For what will it profit a man,
if he gains the whole world,
and forfeits his life?
Or what will a man give in exchange for his life?
For the Son of Man will come in the glory of his Father
with his angels,
and then he will render to everyone
according to his deeds.
Most certainly

I tell you,
there are some standing here
 who will in no way taste of death,
until they see the Son of Man coming in his Kingdom." 16:24-28

---

---

**"Get up,**
and don't be afraid." 17:7

"Don't tell anyone what you saw,
until the Son of Man
has risen from the dead." 17:9

"Elijah indeed comes first, and will restore all things,
but I tell you
that Elijah has come already,
and they didn't recognize him,
but did to him
whatever they wanted to.
Even so
the Son of Man will also suffer by them." 17:11-12

"Faithless and perverse generation!
How long will I be with you?
How long will I bear with you?
Bring him here to me." 17:17

"Because of your unbelief.
For most certainly
I tell you,
if you have faith as a grain of mustard seed,
you will tell this mountain,
'Move from here to there,'
and it will move;
and nothing will be impossible for you.
But this kind doesn't go out except by prayer and fasting." 17:20-21

"The Son of Man is about to be delivered up
into the hands of men,
and they will kill him,

and the third day
he will be raised up."                                                              17:22-23

"What do you think, Simon?
From whom do the kings of the earth receive toll or tribute?
From their children, or from strangers?"                                            17:25

"Therefore the children are exempt.
But, lest we cause them to stumble,
go to the sea, cast a hook,
and take up the first fish that comes up.
When you have opened its mouth,
you will find a stater coin.
Take that, and give it to them for me and you."                                     17:26-27

---

## MATTHEW 18

---

**"Most certainly**
I tell you,
unless you turn,
and become as little children,
you will in no way enter into the Kingdom of Heaven.
Whoever
therefore humbles himself
as this little child,
the same is the greatest in the Kingdom of Heaven.
Whoever
receives one such little child
in my name
receives me,
but whoever
causes one of these little ones who believe in me
to stumble,
it would be better for him
that a huge millstone should be hung around his neck,
and that he should be sunk in the depths of the sea."                               18:3-6

"Woe to the world
because of occasions of stumbling!
For it must be that the occasions come,
but woe to that person

through whom the occasion comes!
If your hand or your foot causes you to stumble,
cut it off,
and cast it from you.
It is better for you to enter into life maimed or crippled,
rather than having two hands or two feet
to be cast into the eternal fire.
If your eye causes you to stumble,
pluck it out,
and cast it from you.
It is better for you to enter into life with one eye,
rather than having two eyes
to be cast into the Gehenna of fire.
See that you don't despise one of these little ones,
for I tell you
that in heaven their angels always see
the face of my Father who is in heaven.
For the Son of Man
came to save
that which was lost."                                        18:7-11

"What do you think?
If a man has one hundred sheep,
and one of them goes astray,
doesn't he leave the ninety-nine,
go to the mountains,
and seek that which has gone astray?
If he finds it,
most certainly
I tell you,
he rejoices over it
more than over the ninety-nine which have not gone astray.
Even so
it is not the will of your Father who is in heaven
that one
of these little ones should perish."                         18:12-14

"If your brother sins against you,
go,
show him his fault
between you and him alone.

If he listens to you,
you have gained back your brother.
But if he doesn't listen,
take one or two more with you,
that at the mouth of two or three witnesses
every word may be established.
If he refuses to listen to them,
tell it to the assembly.
If he refuses to hear the assembly also,
let him be to you as a Gentile or a tax collector.
Most certainly
I tell you,
whatever things you bind on earth
will have been bound in heaven,
and whatever things you release on earth
will have been released in heaven.
Again,
assuredly
I tell you,
that if two of you will agree on earth
concerning anything that they will ask,
it will be done for them
by my Father who is in heaven.
For where two or three are gathered together
in my name,
there I am
in their midst."

18:15-20

"I don't tell you until seven times,
but, until seventy times seven.
Therefore the Kingdom of Heaven
is like a certain king, who wanted to reconcile accounts with his servants.
When he had begun to reconcile,
one was brought to him who owed him ten thousand talents.
But because he couldn't pay,
his lord commanded him to be sold,
with his wife, his children, and all that he had,
and payment to be made.
The servant therefore fell down and kneeled before him, saying,
'Lord, have patience with me,
and I will repay you all!'

The lord of that servant, being moved with compassion,
released him, and forgave him the debt."                                    18:22-27

"But that servant went out,
and found one of his fellow servants,
who owed him one hundred denarii,
and he grabbed him,
and took him by the throat, saying,
'Pay me what you owe!'"                                                          18:28

"So his fellow servant fell down at his feet and begged him, saying,
'Have patience with me,
and I will repay you!'
He would not,
but went and cast him into prison,
until he should pay back that which was due.
So when his fellow servants saw what was done,
they were exceedingly sorry,
and came and told to their lord all that was done.
Then his lord called him in, and said to him,
'You wicked servant!
I forgave you all that debt,
because you begged me.
Shouldn't you also have had mercy on your fellow servant,
even as I had mercy on you?'
His lord was angry,
and delivered him to the tormentors,
until he should pay all that was due to him.
So my heavenly Father will also do to you,
if you don't each forgive your brother from your hearts
for his misdeeds."                                                              18:29-35

--------------------------------------------------------------------------------
MATTHEW 19
--------------------------------------------------------------------------------

**"Haven't you read**
that he who made them
from the beginning
made them male and female,
and said,
'For this cause a man shall leave his father and mother,
and shall join to his wife;
and the two shall become one flesh?'

So that they are no more two,
but one flesh.
What therefore God has joined together,
don't let man tear apart."                                          19:4-6

"Moses, because of the hardness of your hearts,
allowed you to divorce your wives,
but from the beginning
it has not been so.
I tell you
that whoever divorces his wife,
except for sexual immorality,
and marries another,
commits adultery;
and he who marries her
when she is divorced
commits adultery."                                                  19:8-9

"Not all men can receive this saying,
but those to whom it is given.
For there are eunuchs who were born that way from their mother's womb,
and there are eunuchs who were made eunuchs by men;
and there are eunuchs who made themselves eunuchs
for the Kingdom of Heaven's sake.
He who is able to receive it,
let him receive it."                                                19:11-12

"Allow the little children,
and don't forbid them to come to me;
for the Kingdom of Heaven belongs to ones like these."             19:14

"Why do you call me good?
No one is good but one,
that is, God.
But if you want to enter into life,
keep the commandments."                                            19:17

"'You shall not murder.'
'You shall not commit adultery.'
'You shall not steal.'
'You shall not offer false testimony.'
'Honor your father and mother.'

And, 'You shall love your neighbor as yourself.'"  19:18-19

"If you want to be perfect,
go,
sell what you have,
and give to the poor,
and you will have treasure in heaven;
and come,
follow me."  19:21

"Most certainly
I say to you,
a rich man will enter into the Kingdom of Heaven
with difficulty.
Again
I tell you,
it is easier for a camel
to go through a needle's eye,
than for a rich man
to enter into the Kingdom of God."  19:23-24

"With men this is impossible,
but with God
all things are possible."  19:26

"Most certainly
I tell you
that you who have followed me,
in the regeneration
when the Son of Man will sit on the throne of his glory,
you also will sit on twelve thrones,
judging the twelve tribes of Israel.
Everyone who has left
houses,
or brothers,
or sisters,
or father,
or mother,
or wife,
or children,
or lands,

for my name's sake,
will receive one hundred times,
and will inherit eternal life.
But many will be last who are first;
and first who are last."

19:28-30

---

MATTHEW 20

---

**"For the Kingdom of Heaven is like a man**
who was the master of a household,
who went out early in the morning
to hire laborers for his vineyard.
When he had agreed with the laborers for a denarius a day,
he sent them into his vineyard.
He went out about the third hour,
and saw others standing idle in the marketplace.
To them he said,
'You also go into the vineyard,
and whatever is right I will give you.'
So they went their way.
Again he went out about the sixth and the ninth hour,
and did likewise.
About the eleventh hour
he went out, and found others standing idle.
He said to them,
'Why do you stand here all day idle?'"

20:1-6

"They said to him, 'Because no one has hired us.'
"He said to them,
'You also go into the vineyard,
and you will receive whatever is right.'
When evening had come,
the lord of the vineyard said to his manager,
'Call the laborers and pay them their wages,
beginning from the last to the first.'"

20:7-8

"When those who were hired at about the eleventh hour came,
they each received a denarius.
When the first came,
they supposed that they would receive more;
and they likewise each received a denarius.

When they received it,
they murmured against the master of the household,
saying, 'These last have spent one hour,
and you have made them equal to us,
who have borne the burden of the day and the scorching heat!'"                    20:9-12

"But he answered
one of them,
'Friend,
I am doing you no wrong.
Didn't you agree with me for a denarius?
Take that which is yours,
and go your way.
It is my desire to give to this last
just as much as to you.
Isn't it lawful for me
to do what I want to
with what I own?
Or is your eye evil,
because I am good?'
So the last will be first,
and the first last.
For many are called,
but few are chosen."                                                               20:13-16

"Behold,
we are going up to Jerusalem,
and the Son of Man will be delivered
to the chief priests and scribes,
and they will condemn him to death,
and will hand him over to the Gentiles
to mock, to scourge, and to crucify;
and the third day he will be raised up."                                           20:18-19

"What do you want?"                                                                20:21

"You don't know what you are asking.
Are you able to drink the cup that I am about to drink,
and be baptized with the baptism that I am baptized with?"                         20:22

"You will indeed drink my cup,
and be baptized with the baptism that I am baptized with,

but to sit on my right hand and on my left hand
is not mine to give;
but it is for whom
it has been prepared by my Father."                                            20:23

"You know that the rulers of the nations
lord it over them,
and their great ones exercise authority over them.
It shall not be so among you,
but whoever desires to become great
among you
shall be your servant.
Whoever desires to be first
among you
shall be your bondservant,
even as the Son of Man
came not to be served,
but to serve,
and to give his life
as a ransom for many."                                                     20:25-28

"What do you want me to do for you?"                                          20:32

---

MATTHEW 21

---

**"Go into the village that is opposite you,**
and immediately
you will find a donkey tied,
and a colt with her.
Untie them, and bring them to me.
If anyone says anything to you,
you shall say, 'The Lord needs them,'
and immediately
he will send them."                                                          21:1-3

"It is written,
'My house shall be called a house of prayer,
but you have made it a den of robbers!"                                       21:13

"Yes.
Did you never read,

'Out of the mouth of babes and nursing babies
you have perfected praise?'"                                    21:16

"Let there be no fruit from you forever!"                       21:19

"Most certainly
I tell you,
if you have faith,
and don't doubt,
you will not only do what was done to the fig tree,
but even if you told this mountain,
'Be taken up and cast into the sea,'
it would be done.
All things,
whatever you ask in prayer,
believing,
you will receive."                                             21:21-22

"I also will ask you
one question,
which if you tell me,
I likewise will tell you
by what authority
I do these things.
The baptism of John,
where was it from?
From heaven
or from men?"                                                  21:24-25

"Neither will I tell you
by what authority
I do these things.
But what do you think?
A man had two sons,
and he came to the first, and said,
'Son, go work today in my vineyard.'
He answered, 'I will not,'
but afterward he changed his mind,
and went.
He came to the second,
and said the same thing.

He answered, 'I go, sir,'
but he didn't go.
Which of the two did the will of his father?"                    21:27-31


"Most certainly
I tell you
that the tax collectors
and the prostitutes
are entering into the Kingdom of God
before you.
For John came to you in the way of righteousness,
and you didn't believe him,
but the tax collectors and the prostitutes believed him.
When you saw it,
you didn't even repent afterward,
that you might believe him."                                     21:31-32


"Hear another parable.
There was a man who was a master of a household,
who planted a vineyard,
set a hedge about it,
dug a winepress in it,
built a tower,
leased it out to farmers,
and went into another country.
When the season for the fruit drew near,
he sent his servants to the farmers,
to receive his fruit.
The farmers took his servants,
beat one,
killed another,
and stoned another.
Again, he sent other servants more than the first:
and they treated them the same way.
But afterward he sent to them his son, saying,
'They will respect my son.'
But the farmers, when they saw the son,
said among themselves,
'This is the heir.
Come, let's kill him,
and seize his inheritance.'

So they took him,
and threw him out of the vineyard,
and killed him.
When therefore the lord of the vineyard comes,
what will he do to those farmers?"                                         21:33-40

"Did you never read in the Scriptures,
'The stone which the builders rejected,
the same was made the head of the corner.
This was from the Lord.
It is marvelous in our eyes?'
Therefore I tell you,
the Kingdom of God will be taken away from you,
and will be given to a nation
bringing forth its fruit.
He who falls on this stone
will be broken to pieces,
but on whomever it will fall,
it will scatter him as dust."                                             21:42-44

-----------------------------------------------------------------------------------
MATTHEW 22
-----------------------------------------------------------------------------------

**"The Kingdom of Heaven**
is like a certain king,
who made a marriage feast for his son,
and sent out his servants to call those
who were invited to the marriage feast,
but they would not come.
Again he sent out other servants, saying,
'Tell those who are invited,
"Behold, I have prepared my dinner.
My cattle and my fatlings are killed,
and all things are ready.
Come to the marriage feast!"'
But they made light of it,
and went their ways,
one to his own farm,
another to his merchandise,
and the rest grabbed his servants,
and treated them shamefully,
and killed them.

When the king heard that, he was angry,
and sent his armies, destroyed those murderers,
and burned their city.'"                                            22:1-7

"Then he said to his servants,
'The wedding is ready,
but those who were invited weren't worthy.
Go therefore to the intersections of the highways,
and as many as you may find,
invite to the marriage feast.'
Those servants went out into the highways,
and gathered together as many as they found,
both bad and good.
The wedding was filled with guests.
But when the king came in to see the guests,
he saw there a man who didn't have on wedding clothing,
and he said to him,
'Friend,
how did you come in here not wearing wedding clothing?'
He was speechless.
Then the king said to the servants,
'Bind him hand and foot,
take him away,
and throw him into the outer darkness;
there is where the weeping and grinding of teeth will be.'
For many are called,
but few chosen."                                                    22:8-14

"Why do you test me,
you hypocrites?
Show me the tax money."                                             22:18-19

"Whose is this image and inscription?"                              22:20

"Give therefore to Caesar the things that are Caesar's,
and to God the things that are God's."                              22:21

"You are mistaken,
not knowing the Scriptures,
nor the power of God.
For in the resurrection they neither marry,

nor are given in marriage,
but are like God's angels in heaven.
But concerning the resurrection of the dead,
haven't you read that which was spoken to you by God, saying,
'I am
the God
of Abraham,
and the God of Isaac,
and the God of Jacob?'
God is not the God of the dead,
but of the living."                                                              22:29-32

"'You shall love
the Lord
your God
with all your heart,
with all your soul,
and with all your mind.'
This is the first
and great commandment.
A second likewise is this,
'You shall love
your neighbor
as yourself.'
The whole law and the prophets
depend
on these two commandments."                                                      22:37-40

"What do you think of the Christ?
Whose son is he?"                                                                22:42

"How then does David
in the Spirit
call him Lord, saying,
'The Lord said to my Lord,
sit on my right hand,
until I make your enemies a footstool for your feet?'
"If then David calls him Lord,
how is he his son?"                                                              22:43-45

**"The scribes and the Pharisees sat on Moses' seat.**
All things therefore whatever they tell you to observe, observe and do,
but don't do their works;
for they say,
and don't do.
For they bind heavy burdens
that are grievous to be borne,
and lay them on men's shoulders;
but they themselves
will not lift a finger to help them.
But all their works
they do to be seen by men.
They make their phylacteries broad,
enlarge the fringes of their garments,
and love the place of honor at feasts,
the best seats in the synagogues,
the salutations in the marketplaces,
and to be called 'Rabbi, Rabbi' by men.
But don't you be called 'Rabbi,'
for one is your teacher, the Christ,
and all of you are brothers.
Call no man on the earth
your father,
for one is your Father,
he who is in heaven.
Neither be called masters,
for one is your master,
the Christ.
But he who is greatest among you
will be your servant.
Whoever exalts himself
will be humbled,
and whoever humbles himself
will be exalted."                                    23:2-12

"Woe to you, scribes and Pharisees,
Hypocrites!
For you devour widows' houses,
And as a pretense you make long prayers.
Therefore you will receive greater condemnation."                     23:13

"But woe to you, scribes and Pharisees,
hypocrites!
Because you shut up the Kingdom of Heaven against men;
for you don't enter in yourselves,
neither do you allow those who are entering in
to enter.
Woe to you, scribes and Pharisees,
hypocrites!
For you travel around by sea and land
to make one proselyte;
and when he becomes one,
you make him twice as much
of a son of Gehenna as yourselves."                                    23:14-15

"Woe to you, you blind guides,
who say,
'Whoever swears by the temple,
it is nothing;
but whoever swears by the gold of the temple,
he is obligated.'
You blind fools!
For which is greater,
the gold,
or the temple that sanctifies the gold?
'Whoever swears by the altar, it is nothing;
but whoever swears by the gift that is on it,
he is obligated?'
You blind fools!
For which is greater,
the gift,
or the altar that sanctifies the gift?
He therefore who swears by the altar,
swears by it, and by everything on it.
He who swears by the temple,
swears by it, and by him who was living in it.
He who swears by heaven,
swears by the throne of God, and by him who sits on it."               23:16-22

"Woe to you, scribes and Pharisees,
hypocrites!
For you tithe

mint, dill, and cumin,
and have left undone
the weightier matters of the law:
justice, mercy, and faith.
But you ought to have done these,
and not to have left the other undone.
You blind guides,
who strain out a gnat, and swallow a camel!"                    23:23-24

"Woe to you, scribes and Pharisees,
hypocrites!
For you clean the outside of the cup and of the platter,
but within
they are full of extortion and unrighteousness.
You blind Pharisee,
first clean the inside of the cup and of the platter,
that its outside may become clean also."                        23:25-26

"Woe to you, scribes and Pharisees,
hypocrites!
For you are like whitened tombs,
which outwardly appear beautiful,
but inwardly are full of dead men's bones,
and of all uncleanness.
Even so
you also outwardly appear righteous to men,
but inwardly
you are full of hypocrisy and iniquity."                        23:27-28

"Woe to you, scribes and Pharisees,
hypocrites!
For you build the tombs of the prophets,
and decorate the tombs of the righteous,
and say,
'If we had lived in the days of our fathers,
we wouldn't have been partakers with them
in the blood of the prophets.'
Therefore you testify to yourselves
that you are children of those
who killed the prophets.
Fill up, then,

the measure of your fathers.
You serpents,
you offspring of vipers,
how will you escape the judgment of Gehenna?
Therefore,
behold,
I send to you prophets,
wise men,
and scribes.
Some of them you will kill and crucify;
and some of them you will scourge in your synagogues,
and persecute from city to city;
that on you may come
all the righteous blood shed on the earth,
from the blood of righteous Abel
to the blood of Zachariah son of Barachiah,
whom you killed
between the sanctuary and the altar.
Most certainly
I tell you,
all these things
will come
upon this generation."                                             23:29-36

"Jerusalem,
Jerusalem,
who kills the prophets,
and stones those who are sent to her!
How often I would have gathered your children together,
even as a hen gathers her chicks
under her wings,
and you would not!
Behold,
your house is left to you desolate.
For I tell you,
you will not see me from now on,
until you say,
'Blessed is he who comes in the name of the Lord!'"               23:37-39

## "You see all of these things, don't you?
Most certainly
I tell you,
there will not be left here one stone
on another,
that will not be thrown down."

24:2

"Be careful
that no one leads you astray.
For many will come
in my name,
saying, 'I am the Christ,'
and will lead many astray.
You will hear of wars
and rumors of wars.
See that you aren't troubled,
for all this must happen,
but the end is not yet.
For nation will rise against nation,
and kingdom against kingdom;
and there will be famines, plagues,
and earthquakes in various places.
But all these things are the beginning of birth pains.
Then they will deliver you up
to oppression,
and will kill you.
You will be hated
by all of the nations
for my name's sake.
Then many will stumble,
and will deliver up one another,
and will hate one another.
Many false prophets
will arise,
and will lead many astray.
Because iniquity will be multiplied,
the love of many will grow cold.
But he
who endures

to the end,
the same
will
be saved.
This Good News of the Kingdom
will be preached
in the whole world
for a testimony to all the nations,
and then
the end
will come."

24:4-14

"When, therefore,
you see the abomination of desolation,
which was spoken of through Daniel the prophet,
standing in the holy place
(let the reader understand),
then let those
who are in Judea
flee to the mountains.
Let him
who is on the housetop
not go down
to take out things
that are in his house.
Let him
who is in the field
not return back
to get his clothes.
But woe to those
who are with child
and to nursing mothers
in those days!
Pray
that your flight
will not be
in the winter,
nor on a Sabbath,
for then there will be
great oppression,
such as has not been

from the beginning of the world
until now,
no,
nor ever will be.
Unless those days
had been shortened,
no flesh
would have been saved.
But for the sake of the chosen ones,
those days will be shortened."

24:15-22

"Then
if any man
tells you,
'Behold,
here is the Christ,'
or,
'There,'
don't
believe
it.
For there will arise
false christs,
and false prophets,
and they will show
great signs
and wonders,
so as to lead astray,
if possible,
even the chosen ones."

24:23-24

"Behold,
I have told you
beforehand.
If therefore they tell you,
'Behold,
he is in the wilderness,'
don't
go
out;
'Behold,

he is in the inner rooms,'
don't
believe
it.
For as the lightning flashes from the east,
and is seen even to the west,
so will be
the coming of the Son of Man.
For wherever the carcass is,
there is where the vultures gather together.
But immediately
after the oppression of those days,
the sun will be darkened,
the moon will not give its light,
the stars will fall from the sky,
and the powers of the heavens will be shaken;
and then the sign of the Son of Man
will appear in the sky.
Then all the tribes of the earth will mourn,
and they will see the Son of Man
coming on the clouds of the sky
with power and great glory.
He will send out his angels
with a great sound of a trumpet,
and they will gather together his chosen ones
from the four winds,
from one end of the sky to the other."

24:25-31

"Now from the fig tree learn this parable.
When its branch has now become tender, and puts forth its leaves,
you know that the summer is near.
Even so you also, when you see all these things,
know that it is near,
even at the doors.
Most certainly
I tell you,
this generation will not pass away,
until all these things are accomplished.
Heaven and earth will pass away,
but my words
will not

pass away.
But no one knows
of that day and hour,
not even the angels of heaven,
but my Father only."                                         24:32-36

"As the days of Noah were,
so will be the coming of the Son of Man.
For as in those days which were before the flood
they were eating and drinking,
marrying and giving in marriage,
until the day that Noah entered into the ship,
and they didn't know until the flood came,
and took them all away,
so will be the coming of the Son of Man.
Then two men will be in the field:
one will be taken and one will be left;
two women grinding at the mill,
one will be taken and one will be left.
Watch therefore,
for you don't know
in what hour
your Lord comes.
But know this,
that if the master of the house had known
in what watch of the night
the thief was coming,
he would have watched,
and would not have allowed his house to be broken into.
Therefore also be ready,
for in an hour
that you don't expect,
the Son of Man will come."                                   24:37-44

"Who then is the faithful and wise servant,
whom his lord has set over his household,
to give them their food in due season?
Blessed is that servant
whom his lord finds doing so
when he comes.
Most certainly

I tell you
that he will set him
over all that he has.
But if that evil servant
should say in his heart,
'My lord is delaying his coming,'
and begins to beat his fellow servants,
and eat and drink with the drunkards,
the lord of that servant will come in a day
when he doesn't expect it,
and in an hour when he doesn't know it,
and will cut him in pieces,
and appoint his portion
with the hypocrites.
There is where the weeping and grinding of teeth will be."                    24:45-51

------------------------------------------------------------------------

MATTHEW 25
------------------------------------------------------------------------

## "Then the Kingdom of Heaven

will be like ten virgins, who took their lamps,
and went out to meet the bridegroom.
Five of them were foolish,
and five were wise.
Those who were foolish,
when they took their lamps,
took no oil with them,
but the wise
took oil in their vessels with their lamps.
Now while the bridegroom delayed,
they all slumbered and slept.
But at midnight there was a cry,
'Behold!
The bridegroom is coming!
Come out to meet him!'
Then all those virgins arose,
and trimmed their lamps.
The foolish said to the wise,
'Give us some of your oil, for our lamps are going out.'
But the wise answered, saying,
'What if there isn't enough for us and you?
You go rather to those who sell, and buy for yourselves.'

While they went away to buy,
the bridegroom came,
and those who were ready
went in with him to the marriage feast,
and the door was shut.
Afterward the other virgins also came,
saying, 'Lord, Lord,
open to us.'
But he answered,
'Most certainly
I tell you,
I don't know you.'
Watch therefore,
for you don't know
the day nor the hour
in which the Son of Man is coming."                                      25:1-13

"For it is like a man, going into another country,
who called his own servants,
and entrusted his goods to them.
To one he gave five talents,
to another two,
to another one;
to each according to his own ability.
Then he went on his journey.
Immediately
he who received the five talents
went and traded with them,
and made another five talents.
In the same way,
he also who got the two
gained another two.
But he who received the one
went away
and dug in the earth,
and hid his lord's money."                                               25:14-18

"Now after a long time
the lord of those servants came,
and reconciled accounts with them.
He who received the five talents came and brought another five talents,
saying, 'Lord, you delivered to me five talents.

Behold, I have gained another five talents besides them.'"          25:19-20

"His lord said to him,
'Well done, good and faithful servant.
You have been faithful over a few things,
I will set you over many things.
Enter into the joy of your lord.'"          25:21

"He also who got the two talents came and said,
'Lord, you delivered to me two talents.
Behold, I have gained another two talents besides them.'"          25:22

"His lord said to him,
'Well done, good and faithful servant.
You have been faithful over a few things,
I will set you over many things.
Enter into the joy of your lord.'"          25:23

"He also who had received the one talent came and said,
'Lord, I knew you that you are a hard man,
reaping where you did not sow,
and gathering where you did not scatter.
I was afraid,
and went away and hid your talent in the earth.
Behold, you have what is yours.'"          25:24-25

"But his lord answered him,
'You wicked and slothful servant.
You knew that I reap where I didn't sow,
and gather where I didn't scatter.
You ought therefore to have deposited
my money with the bankers,
and at my coming
I should have received back my own with interest.
Take away therefore the talent from him,
and give it to him who has the ten talents.
For to everyone who has will be given,
and he will have abundance,
but from him who doesn't have,
even that which he has will be taken away.
Throw out the unprofitable servant into the outer darkness,
where there will be weeping and gnashing of teeth.'"          25:26-30

"But when the Son of Man comes in his glory,
and all the holy angels with him,
then he will sit on the throne of his glory.
Before him all the nations will be gathered,
and he will separate them
one from another,
as a shepherd separates the sheep from the goats.
He will set the sheep on his right hand,
but the goats on the left.
Then the King will tell those on his right hand,
'Come, blessed of my Father,
inherit the Kingdom
prepared for you from the foundation of the world;
for I was hungry,
and you gave me food to eat.
I was thirsty,
and you gave me drink.
I was a stranger,
and you took me in.
I was naked,
and you clothed me.
I was sick,
and you visited me.
I was in prison,
and you came to me.'"                                              25:31-36

"Then the righteous will answer him, saying,
'Lord,
when did we see you hungry, and feed you;
or thirsty, and give you a drink?
When did we see you as a stranger,
and take you in; or naked, and clothe you?
When did we see you sick, or in prison, and come to you?'"        25:37-39

"The King will answer them,
'Most certainly
I tell you,
inasmuch as you did it to one of the least of these my brothers,
you did it to me.'
Then he will say also to those on the left hand,
'Depart from me,
you cursed,

into the eternal fire which is
prepared for the devil and his angels;
for I was hungry,
and you didn't give me food to eat;
I was thirsty,
and you gave me no drink;
I was a stranger,
and you didn't take me in;
naked,
and you didn't clothe me;
sick, and in prison,
and you didn't visit me.'"                                                       25:40-43

"Then they will also answer, saying,
'Lord,
when did we see you hungry,
or thirsty,
or a stranger,
or naked,
or sick,
or in prison,
and didn't help you?'"                                                           25:44

"Then he will answer them, saying,
'Most certainly
I tell you,
inasmuch as you didn't do it
to one of the least of these,
you didn't do it to me.'
These will go away into eternal punishment,
but the righteous into eternal life."                                            25:45-46

--------------------------------------------------------------------------------
MATTHEW 26
--------------------------------------------------------------------------------

**"You know that after two days**
the Passover is coming,
and the Son of Man
will be delivered up to be crucified."                                           26:2

"Why do you trouble the woman?
Because she has done a good work for me.

For you always have the poor with you;
but you don't always have me.
For in pouring this ointment on my body,
she did it to prepare me for burial.
Most certainly
I tell you,
wherever this Good News is preached in the whole world,
what this woman has done
will also be spoken of
as a memorial of her."                                          26:10-13

"Go into the city to a certain person,
and tell him, 'The Teacher says,
"My time is at hand.
I will keep the Passover
at your house
with my disciples."'"                                           26:18

"Most certainly
I tell you
that one of you will betray me."                                26:21

"He who dipped his hand with me in the dish,
the same will betray me.
The Son of Man goes,
even as it is written of him,
but woe to that man through whom the Son of Man is betrayed!
It would be better for that man if he had not been born."       26:23-24

"You said it."                                                  26:25

"Take,
eat;
this is my body"…
"All of you
drink it,
for this is my blood of the new covenant,
which is poured out for many
for the remission of sins.
But I tell you that
I will not drink of this fruit of the vine

from now on,
until that day
when I drink it anew with you in my Father's Kingdom."                    26:26-29

"All of you will be made to stumble
because of me tonight,
for it is written,
'I will strike the shepherd,
and the sheep of the flock will be scattered.'
But after I am raised up,
I will go before you into Galilee."                                       26:31-32

"Most certainly
I tell you
that tonight,
before the rooster crows,
you will deny me three times."                                            26:34

"Sit here,
while I go there and pray."                                                26:36

"My soul is exceedingly sorrowful,
even to death.
Stay here,
and watch with me."                                                       26:38

"My Father,
if it is possible,
let this cup pass away from me;
nevertheless,
not what I desire,
but what you desire."                                                     26:39

"What, couldn't you watch with me for one hour?
Watch and pray,
that you don't enter into temptation.
The spirit indeed is willing,
but the flesh is weak."                                                   26:40-41

"My Father,
if this cup can't pass away from me
unless I drink it,
your desire be done."                                   26:42

"Sleep on now, and take your rest.
Behold,
the hour is at hand,
and the Son of Man is betrayed into the hands of sinners.
Arise,
let's be going.
Behold,
he who betrays me is at hand."                          26:45-46

"Friend,
why are you here?"                                      26:50

"Put your sword back into its place,
for all those who take the sword
will die by the sword.
Or do you think that I couldn't ask my Father,
and he would
even now
send me
more than twelve legions of angels?
How then would the Scriptures be fulfilled
that it must be so?"                                    26:52-54

"Have you come out as against a robber
with swords and clubs to seize me?
I sat daily in the temple teaching,
and you didn't arrest me.
But all this has happened,
that the Scriptures of the prophets might be fulfilled." 26:55-56

"You have said it.
Nevertheless,
I tell you,
after this
you will see the Son of Man
sitting at the right hand of Power,
and coming on the clouds of the sky."                   26:64

## "So you say." 27:11

"Eli,
Eli,
lima sabachthani?"...
"My God,
my God,
why have you forsaken me?" 27:46

## "Rejoice!" 28:9

"Don't be afraid.
Go
tell my brothers that they should go into Galilee,
and there they will see me." 28:10

"All authority has been given to me
in heaven
and on earth.
Go,
and make disciples
of all nations,
baptizing them
in the name of the Father
and of the Son
and of the Holy Spirit,
teaching them
to observe
all things
that I commanded you.
Behold,
I am with you always,
even to the end of the age." 28:18-20

# THE GOOD NEWS ACCORDING TO *Mark*

## CHAPTER 1

**"The time is fulfilled,**
and the Kingdom of God is at hand!
Repent, and believe in the Good News."

1:15

"Come
after me,
and I will make you into fishers for men."

1:17

"Be quiet,
and come out of him!"

1:25

"Let's go elsewhere
into the next towns,
that I may preach there also,
because I came out for this reason."

1:38

"I want to.
Be made clean."

1:41

"See you say nothing to anybody,
but go
show yourself to the priest,
and offer for your cleansing
the things which Moses commanded,
for a testimony to them."

1:44

-----------------------------------------------------------

MARK 2

-----------------------------------------------------------

**"Son,**
your sins are forgiven you."

2:5

"Why do you reason these things in your hearts?
Which is easier,
to tell the paralytic,
'Your sins are forgiven;'
or to say, 'Arise,

and take up your bed, and walk?'
But that you may know
that the Son of Man
has authority on earth
to forgive sins"                                                                        2:8-10

"I tell you,
arise,
take up your mat, and
go to your house."                                                                      2:11

"Follow me."                                                                            2:14

"Those who are healthy have no need for a physician,
but those who are sick.
I came not to call the righteous,
but sinners to repentance."                                                            2:17

"Can the groomsmen fast while the bridegroom is with them?
As long as they have the bridegroom with them, they can't fast.
But the days will come
when the bridegroom will be taken away from them,
and then will they fast in that day.
No one sews a piece of unshrunk cloth on an old garment,
or else the patch shrinks and the new tears away from the old,
and a worse hole is made.
No one puts new wine
into old wineskins,
or else the new wine will burst the skins,
and the wine pours out,
and the skins will be destroyed;
but they put
new wine
into fresh wineskins."                                                                 2:19-22

"Did you never read
what David did,
when he had need, and was hungry
– he, and those who were with him?
How he entered into God's house
when Abiathar was high priest,

and ate the show bread,
which is not lawful to eat except for the priests,
and gave also to those who were with him?"                    2:25-26

"The Sabbath was made for man,
not man for the Sabbath.
Therefore the
Son of Man
is lord
even of the Sabbath."                                         2:27-28

---

MARK 3

---

## "Stand up."                                                 3:3

"Is it lawful on the Sabbath day
to do good, or to do harm?
To save a life, or to kill?"                                   3:4

"Stretch out your hand."                                       3:5

"How can Satan cast out Satan?
If a kingdom is divided against itself,
that kingdom cannot stand.
If a house is divided against itself,
that house cannot stand.
If Satan has risen up against himself,
and is divided,
he can't stand,
but has an end.
But no one can enter into the house of the strong man to plunder,
unless he first binds the strong man;
and then he will plunder his house.
Most certainly
I tell you,
all sins of the descendants of man
will be forgiven,
including their blasphemies with which they may blaspheme;
but
whoever
may blaspheme

against the Holy Spirit
never has forgiveness,
but is guilty
of an eternal sin"                                                        3:23-29

"Who are my mother and my brothers?"                                      3:33

"Behold, my mother and my brothers!
For whoever does the will of God,
the same is my brother, and my sister, and mother."                      3:34-35

- - - - - - - - - - - - - - - - - - - - - - - - - - - - - - - - - - - - - - - - - - - - - - - - - - - - - - - - - - -

MARK 4

- - - - - - - - - - - - - - - - - - - - - - - - - - - - - - - - - - - - - - - - - - - - - - - - - - - - - - - - - - -

**"Listen!**
Behold,
the farmer went out to sow,
and it happened, as he sowed,
some seed fell by the road,
and the birds came and devoured it.
Others fell on the rocky ground,
where it had little soil,
and immediately it sprang up,
because it had no depth of soil.
When the sun had risen,
it was scorched;
and because it had no root,
it withered away.
Others fell among the thorns,
and the thorns grew up,
and choked it,
and it yielded no fruit.
Others fell into the good ground,
and yielded fruit,
growing up and increasing.
Some brought forth thirty times,
some sixty times,
and some one hundred times as much."...
"Whoever has ears to hear, let him hear."                                4:3-8, 9

"To you is given
the mystery

of the Kingdom of God,
but to those who are outside,
all things are done in parables,
that 'seeing they may see,
and not perceive;
and hearing they may hear,
and not understand;
lest perhaps they should turn again,
and their sins should be forgiven them.'"                                    4:11-12

"Don't you understand this parable?
How will you understand all of the parables?
The farmer sows the word.
The ones by the road are the ones
where the word is sown;
and when they have heard,
immediately Satan comes,
and takes away the word
which has been sown in them.
These in the same way are those who are sown on the rocky places,
who, when they have heard the word,
immediately receive it with joy.
They have no root in themselves,
but are short-lived.
When oppression or persecution arises
because of the word,
immediately they stumble.
Others are those who are sown among the thorns.
These are those who have heard the word,
and the cares of this age,
and the deceitfulness of riches,
and the lusts of other things entering in
choke the word,
and it becomes unfruitful.
Those which were sown on the good ground
are those who hear the word,
and accept it,
and bear fruit,
some thirty times,
some sixty times,
and some one hundred times."                                                   4:13-20

"Is the lamp brought to be put under a basket or under a bed?
Isn't it put on a stand?
For there is nothing hidden,
except that it should be made known;
neither was anything made secret,
but that it should come to light.
If any man has ears to hear, let him hear."                             4:21-23

"Take heed what you hear.
With whatever measure you measure,
it will be measured to you,
and more will be given to you who hear.
For whoever has,
to him will more be given,
and he who doesn't have,
even that which he has
will be taken away from him."                                           4:24-25

"The Kingdom of God is as if
a man should cast seed on the earth,
and should sleep and rise night and day,
and the seed should spring up and grow,
he doesn't know how.
For the earth bears fruit:
first the blade,
then the ear,
then the full grain in the ear.
But when the fruit is ripe,
immediately he puts forth the sickle,
because the harvest has come."                                          4:26-27

"How will we liken the Kingdom of God?
Or with what parable will we illustrate it?
It's like a grain of mustard seed,
which, when it is sown in the earth,
though it is less than
all the seeds that are on the earth,
yet when it is sown,
grows up,
and becomes greater than all the herbs,
and puts out great branches,

so that the birds of the sky can lodge under its shadow."

4:30-32

"Let's go over to the other side."

4:35

"Peace!
Be still!"

4:39

"Why are you so afraid?
How is it that you have no faith?"

4:40

---

MARK 5

---

**"Come out of the man, you unclean spirit!"**

5:8

"What is your name?"

5:9

"Go
to your house,
to your friends,
and tell them
what great things
the Lord has done for you,
and how he had mercy on you."

5:19

"Who touched my clothes?"

5:30

"Daughter,
your faith has made you well.
Go in peace,
and be cured
of your disease."

5:34

"Don't be afraid,
only believe."…
"Why do you make an uproar and weep?
The child is not dead, but is asleep."

5:36,39

"Talitha cumi!"…
"Girl,
I tell you,
get up!"

5:41

**"A prophet is not without honor,**
except in his own country,
and among his own relatives,
and in his own house."                                                   6:4

"Wherever you enter into a house,
stay there
until you depart from there.
Whoever will not receive you
nor hear you,
as you depart from there,
shake off the dust that is under your feet
for a testimony against them.
Assuredly,
I tell you,
it will be more tolerable for Sodom and Gomorrah
in the day of judgment than for that city!"                              6:10-11

"You come apart
into a deserted place,
and rest awhile."                                                        6:31

"You give them something to eat."                                        6:37

"How many loaves do you have?
Go see."                                                                 6:38

"Cheer up!
It is I!
Don't be afraid."                                                        6:50

**"Well did Isaiah prophesy of you hypocrites, as it is written,**
'This people honors me with their lips,
but their heart is far from me.
But in vain do they worship me,
teaching as doctrines the commandments of men.'                          7:6-7

"For you set aside the commandment of God,
and hold tightly to the tradition of men—
the washing of pitchers and cups,
and you do many other such things."                                    7:8

"Full well do you reject the commandment of God,
that you may keep your tradition.
For Moses said, 'Honor your father and your mother;'
and, 'He who speaks evil of father or mother,
let him be put to death.'
But you say, 'If a man tells his father or his mother,
"Whatever profit you might have received from me is Corban,
that is to say, given to God;"
then you no longer allow him to do anything
for his father or his mother,
making void the word of God
by your tradition,
which you have handed down.
You do many things like this."                                         7:9-13

"Hear me,
all of you,
and understand.
There is nothing from outside of the man,
that going into him
can defile him;
but the things which proceed out of the man
are those that defile the man.
If anyone has ears to hear, let him hear!"                             7:14-16

"Are you thus without understanding also?
Don't you perceive
that whatever goes into the man from outside
can't defile him,
because it doesn't go into his heart,
but into his stomach,
then into the latrine, thus purifying all foods?"                      7:18-19

"That which proceeds out of the man,
that defiles the man.
For from within,

out of the hearts of men,
proceed evil thoughts,
adulteries, sexual sins,
murders, thefts,
covetings, wickedness,
deceit, lustful desires,
an evil eye,
blasphemy,
pride, and foolishness.
All these evil things come from within,
and defile the man."                                                7:20-23

"Let the children be filled first,
for it is not appropriate to take the children's bread
and throw it to the dogs."                                          7:27

"For this saying,
go your way.
The demon has gone out of your daughter."                           7:29

"Ephphatha!"...
"Be opened!"                                                        7:34

---

MARK 8

---

**"I have compassion**
on the multitude,
because they have stayed with me now three days,
and have nothing to eat.
If I send them away fasting to their home,
they will faint on the way,
for some of them have come a long way."                             8:2-3

"How many loaves do you have?"                                      8:5

"Why does this generation seek a sign?
Most certainly
I tell you,
no sign will be given to this generation."                         8:12

"Take heed:
beware
of the yeast of the Pharisees and the yeast of Herod."                    8:15

"Why do you reason that it's because you have no bread?
Don't you perceive yet, neither understand?
Is your heart still hardened?
Having eyes,
don't you see?
Having ears,
don't you hear?
Don't you remember?
When I broke the five loaves among the five thousand,
how many baskets full of broken pieces did you take up?"             8:17-19

"When the seven loaves fed the four thousand,
how many baskets full of broken pieces did you take up?"              8:20

"Don't you understand, yet?"                                          8:21

"Don't enter into the village,
nor tell anyone in the village."                                     8:26

"Who do men say that I am?"                                          8:27

"But who do you say that I am?"                                      8:29

"Get behind me, Satan!
For you have in mind not the things of God,
but the things of men."                                             8:33

"Whoever wants to come after me,
let him deny himself,
and take up his cross,
and follow me.
For whoever
wants to save his life
will lose it;
and whoever
will lose his life
for my sake

and the sake of the Good News
will save it.
For what does it profit a man,
to gain the whole world,
and forfeit his life?
For what will a man give
in exchange for his life?
For whoever will be ashamed of me
and of my words
in this adulterous and sinful generation,
the Son of Man also will be ashamed of him,
when he comes in the glory of his Father with the holy angels."                8:34-38

---

## "Most certainly

I tell you,
there are some standing here who will in no way taste death
until they see the Kingdom of God come with power."                             9:1

"Elijah indeed comes first, and restores all things.
How is it written
about the Son of Man,
that he should suffer many things
and be despised?
But I tell you
that Elijah has come,
and they have also done to him whatever they wanted to,
even as it is written about him."                                              9:12-13

"What are you asking them?"                                                     9:16

"Unbelieving generation,
how long shall I be with you?
How long shall I bear with you?
Bring him to me."                                                              9:19

"How long
has it been
since this has come to him?"                                                   9:21

"If you can believe,
all things are possible to him who believes."                    9:23

"You mute and deaf spirit,
I command you,
come out of him,
and never enter him again!"                                      9:25

"This kind can come out by nothing,
except by prayer and fasting."                                   9:29

"The Son of Man
is being handed over to the hands of men,
and they will kill him;
and when he is killed,
on the third day
he will rise again."                                             9:31

"What were you arguing among yourselves on the way?"             9:33

"If any man wants to be first,
he shall be last of all,
and servant of all."                                             9:35

"Whoever receives one such little child in my name,
receives me,
and whoever receives me,
doesn't receive me,
but him who sent me."                                            9:37

"Don't forbid him,
for there is no one who will do a mighty work in my name,
and be able quickly to speak evil of me.
For whoever is not against us is on our side.
For whoever will give you a cup of water to drink in my name,
because you are Christ's,
most certainly
I tell you,
he will in no way lose his reward.
Whoever
will cause one of these little ones who believe in me to stumble,

it would be better for him if he were thrown into the sea
with a millstone hung around his neck.
If your hand causes you to stumble,
cut it off.
It is better for you to enter into life maimed,
rather than having your two hands to go into Gehenna,
into the unquenchable fire,
'where their worm doesn't die, and the fire is not quenched.'
If your foot causes you to stumble,
cut it off.
It is better for you to enter into life lame,
rather than having your two feet to be cast into Gehenna,
into the fire that will never be quenched—
'where their worm doesn't die, and the fire is not quenched.'
If your eye causes you to stumble,
cast it out.
It is better for you to enter into the Kingdom of God with one eye,
rather than having two eyes to be cast into the Gehenna of fire,
'where their worm doesn't die, and the fire is not quenched.'
For everyone will be salted with fire,
and every sacrifice will be seasoned with salt.
Salt is good,
but if the salt has lost its saltiness,
with what will you season it?
Have salt in yourselves,
and be at peace with one another."

9:39-50

---

## "What did Moses command you?"

10:3

"For your hardness of heart,
he wrote you this commandment.
But from the beginning of the creation,
God made them male and female.
For this cause
a man will leave his father and mother,
and will join to his wife,
and the two will become one flesh,
so that they are no longer two,
but one flesh.

What therefore God has joined together,
let no man separate."

10:5-9

"Whoever divorces his wife,
and marries another,
commits adultery against her.
If a woman herself divorces her husband,
and marries another,
she commits adultery."

10:11-12

"Allow the little children to come to me!
Don't forbid them,
for the Kingdom of God belongs to such as these.
Most certainly
I tell you,
whoever will not receive the Kingdom of God
like a little child,
he will in no way enter into it."

10:14-15

"Why do you call me good?
No one is good
except one – God.
You know the commandments:
'Do not murder,'
'Do not commit adultery,'
'Do not steal,'
'Do not give false testimony,'
'Do not defraud,'
'Honor your father and mother.'"

10:18-19

"One thing you lack.
Go,
sell whatever you have,
and give to the poor,
and you will have treasure in heaven;
and come,
follow me,
taking up the cross."

10:21

"How difficult it is for those who have riches
to enter into the Kingdom of God!"

10:23

"Children,
how hard is it for those who trust in riches
to enter into the Kingdom of God!
It is easier for a camel
to go through a needle's eye
than for a rich man to enter into the Kingdom of God."

10:24-25

"With men it is impossible,
but not with God,
for all things are possible with God."

10:27

"Most certainly
I tell you,
there is no one who has left house,
or brothers, or sisters,
or father, or mother,
or wife, or children,
or land,
for my sake, and for the sake of the Good News,
but he will receive one hundred times more
now in this time,
houses, brothers, sisters, mothers, children, and land,
with persecutions;
and in the age to come eternal life.
But many who are first will be last;
and the last first."

10:29-31

"Behold,
we are going up to Jerusalem.
The Son of Man
will be delivered
to the chief priests and the scribes.
They will condemn him to death,
and will deliver him to the Gentiles.
They will mock him,
spit on him,
scourge him, and kill him.
On the third day he will rise again."

10:33-34

"What do you want me to do for you?"

10:36

"You don't know what you are asking.

Are you able to drink the cup that I drink,
and to be baptized with the baptism that I am baptized with?"

10:38

"You shall indeed drink the cup that I drink,
and you shall be baptized with the baptism that I am baptized with;
but to sit at my right hand and at my left hand
is not mine to give,
but for whom it has been prepared."

10:39-40

"You know
that they who are recognized as rulers over the nations
lord it over them,
and their great ones exercise authority over them.
But it shall not be so among you,
but whoever
wants
to become great among you
shall be your servant.
Whoever of you
wants
to become first among you,
shall be bondservant of all.
For the Son of Man
also came not to be served,
but to serve,
and to give his life
as a ransom for many."

10:42-45

"Call him."

10:49

"What do you want me to do for you?"

10:51

"Go your way.
Your faith has made you well."

10:52

**"Go your way into the village that is opposite you.**
Immediately as you enter into it,
you will find a young donkey tied,
on which no one has sat.
Untie him, and bring him.
If anyone asks you, 'Why are you doing this?'
say, 'The Lord needs him;'
and immediately he will send him back here."  11:2-3

"May no one ever eat fruit from you again!"  11:14

"Isn't it written,
'My house will be called a house of prayer for all the nations?'
But you have made it a den of robbers!"  11:17

"Have faith in God.
For most certainly
I tell you,
whoever may tell this mountain,
'Be taken up and cast into the sea,'
and doesn't doubt in his heart,
but believes
that what he says is happening;
he shall have whatever he says.
Therefore I tell you,
all things whatever you pray and ask for,
believe
that you have received them,
and you shall have them.
Whenever you stand praying,
forgive,
if you have anything against anyone;
so that your Father, who is in heaven,
may also forgive you your transgressions.
But if you do not forgive,
neither will your Father in heaven
forgive your transgressions."  11:22-26

"I will ask you one question.
Answer me,

and I will tell you
by what authority
I do these things.
The baptism of John —
was it from heaven,
or from men?
Answer me."                                              11:29-30

"Neither do I tell you
by what authority
I do these things."                                       11:33

- - - - - - - - - - - - - - - - - - - - - - - - - - - - - - - - - - - - - - - - - - - - - - - - - - - - - - - - - - - - - -

MARK 12
- - - - - - - - - - - - - - - - - - - - - - - - - - - - - - - - - - - - - - - - - - - - - - - - - - - - - - - - - - - - - -

**"A man planted a vineyard,**
put a hedge around it,
dug a pit for the winepress,
built a tower,
rented it out to a farmer,
and went into another country.
When it was time,
he sent a servant to the farmer
to get from the farmer his share
of the fruit of the vineyard.
They took him,
beat him,
and sent him away empty.
Again, he sent another servant to them;
and they threw stones at him,
wounded him in the head,
and sent him away shamefully treated.
Again he sent another;
and they killed him;
and many others,
beating some,
and killing some.
Therefore still having one,
his beloved son,
he sent him last to them, saying,
'They will respect my son.'
But those farmers said among themselves,

'This is the heir.
Come, let's kill him, and the inheritance will be ours.'
They took him, killed him,
and cast him out of the vineyard.
What therefore will the lord of the vineyard do?
He will come
and destroy the farmers, and will give the vineyard to others.
Haven't you even read this Scripture:
'The stone which the builders rejected,
the same was made the head of the corner.
This was from the Lord,
it is marvelous in our eyes'?"                                            12:1-11

"Why do you test me?
Bring me a denarius, that I may see it."                                    12:15

"Whose is this image and inscription?"                                      12:16

"Render to Caesar the things that are Caesar's,
and to God the things that are God's."                                      12:17

"Isn't this because you are mistaken,
not knowing the Scriptures,
nor the power of God?
For when they will rise from the dead,
they neither marry, nor are given in marriage,
but are like angels in heaven.
But about the dead, that they are raised;
haven't you read in the book of Moses,
about the Bush,
how God spoke to him, saying,
'I am
the God of Abraham, the God of Isaac, and the God of Jacob'?
He is not the God of the dead, but of the living.
You are therefore badly mistaken."                                         12:24-27

"The greatest is,
'Hear, Israel,
the Lord our God,
the Lord is one:
you shall love the Lord your God

with all your heart,
and with all your soul,
and with all your mind,
and with all your strength.'
This is the first commandment.
The second is like this,
'You shall love your neighbor as yourself.'
There is no other commandment greater than these."                    12:29-31

"You are not far from the Kingdom of God."                             12:34

"How is it that the scribes say
that the Christ is the son of David?
For David himself said in the Holy Spirit,
'The Lord said to my Lord,
"Sit at my right hand,
until I make your enemies the footstool of your feet."'
Therefore David himself calls him Lord,
so how can he be his son?"                                             12:35-37

"Beware of the scribes,
who like to walk in long robes,
and to get greetings in the marketplaces,
and the best seats in the synagogues,
and the best places at feasts:
those who devour widows' houses,
and for a pretense make long prayers.
These will receive greater condemnation."                             12:38-40

"Most certainly
I tell you,
this poor widow
gave more than all those who are giving into the treasury,
for they all gave out of their abundance,
but she,
out of her poverty,
gave all that she had to live on."                                    12:43-44

**"Do you see these great buildings?**
There will not be left here one stone on another,
which will not be thrown down."                                                13:2

"Be careful
that no one leads you astray.
For many will come
in my name,
saying,
'I am he!'
and will lead many astray."                                                    13:5-6

"When you hear of wars and rumors of wars,
don't be troubled.
For those must happen,
but the end is not yet.
For nation will rise against nation,
and kingdom against kingdom.
There will be earthquakes in various places.
There will be famines and troubles.
These things are the beginning of birth pains.
But watch yourselves,
for they will deliver you up to councils.
You will be beaten in synagogues.
You will stand before rulers and kings
for my sake,
for a testimony to them.
The Good News must first be preached to all the nations.
When they lead you away and deliver you up,
don't be anxious beforehand,
or premeditate what you will say,
but say whatever will be given you in that hour.
For it is not you who speak,
but the Holy Spirit."                                                          13:7-11

"Brother will deliver up brother to death,
and the father his child.
Children will rise up against parents,
and cause them to be put to death.

You will be hated by all men for my name's sake,
but he who endures to the end, the same will be saved.
But when you see the abomination of desolation,
spoken of by Daniel the prophet,
standing where it ought not
(let the reader understand),
then let those who are in Judea flee to the mountains,
and let him who is on the housetop not go down,
nor enter in, to take anything out of his house.
Let him who is in the field not return back to take his cloak.
But woe to those who are with child
and to those who nurse babies in those days!
Pray
that your flight won't be in the winter.
For in those days there will be oppression,
such as there has not been the like from the beginning
of the creation which God created
until now,
and never will be.
Unless the Lord had shortened the days,
no flesh would have been saved;
but for the sake of the chosen ones, whom he picked out,
he shortened the days.
Then if anyone tells you,
'Look,
here is the Christ!'
or,
'Look,
there!'
don't
believe it.
For there will arise false christs and false prophets,
and will show signs and wonders,
that they may lead astray,
if possible,
even the chosen ones.
But you watch."

"Behold, I have told you all things beforehand.
But in those days, after that oppression,
the sun will be darkened, the moon will not give its light,

the stars will be falling from the sky,
and the powers that are in the heavens will be shaken.
Then they will see the Son of Man coming in clouds
with great power and glory.
Then he will send out his angels,
and will gather together his chosen ones
from the four winds, from the ends of the earth
to the ends of the sky."                                                    13:23-27


"Now from the fig tree, learn this parable.
When the branch has now become tender, and puts forth its leaves,
you know that the summer is near;
even so you also, when you see these things coming to pass,
know that it is near, at the doors.
Most certainly
I say to you,
this generation will not pass away
until all these things happen.
Heaven and earth will pass away,
but my words will not pass away.
But of that day or that hour no one knows,
not even the angels in heaven,
nor the Son,
but only the Father.
Watch,
keep alert, and
pray;
for you don't know when the time is."                                       13:28-33


"It is like a man, traveling to another country,
having left his house, and given authority to his servants,
and to each one his work,
and also commanded the doorkeeper to keep watch.
Watch therefore,
for you don't know
when the lord of the house is coming,
whether at evening, or at midnight,
or when the rooster crows, or in the morning;
lest coming suddenly he might find you sleeping.
What I tell you,
I tell all:
Watch."                                                                     13:34-37

---
---

**"Leave her alone.**
Why do you trouble her?
She has done a good work for me.
For you always have the poor with you,
and whenever you want to, you can do them good;
but you will not always have me.
She has done what she could.
She has anointed my body beforehand for the burying.
Most certainly
I tell you,
wherever this Good News may be preached
throughout the whole world,
that which this woman has done
will also be spoken of for a memorial of her."                     14:6-9

"Go into the city,
and there you will meet a man carrying a pitcher of water.
Follow him, and wherever he enters in, tell the master of the house,
'The Teacher says,
"Where is the guest room,
where I may eat the Passover with my disciples?"'
He will himself show you a large upper room furnished and ready.
Get ready for us there."                                           14:13-15

"Most certainly
I tell you,
one of you will betray me—
he who eats with me."                                               14:18

"It is one of the twelve,
he who dips with me in the dish.
For the Son of Man goes, even as it is written about him,
but woe to that man by whom the Son of Man is betrayed!
It would be better for that man if he had not been born."          14:20-21

"Take, eat. This is my body."                                      14:22

"This is my blood of the new covenant,
which is poured out for many.

Most certainly
I tell you,
I will no more drink of the fruit of the vine,
until that day when I drink it anew in the Kingdom of God."                    14:24-25

"All of you will be made to stumble because of me tonight,
for it is written,
'I will strike the shepherd,
and the sheep will be scattered.'
However, after I am raised up,
I will go before you into Galilee."                                            14:27-28

"Most certainly
I tell you,
that you today, even this night,
before the rooster crows twice,
you will deny me three times."                                                 14:30

"Sit here, while I pray."                                                       14:32

"My soul is exceedingly sorrowful,
even to death.
Stay here, and watch."                                                         14:34

"Abba, Father,
all things are possible to you.
Please remove this cup from me.
However, not what I desire,
but what you desire."                                                          14:36

"Simon,
are you sleeping?
Couldn't you watch one hour?
Watch
and pray,
that you may not enter into temptation.
The spirit indeed is willing,
but the flesh is weak."                                                        14:37-38

"Sleep on now, and take your rest.
It is enough.

The hour has come.
Behold,
the Son of Man is betrayed
into the hands of sinners.
Arise,
let us be going.
Behold,
he who betrays me is at hand." 14:41-42

"Have you come out, as against a robber,
with swords and clubs to seize me?
I was daily with you
in the temple teaching, and you didn't arrest me.
But this is so that the Scriptures might be fulfilled." 14:48-49

"I am.
You will see the Son of Man
sitting at the right hand of Power,
and coming with the clouds of the sky." 14:62

"Before the rooster crows twice,
you will deny me
three times." 14:72

---

MARK 15

---

**"So you say."** 15:2

"Eloi,
Eloi,
lama sabachthani?"…
"My God,
my God,
why have you forsaken me?" 15:34

---

---

**"Go into all the world,**
and preach the Good News to the whole creation.
He who believes and is baptized will be saved;
but he who disbelieves will be condemned.
These signs will accompany those who believe:
in my name they will cast out demons;
they will speak with new languages;
they will take up serpents;
and if they drink any deadly thing,
it will in no way hurt them;
they will lay hands on the sick,
and they will recover."                                                16:15-18

# THE GOOD NEWS ACCORDING TO *Luke*

## CHAPTER 2

**"Why were you looking for me?**
Didn't you know that
I must be in my Father's house?"                                              2:49

---

---

**"It is written,**
'Man shall not live by bread alone,
but by every word of God.'"                                                    4:4

"Get behind me Satan!
For it is written,
'You shall worship the Lord your God,
and you shall serve him only.'"                                                4:8

"It has been said,
'You shall not tempt the Lord your God.'"                                      4:12

"The Spirit of the Lord is on me,
because he has anointed me
to preach good news to the poor.
He has sent me to heal the brokenhearted,
to proclaim release to the captives,
recovering of sight to the blind,
to deliver those who are crushed,
and to proclaim the acceptable year of the Lord."                              4:18-19

"Today, this Scripture has been fulfilled in your hearing."                    4:21

"Doubtless you will tell me this parable,
'Physician, heal yourself!
Whatever we have heard done at Capernaum,
do also here in your hometown.'"                                               4:23

"Most certainly
I tell you,
no prophet is acceptable in his hometown.

But truly
I tell you,
there were many widows in Israel in the days of Elijah,
when the sky was shut up three years and six months,
when a great famine came over all the land.
Elijah was sent to none of them,
except to Zarephath, in the land of Sidon,
to a woman who was a widow.
There were many lepers in Israel
in the time of Elisha the prophet,
yet not one of them was cleansed,
except Naaman, the Syrian."

4:24-27

"Be silent,
and come out of him!"

4:35

"I must preach the good news of the Kingdom of God
to the other cities also.
For this reason I have been sent."

4:43

---

LUKE 5

---

**"Put out into the deep,**
and let down your nets for a catch."

5:4

"Don't be afraid.
From now on you will be catching people alive."

5:10

"I want to.
Be made clean."

5:13

"But go your way,
and show yourself to the priest,
and offer for your cleansing according to what Moses commanded,
for a testimony to them."

5:14

"Man,
your sins are forgiven you."

5:20

"Why are you reasoning so in your hearts?
Which is easier to say,
'Your sins are forgiven you;'
or to say, 'Arise and walk?'
But that you may know that
the Son of Man
has authority on earth
to forgive sins"...
"I tell you,
arise,
and take up your cot,
and go to your house."                                        5:22-24

"Follow me!"                                                   5:27

"Those who are healthy have no need for a physician,
but those who are sick do.
I have not come to call the righteous,
but sinners to repentance."                                   5:31-32

"Can you make the friends of the bridegroom fast,
while the bridegroom is with them?
But the days will come
when the bridegroom will be taken away from them.
Then they will fast in those days."                           5:34-35

"No one puts a piece from a new garment
on an old garment,
or else he will tear the new,
and also the piece from the new will not match the old.
No one puts new wine into old wineskins,
or else the new wine will burst the skins,
and it will be spilled, and the skins will be destroyed.
But new wine must be put into fresh wineskins,
and both are preserved.
No man having drunk old wine immediately desires new,
for he says, 'The old is better.'"                            5:36-39

**"Haven't you read what David did**
when he was hungry, he, and those who were with him;
how he entered into God's house,
and took and ate the show bread,
and gave also to those who were with him,
which is not lawful to eat except for the priests alone?"…
"The Son of Man is lord of the Sabbath."                                6:3-4,5

"Rise up, and stand in the middle."                                     6:8

"I will ask you something: Is it lawful on the Sabbath
to do good, or to do harm?
To save a life, or to kill?"                                            6:9

"Stretch out your hand."                                                6:10

"Blessed are you who are poor,
for yours is the Kingdom of God.
Blessed are you who hunger now,
for you will be filled.
Blessed are you who weep now,
for you will laugh.
Blessed are you when men shall hate you,
and when they shall exclude and mock you,
and throw out your name as evil,
for the Son of Man's sake.
Rejoice in that day, and leap for joy,
for behold,
your reward is great in heaven,
for their fathers did the same thing to the prophets.
"But woe to you who are rich!
For you have received your consolation.
Woe to you, you who are full now,
for you will be hungry.
Woe to you who laugh now,
for you will mourn and weep.
Woe when men speak well of you,
for their fathers did the same thing to the false prophets."            6:20-26

"But I tell you who hear:
love your enemies,
do good to those who hate you,
bless those who curse you,
and pray for those who mistreat you.
To him who strikes you on the cheek,
offer also the other;
and from him who takes away your cloak,
don't withhold your coat also.
Give to everyone who asks you,
and don't ask him who takes away your goods
to give them back again."                                              6:27-30

"As you would like people to do to you, do exactly so to them.
If you love those who love you,
what credit is that to you?
For even sinners love those who love them.
If you do good to those who do good to you,
what credit is that to you?
For even sinners do the same.
If you lend to those from whom you hope to receive,
what credit is that to you?
Even sinners lend to sinners, to receive back as much.
But love your enemies,
and do good, and lend,
expecting nothing back;
and your reward will be great,
and you will be children of the Most High;
for he is kind toward the unthankful and evil."                        6:31-35

"Therefore be merciful,
even as your Father is also merciful.
Don't judge,
and you won't be judged.
Don't condemn,
and you won't be condemned.
Set free,
and you will be set free."                                             6:36-37

"Give,
and it will be given to you:

good measure,
pressed down,
shaken together,
and running over,
will be given to you.
For with the same measure you measure
it will be measured back to you."                                                6:38

"Can the blind guide the blind?
Won't they both fall into a pit?
A disciple is not above his teacher,
but everyone when he is fully trained will be like his teacher.
Why do you see the speck of chaff that is in your brother's eye,
but don't consider the beam that is in your own eye?
Or how can you tell your brother,
'Brother, let me remove the speck of chaff that is in your eye,'
when you yourself don't see the beam that is in your own eye?
You hypocrite!
First remove the beam from your own eye,
and then you can see clearly
to remove the speck of chaff that is in your brother's eye.
For there is no good tree that brings forth rotten fruit;
nor again a rotten tree that brings forth good fruit.
For each tree is known by its own fruit.
For people don't gather figs from thorns,
nor do they gather grapes from a bramble bush.
The good man out of the good treasure of his heart
brings out that which is good,
and the evil man out of the evil treasure of his heart
brings out that which is evil,
for out of the abundance of the heart,
his mouth speaks."                                                               6:39-45

"Why do you call me, 'Lord, Lord,' and don't do the things which I say?
Everyone who comes to me, and hears my words, and does them,
I will show you who he is like.
He is like a man building a house, who dug and went deep,
and laid a foundation on the rock.
When a flood arose, the stream broke against that house,
and could not shake it, because it was founded on the rock.
But he who hears, and doesn't do,

is like a man who built a house on the earth without a foundation,
against which the stream broke,
and immediately it fell, and the ruin of that house was great."

6:46-49

---

---

**"I tell you,**
I have not found such great faith, no, not in Israel."

7:9

"Don't cry."

7:13

"Young man,
I tell you,
arise!"

7:14

"Go
and tell John
the things
which you have seen and heard:
that the blind receive their sight,
the lame walk,
the lepers are cleansed,
the deaf hear,
the dead are raised up,
and the poor have good news preached to them.
Blessed is he
who finds no occasion for stumbling
in me."

7:22-23

"What did you go out into the wilderness to see?
A reed shaken by the wind?
But what did you go out to see?
A man clothed in soft clothing?
Behold, those who are gorgeously dressed,
and live delicately, are in kings' courts.
But what did you go out to see?
A prophet?
Yes, I tell you,
and much more than a prophet.
This is he of whom it is written,
'Behold, I send my messenger before your face,

who will prepare your way before you.'
For I tell you,
among those who are born of women
there is not a greater prophet than John the Baptizer,
yet he who is least in the Kingdom of God
is greater than he."                                                                7:24-28

"To what then will I liken the people of this generation?
What are they like?
They are like children
who sit in the marketplace,
and call one to another, saying,
'We piped to you,
and you didn't dance.
We mourned,
and you didn't weep.'
For John the Baptizer came
neither eating bread nor drinking wine,
and you say, 'He has a demon.'
The Son of Man has come
eating and drinking,
and you say,
'Behold, a gluttonous man, and a drunkard;
a friend of tax collectors and sinners!'
Wisdom is justified by all her children."                                           7:31-35

"Simon,
I have something to tell you."                                                      7:40

"A certain lender had two debtors.
The one owed five hundred denarii,
and the other fifty.
When they couldn't pay,
he forgave them both.
Which of them therefore will love him most?"                                        7:41-42

"You have judged correctly."                                                         7:43

"Do you see this woman?
I entered into your house,

and you gave me no water for my feet,
but she has wet my feet with her tears,
and wiped them with the hair of her head.
You gave me no kiss,
but she,
since the time I came in, has not ceased to kiss my feet.
You didn't anoint my head with oil,
but she has anointed my feet with ointment.
Therefore I tell you,
her sins, which are many, are forgiven,
for she loved much.
But to whom little is forgiven,
the same loves little."                                      7:44-47

"Your sins are forgiven."                                    7:48

"Your faith has saved you.
Go in peace."                                                7:50

------------------------------------------------------------------
LUKE 8
------------------------------------------------------------------

**"The farmer went out to sow his seed.**
As he sowed, some fell along the road,
and it was trampled under foot,
and the birds of the sky devoured it.
Other seed fell on the rock,
and as soon as it grew,
it withered away,
because it had no moisture.
Other fell amid the thorns,
and the thorns grew with it,
and choked it.
Other fell into the good ground,
and grew, and brought forth fruit
one hundred times...
He who has ears to hear, let him hear!"                      8:5-8

"To you it is given
to know the mysteries
of the Kingdom of God,
but to the rest in parables;

that 'seeing
they may not see,
and hearing
they may not understand.'
Now the parable is this:
The seed is the word of God.
Those along the road
are those who hear,
then the devil comes,
and takes away the word from their heart,
that they may not believe and be saved.
Those on the rock
are they who,
when they hear,
receive the word with joy;
but these have no root,
who believe for a while,
then fall away in time of temptation.
That which fell among the thorns,
these are those who have heard,
and as they go on their way
they are choked with cares, riches, and pleasures of life,
bring no fruit to maturity.
That in the good ground,
these are such as in an honest and good heart,
having heard the word,
hold it tightly,
and bring forth fruit with patience."                           8:10-15


"No one, when he has lit a lamp,
covers it with a container,
or puts it under a bed;
but puts it on a stand,
that those who enter in may see the light.
For nothing is hidden, that will not be revealed;
nor anything secret, that will not be known and come to light.
Be careful therefore how you hear.
For whoever has, to him will be given;
and whoever doesn't have, from him will be taken away
even that which he thinks he has."                              8:16-18

"My mother and my brothers
are these
who hear the word of God,
and do it."                                     8:21

"Let's go over to the other side
of the lake."                                   8:22

"Where is your faith?"                          8:25

"What is your name?"                            8:30

"Return to your house,
and declare what great things God has done for you."     8:39

"Who touched me?"…
"'Who touched me?'"                             8:45

"Someone did touch me,
for I perceived that power has gone out of me."          8:46

"Daughter,
cheer up.
Your faith has made you well.
Go in peace."                                   8:48

"Don't be afraid.
Only believe,
and she will be healed."                        8:50

"Don't weep.
She isn't dead,
but sleeping."                                  8:52

"Child,
arise!"                                         8:54

**"Take nothing for your journey —**
neither staffs, nor wallet, nor bread, nor money;
neither have two coats apiece.
Into whatever house you enter,
stay there, and depart from there.
As many as don't receive you,
when you depart from that city,
shake off even the dust from your feet
for a testimony against them."                                    9:3-5

"You give them something to eat."                                 9:13

"Make them sit down in groups of about fifty each."              9:14

"Who do the multitudes say that I am?"                            9:18

"But who do you say that I am?"                                   9:20

"The Son of Man
must suffer many things, and
be rejected by the elders, chief priests, and scribes, and
be killed,
and the third day
be raised up."                                                    9:22

"If anyone desires to come after me,
let him deny himself,
take up his cross,
and follow me.
For whoever
desires to save his life
will lose it,
but whoever will lose his life
for my sake,
the same will save it.
For what does it profit a man
if he gains the whole world,
and loses or forfeits his own self?
For whoever will be ashamed of me
and of my words,

of him will the Son of Man be ashamed,
when he comes in his glory,
and the glory of the Father,
and of the holy angels.
But I tell you the truth:
There are some of those who stand here,
who will in no way taste of death,
until they see the Kingdom of God."                                          9:23-27

"Faithless and perverse generation,
how long shall I be with you and bear with you?
Bring your son here."                                                              9:41

"Let these words
sink into your ears,
for the Son of Man
will be delivered up into the hands of men."                                 9:44

"Whoever receives this little child in my name
receives me.
Whoever receives me
receives him who sent me.
For whoever is least among you all,
this one will be great."                                                           9:48

"Don't forbid him,
for he who is not against us
is for us."                                                                          9:50

"You don't know of what kind of spirit you are.
For the Son of Man didn't come to destroy men's lives,
but to save them."                                                              9:55-56

"The foxes have holes,
and the birds of the sky have nests,
but the Son of Man
has no place to lay his head."                                                    9:58

"Follow me!"                                                                          9:59

"Leave the dead to bury their own dead,

but you go
and announce the Kingdom of God."                                                            9:60

"No one,
having put his hand to the plow,
and looking back,
is fit for the Kingdom of God."                                                              9:62

---

---

## "The harvest is indeed plentiful,
but the laborers are few.
Pray therefore to the Lord of the harvest,
that he may send out laborers into his harvest.
Go your ways.
Behold,
I send you out as lambs among wolves.
Carry no purse, nor wallet, nor sandals.
Greet no one on the way.
Into whatever house you enter,
first say, 'Peace be to this house.'
If a son of peace is there,
your peace will rest on him;
but if not, it will return to you.
Remain in that same house,
eating and drinking the things they give,
for the laborer is worthy of his wages.
Don't go from house to house.
Into whatever city you enter, and they receive you,
eat the things that are set before you.
Heal the sick who are therein,
and tell them, 'The Kingdom of God has come near to you.'
But into whatever city you enter, and they don't receive you,
go out into its streets and say,
'Even the dust from your city that clings to us,
we wipe off against you.
Nevertheless know this,
that the Kingdom of God
has come near to you.'
I tell you,
it will be more tolerable in that day for Sodom
than for that city."                                                                        10:2-12

"Woe to you, Chorazin!
Woe to you, Bethsaida!
For if the mighty works had been done in Tyre and Sidon
which were done in you,
they would have repented long ago,
sitting in sackcloth and ashes.
But it will be more tolerable for Tyre and Sidon
in the judgment than for you.
You, Capernaum,
who are exalted to heaven,
will be brought down to Hades.
Whoever listens to you
listens to me,
and whoever rejects you
rejects me.
Whoever rejects me
rejects him who sent me."                                                      10:13-16

"I saw Satan having fallen like lightning from heaven.
Behold,
I give you authority
to tread on serpents and scorpions,
and over all the power of the enemy.
Nothing will in any way hurt you.
Nevertheless,
don't rejoice in this,
that the spirits are subject to you,
but rejoice that your names are written in heaven."                          10:18-20

"I thank you, O Father,
Lord of heaven and earth,
that you have hidden these things
from the wise and understanding,
and revealed them to little children.
Yes,
Father,
for so it was well-pleasing in your sight."                                    10:21

"All things
have been delivered to me by my Father.
No one knows who the Son is,

except the Father,
and who the Father is,
except the Son,
and he
to whomever the Son desires to reveal him."                    10:22

"Blessed are the eyes which see
the things that you see,
for I tell you
that many prophets and kings
desired to see the things which you see,
and didn't see them,
and to hear the things which you hear,
and didn't hear them."                                          10:23-24

"What is written in the law?
How do you read it?"                                            10:26

"You have answered correctly.
Do this,
and you will live."                                             10:28

"A certain man was going down from Jerusalem to Jericho,
and he fell among robbers,
who both stripped him and beat him,
and departed,
leaving him half dead.
By chance a certain priest was going down that way.
When he saw him,
he passed by on the other side.
In the same way a Levite also, when he came to the place,
and saw him,
passed by on the other side.
But a certain Samaritan, as he traveled, came where he was.
When he saw him,
he was moved with compassion,
came to him,
and bound up his wounds,
pouring on oil and wine.
He set him on his own animal,
and brought him to an inn,
and took care of him.

On the next day, when he departed,
he took out two denarii, and gave them to the host,
and said to him, 'Take care of him.
Whatever you spend beyond that,
I will repay you when I return.'
Now which of these three do you think
seemed to be a neighbor to him
who fell among the robbers?"                                                      10:30-36

"Go and do likewise."                                                                   10:37

"Martha,
Martha,
you are anxious and troubled
about many things,
but one thing is needed.
Mary has chosen the good part,
which will not be taken away from her."                                        10:41-42

---

---

**"When you pray, say,**
'Our Father in heaven,
may your name be kept holy.
May your Kingdom come.
May your will be done on earth,
as it is in heaven.
Give us day by day our daily bread.
Forgive us our sins,
for we ourselves also forgive everyone who is indebted to us.
Bring us not into temptation,
but deliver us from the evil one.'"                                               11:2-4

"Which of you, if you go to a friend
at midnight, and tell him,
'Friend, lend me three loaves of bread,
for a friend of mine has come to me from a journey,
and I have nothing to set before him,'
and he from within will answer and say,
'Don't bother me.
The door is now shut,

and my children are with me in bed.
I can't get up and give it to you'?
I tell you,
although he will not rise and give it to him
because he is his friend,
yet because of his persistence,
he will get up
and give him
as many as he needs."                                                    11:5-8

"I tell you,
keep asking, and it will be given you.
Keep seeking, and you will find.
Keep knocking, and it will be opened to you.
For everyone who asks receives.
He who seeks finds.
To him who knocks it will be opened."                                    11:9-10

"Which of you fathers,
if your son asks for bread,
will give him a stone?
Or if he asks for a fish,
he won't give him a snake instead of a fish, will he?
Or if he asks for an egg,
he won't give him a scorpion, will he?
If you then, being evil,
know how to give good gifts to your children,
how much more will your heavenly Father
give the Holy Spirit to those who ask him?"                              11:11-13

"Every kingdom divided against itself is
brought to desolation.
A house divided against itself
falls.
If Satan also is divided against himself,
how will his kingdom stand?
For you say that I cast out demons by Beelzebul.
But if I cast out demons by Beelzebul,
by whom do your children cast them out?
Therefore will they be your judges.
But if I by the finger of God cast out demons,
then the Kingdom of God has come to you."                                11:17-20

"When the strong man,
fully armed,
guards his own dwelling, his goods are safe.
But when someone stronger attacks him and overcomes him,
he takes from him his whole armor
in which he trusted,
and divides his spoils."                                              11:21-22

"He that is not with me is against me.
He who doesn't gather with me scatters.
The unclean spirit, when he has gone out of the man,
passes through dry places, seeking rest, and finding none,
he says, 'I will turn back to my house from which I came out.'
When he returns,
he finds it swept and put in order.
Then he goes, and takes seven other spirits
more evil than himself,
and they enter in and dwell there.
The last state of that man
becomes worse than the first."                                        11:23-26

"On the contrary,
blessed are those
who hear the word of God,
and keep it."                                                         11:28

"This is an evil generation.
It seeks after a sign.
No sign will be given to it
but the sign of Jonah, the prophet.
For even as Jonah became a sign to the Ninevites,
so will also
the Son of Man be
to this generation.
The Queen of the South
will rise up in the judgment
with the men of this generation,
and will condemn them:
for she came from the ends of the earth
to hear the wisdom of Solomon;
and behold,

one greater
than Solomon is here.
The men of Nineveh will stand up in the judgment with this generation,
and will condemn it:
for they repented at the preaching of Jonah,
and behold,
one greater
than Jonah is here."                                          11:29-32

"No one, when he has lit a lamp,
puts it in a cellar or under a basket,
but on a stand,
that those who come in may see the light.
The lamp of the body is the eye.
Therefore when your eye is good,
your whole body is also full of light;
but when it is evil,
your body also is full of darkness.
Therefore see
whether the light that is in you isn't darkness.
If therefore your whole body is full of light,
having no part dark,
it will be wholly full of light,
as when the lamp with its bright shining gives you light."    11:33-36

"Now you Pharisees cleanse the outside of the cup and of the platter,
but your inward part is full of extortion and wickedness.
You foolish ones,
didn't he who made the outside make the inside also?
But give for gifts to the needy those things which are within,
and behold, all things will be clean to you.
But woe to you Pharisees!
For you tithe mint and rue and every herb,
but you bypass justice and the love of God.
You ought to have done these,
and not to have left the other undone.
Woe to you Pharisees!
For you love the best seats in the synagogues,
and the greetings in the marketplaces.
Woe to you, scribes and Pharisees, hypocrites!
For you are like hidden graves,
and the men who walk over them don't know it."               11:37-44

"Woe to you lawyers also!
For you load men with burdens
that are difficult to carry,
and you yourselves won't even lift one finger
to help carry those burdens.
Woe to you!
For you build the tombs of the prophets,
and your fathers killed them.
So you testify and consent to the works of your fathers.
For they killed them, and you build their tombs.
Therefore also the wisdom of God said,
'I will send to them prophets and apostles;
and some of them they will kill and persecute,
that the blood of all the prophets,
which was shed from the foundation of the world,
may be required of this generation;
from the blood of Abel to the blood of Zachariah,
who perished between the altar and the sanctuary.'
Yes, I tell you, it will be required of this generation.
Woe to you lawyers!
For you took away the key of knowledge.
You didn't enter in yourselves,
and those who were entering in, you hindered."                    11:46-52

- - - - - - - - - - - - - - - - - - - - - - - - - - - - - - - - - - - - - - - - - - - - - - - - - - - - - - - -

LUKE 12

- - - - - - - - - - - - - - - - - - - - - - - - - - - - - - - - - - - - - - - - - - - - - - - - - - - - - - - -

**"Beware of the yeast of the Pharisees,**
which is hypocrisy.
But there is nothing covered up,
that will not be revealed,
nor hidden,
that will not be known.
Therefore whatever you have said in the darkness
will be heard in the light.
What you have spoken in the ear in the inner rooms
will be proclaimed on the housetops."                             12:1-3

"I tell you,
my friends,
don't be afraid
of those who kill the body,

and after that have no more that they can do.
But I will warn you whom you should fear.
Fear him, ·
who after he has killed,
has power to cast into Gehenna.
Yes,
I tell you,
fear him."                                                                        12:4-5

"Aren't five sparrows sold for two assaria coins?
Not one of them is forgotten by God.
But the very hairs of your head are all numbered.
Therefore don't be afraid.
You are of more value than many sparrows."                              12:6-7

"I tell you,
everyone who confesses me before men,
him will the Son of Man
also confess
before the angels of God;
but he who denies me in the presence of men
will be denied
in the presence of the angels of God.
Everyone who speaks a word
against the Son of Man
will be forgiven,
but those who blaspheme against the Holy Spirit
will not be forgiven.
When they bring you
before the synagogues, the rulers, and the authorities,
don't be anxious
how or what you will answer,
or what you will say;
for the Holy Spirit will teach you
in that same hour
what you must say."                                                             12:8-12

"Man, who made me a judge or an arbitrator over you?"                12:14

"Beware!
Keep yourselves from covetousness,

for a man's life
doesn't consist
of the abundance of the things which he possesses." 12:15

"The ground of a certain rich man brought forth abundantly.
He reasoned within himself, saying,
'What will I do,
because I don't have room to store my crops?'
He said,
'This is what I will do.
I will pull down my barns,
and build bigger ones,
and there I will store all my grain and my goods.
I will tell my soul,
"Soul, you have many goods laid up for many years.
Take your ease,
eat, drink, be merry."'" 12:16-19

"But God said to him,
'You foolish one,
tonight
your soul is required of you.
The things which you have prepared—
whose will they be?'
So is he who lays up treasure for himself,
and is not rich toward God." 12:20-21

"Therefore I tell you,
don't be anxious for your life,
what you will eat,
nor yet for your body,
what you will wear.
Life is more than food,
and the body is more than clothing.
Consider the ravens:
they don't sow, they don't reap,
they have no warehouse or barn,
and God feeds them.
How much more valuable are you than birds!
Which of you
by being anxious

can add a cubit to his height?
If then you aren't able to do
even the least things,
why are you anxious about the rest?
Consider the lilies, how they grow.
They don't toil, neither do they spin;
yet I tell you,
even Solomon in all his glory was not arrayed like one of these.
But if this is how God clothes the grass in the field,
which today exists,
and tomorrow is cast into the oven,
how much more will he clothe you,
O you of little faith?
Don't seek
what you will eat or what you will drink;
neither be anxious.
For the nations of the world seek after all of these things,
but your Father knows
that you need these things.
But seek God's Kingdom,
and all these things
will be added to you.
Don't be afraid,
little flock,
for it is your Father's good pleasure to give you the Kingdom.
Sell that which you have,
and give gifts to the needy.
Make for yourselves purses which don't grow old,
a treasure in the heavens that doesn't fail,
where no thief approaches,
neither moth destroys.
For where your treasure is,
there will your heart be also."                                    12:22-34

"Let your waist be dressed
and your lamps burning.
Be like men watching for their lord,
when he returns from the marriage feast;
that, when he comes and knocks,
they may immediately open to him.
Blessed are those servants,

whom the lord will find watching when he comes.
Most certainly
I tell you,
that he will dress himself,
and make them recline,
and will come and serve them.
They will be blessed
if he comes in the second or third watch,
and finds them so.
But know this,
that if the master of the house had known
in what hour the thief was coming,
he would have watched,
and not allowed his house to be broken into.
Therefore be ready also,
for the Son of Man
is coming
in an hour that you don't expect him."                        12:35-40

"Who then is the faithful and wise steward,
whom his lord will set over his household,
to give them their portion of food at the right times?
Blessed is that servant
whom his lord will find doing so when he comes.
Truly I tell you,
that he will set him over all that he has.
But if that servant says in his heart,
'My lord delays his coming,'
and begins to beat the menservants and the maidservants,
and to eat and drink, and to be drunken,
then the lord of that servant will come in a day
when he isn't expecting him, and in an hour that he doesn't know,
and will cut him in two,
and place his portion with the unfaithful.
That servant, who knew his lord's will,
and didn't prepare,
nor do what he wanted,
will be beaten with many stripes,
but he who didn't know,
and did things worthy of stripes,
will be beaten with few stripes.

To whomever much is given,
of him will much be required;
and to whom much was entrusted,
of him more will be asked."                          12:42-48

"I came to throw fire on the earth.
I wish it were already kindled.
But I have a baptism to be baptized with,
and how distressed I am until it is accomplished!
Do you think that I have come to give peace in the earth?
I tell you, no,
but rather division.
For from now on,
there will be five in one house divided,
three against two,
and two against three.
They will be divided,
father against son,
and son against father;
mother against daughter,
and daughter against her mother;
mother-in-law against her daughter-in-law,
and daughter-in-law against her mother-in-law."      12:49-53

"When you see a cloud rising from the west,
immediately you say, 'A shower is coming,' and so it happens.
When a south wind blows, you say, 'There will be a scorching heat,'
and it happens.
You hypocrites!
You know how to interpret
the appearance of the earth and the sky,
but how is it that you don't interpret this time?
Why don't you judge for yourselves what is right?
For when you are going with your adversary before the magistrate,
try diligently
on the way to be released from him,
lest perhaps he drag you to the judge,
and the judge deliver you to the officer,
and the officer throw you into prison.
I tell you,
you will by no means get out of there,
until you have paid the very last penny."            12:54-59

**"Do you think that these Galileans were worse sinners**
than all the other Galileans, because they suffered such things?
I tell you, no,
but unless you repent,
you will all perish in the same way.
Or those eighteen,
on whom the tower in Siloam fell,
and killed them;
do you think that they were worse offenders
than all the men who dwell in Jerusalem?
I tell you, no,
but, unless you repent, you will all perish in the same way."                    13:2-5

"A certain man had a fig tree planted in his vineyard,
and he came seeking fruit on it,
and found none.
He said to the vine dresser,
'Behold, these three years
I have come looking for fruit on this fig tree,
and found none.
Cut it down.
Why does it waste the soil?'
He answered, 'Lord, leave it alone this year also,
until I dig around it, and fertilize it.
If it bears fruit, fine;
but if not, after that, you can cut it down.'"                    13:6-9

"Woman, you are freed from your infirmity."                    13:12

"You hypocrites!
Doesn't each one of you free his ox or his donkey from the stall
on the Sabbath,
and lead him away to water?
Ought not this woman,
being a daughter of Abraham,
whom Satan had bound eighteen long years,
be freed
from this bondage on the Sabbath day?"                    13:15-16

"What is the Kingdom of God like?
To what shall I compare it?
It is like a grain of mustard seed,
which a man took, and put in his own garden.
It grew, and became a large tree,
and the birds of the sky lodged in its branches."

13:18-19

"To what shall I compare the Kingdom of God?
It is like yeast,
which a woman took and hid in three measures of flour,
until it was all leavened."

13:20-21

"Strive to enter in by the narrow door,
for many,
I tell you,
will seek to enter in,
and will not be able.
When once the master of the house has risen up, and has shut the door,
and you begin to stand outside, and to knock at the door, saying,
'Lord, Lord, open to us!'
then he will answer and tell you,
'I don't know you or where you come from.'
Then you will begin to say,
'We ate and drank in your presence,
and you taught in our streets.'
He will say, 'I tell you,
I don't know where you come from.
Depart from me, all you workers of iniquity.'
There will be weeping and gnashing of teeth,
when you see Abraham, Isaac, Jacob,
and all the prophets, in the Kingdom of God,
and yourselves being thrown outside.
They will come from the east, west, north, and south,
and will sit down in the Kingdom of God.
Behold,
there are some who are last
who will be first,
and there are some who are first
who will be last."

13:24-30

"Go and tell that fox,
'Behold,
I cast out demons
and perform cures today
and tomorrow,
and the third day
I complete my mission.
Nevertheless
I must go on my way
today
and tomorrow
and the next day,
for it can't be that a prophet perish outside of Jerusalem.'"                    13:32-33

"Jerusalem, Jerusalem,
that kills the prophets, and stones those who are sent to her!
How often
I wanted
to gather your children together,
like a hen gathers her own brood under her wings,
and you refused!
Behold,
your house is left to you desolate.
I tell you,
you will not see me,
until you say,
'Blessed is he who comes in the name of the Lord!'"                             13:34-35

LUKE 14

## "Is it lawful to heal on the Sabbath?"                                         14:3

"Which of you, if your son or an ox fell into a well,
wouldn't immediately pull him out
on a Sabbath day?"                                                               14:5

"When you are invited by anyone to a marriage feast,
don't sit in the best seat,
since perhaps someone more honorable than you
might be invited by him,
and he who invited both of you would come and tell you,

'Make room for this person.'
Then you would begin, with shame, to take the lowest place.
But when you are invited,
go and sit in the lowest place,
so that when he who invited you comes, he may tell you,
'Friend, move up higher.'
Then you will be honored
in the presence of all who sit at the table with you.
For everyone who exalts himself
will be humbled,
and whoever humbles himself
will be exalted."                                                    14:8-11

"When you make a dinner or a supper,
don't call your friends,
nor your brothers, nor your kinsmen, nor rich neighbors,
or perhaps they might also return the favor, and pay you back.
But when you make a feast,
ask the poor, the maimed, the lame, or the blind;
and you will be blessed,
because they don't have the resources to repay you.
For you will be repaid in the resurrection of the righteous."       14:12-14

"A certain man made a great supper,
and he invited many people.
He sent out his servant at supper time
to tell those who were invited,
'Come, for everything is ready now.'
They all as one began to make excuses.
"The first said to him,
'I have bought a field, and I must go and see it.
Please have me excused.'"                                           14:16-18

"Another said,
'I have bought five yoke of oxen,
and I must go try them out.
Please have me excused.'"                                           14:19

"Another said,
'I have married a wife, and therefore I can't come.'"               14:20

"That servant came, and told his lord these things.
Then the master of the house, being angry,
said to his servant,
'Go out quickly
into the streets and lanes of the city,
and bring in the poor, maimed, blind, and lame.'"

14:21

"The servant said,
'Lord, it is done as you commanded, and there is still room.'"

14:22

"The lord said to the servant,
'Go out into the highways and hedges,
and compel them to come in, that my house may be filled.
For I tell you
that none of those men who were invited
will taste of my supper.'"

14:23-24

"If anyone comes to me,
and doesn't disregard his own father, mother,
wife, children,
brothers, and sisters,
yes,
and his own life also,
he can't be my disciple.
Whoever doesn't bear his own cross,
and come after me,
can't be my disciple.
For which of you, desiring to build a tower,
doesn't first sit down
and count the cost,
to see if he has enough to complete it?
Or perhaps, when he has laid a foundation,
and is not able to finish,
everyone who sees begins to mock him,
saying, 'This man began to build, and wasn't able to finish.'
Or what king, as he goes to encounter another king in war,
will not sit down first
and consider
whether he is able with ten thousand
to meet him who comes against him with twenty thousand?
Or else, while the other is yet a great way off,

he sends an envoy, and asks for conditions of peace.
So therefore
whoever of you
who doesn't renounce all that he has,
he can't be my disciple.
Salt is good,
but if the salt becomes flat and tasteless, with what do you season it?
It is fit neither for the soil nor for the manure pile.
It is thrown out.
He who has ears to hear, let him hear."                                14:26-35

---

## LUKE 15

---

**"Which of you men, if you had one hundred sheep,**
and lost one of them,
wouldn't leave the ninety-nine
in the wilderness,
and go after the one that was lost,
until he found it?
When he has found it,
he carries it on his shoulders, rejoicing.
When he comes home, he calls together his friends and his neighbors,
saying to them,
'Rejoice with me,
for I have found my sheep which was lost!'
I tell you
that even so
there will be more joy in heaven
over one sinner
who repents,
than over ninety-nine righteous people
who need no repentance.
Or what woman, if she had ten drachma coins,
if she lost one drachma coin,
wouldn't light a lamp,
sweep the house,
and seek diligently
until she found it?
When she has found it,
she calls together her friends and neighbors, saying,
'Rejoice with me,

for I have found the drachma which I had lost.'
Even so,
I tell you,
there is joy in the presence of the angels of God
over one sinner repenting."                                                    15:4-10

"A certain man had two sons.
The younger of them said to his father,
'Father, give me my share of your property.'
He divided his livelihood between them.
Not many days after, the younger son gathered all of this together
and traveled into a far country.
There he wasted his property with riotous living.
When he had spent all of it,
there arose a severe famine in that country,
and he began to be in need.
He went and joined himself to one of the citizens of that country,
and he sent him into his fields to feed pigs.
He wanted to fill his belly
with the husks that the pigs ate,
but no one gave him any.
But when he came to himself he said,
'How many hired servants of my father's have bread enough to spare,
and I'm dying with hunger!
I will get up and go to my father, and will tell him,
"Father, I have sinned against heaven, and in your sight.
I am no more worthy to be called your son.
Make me as one of your hired servants."'"                                      15:11-19

"He arose, and came to his father.
But while he was still far off,
his father saw him, and was moved with compassion,
and ran,
and fell on his neck, and kissed him.
The son said to him,
'Father, I have sinned against heaven, and in your sight.
I am no longer worthy to be called your son.'"                                15:20-21

"But the father said to his servants,
'Bring out the best robe, and put it on him.
Put a ring on his hand, and shoes on his feet.

Bring the fattened calf, kill it,
and let us eat, and celebrate;
for this, my son, was dead,
and is alive again.
He was lost,
and is found.'
They began to celebrate."

15:22-24

"Now his elder son was in the field.
As he came near to the house, he heard music and dancing.
He called one of the servants to him, and asked what was going on.
He said to him, 'Your brother has come,
and your father has killed the fattened calf,
because he has received him back
safe and healthy.'
But he was angry, and would not go in.
Therefore his father came out, and begged him.
But he answered his father,
'Behold, these many years I have served you,
and I never disobeyed a commandment of yours,
but you never gave me a goat,
that I might celebrate with my friends.
But when this, your son, came, who has devoured your living
with prostitutes,
you killed the fattened calf for him.'"

15:25-30

"He said to him,
'Son,
you are always with me,
and all that is mine is yours.
But it was appropriate to celebrate and be glad,
for this, your brother, was dead,
and is alive again.
He was lost,
and is found.'"

15:31-32

**"There was a certain rich man who had a manager.**
An accusation was made to him that this man was wasting
his possessions.
He called him, and said to him,
'What is this that I hear about you?
Give an accounting of your management,
for you can no longer be manager.'"                                          16:1-2

"The manager said within himself,
'What will I do,
seeing that my lord is taking away the management position from me?
I don't have strength to dig. I am ashamed to beg.
I know what I will do, so that when I am removed from management,
they may receive me into their houses.'
Calling each one of his lord's debtors to him,
he said to the first, 'How much do you owe to my lord?'
He said, 'A hundred batos of oil.'
He said to him, 'Take your bill,
and sit down quickly and write fifty.'
Then he said to another, 'How much do you owe?'
He said, 'A hundred cors of wheat.'
He said to him,
'Take your bill, and write eighty.'"                                         16:3-7

"His lord commended the dishonest manager
because he had done wisely,
for the children of this world are, in their own generation,
wiser than the children of the light.
I tell you,
make for yourselves friends by means of unrighteous mammon,
so that when you fail,
they may receive you into the eternal tents.
He who is faithful in a very little
is faithful also in much.
He who is dishonest in a very little
is also dishonest in much.
If therefore you have not been faithful in the unrighteous mammon,
who will commit to your trust the true riches?
If you have not been faithful in that which is another's,

who will give you that which is your own?
No servant can serve two masters,
for either he will hate the one,
and love the other;
or else he will hold to one,
and despise the other.
You aren't able to serve God and mammon."

16:8-13

"You are those who justify yourselves in the sight of men,
but God knows your hearts.
For that which is exalted among men
is an abomination in the sight of God.
The law and the prophets were until John.
From that time the Good News of the Kingdom of God
is preached,
and everyone
is forcing
his way
into it.
But it is easier for heaven and earth to pass away,
than for
one
tiny
stroke of a pen in the law to fall.
Everyone who divorces his wife,
and marries another,
commits adultery.
He who marries one
who is divorced from a husband
commits adultery."

16:15-18

"Now there was a certain rich man,
and he was clothed in purple and fine linen,
living in luxury every day.
A certain beggar, named Lazarus, was laid at his gate,
full of sores,
and desiring to be fed with the crumbs that fell from the
rich man's table.
Yes, even the dogs came and licked his sores.
It happened that the beggar died,
and that he was carried away by the angels to Abraham's bosom.

The rich man also died, and was buried.
In Hades, he lifted up his eyes, being in torment,
and saw Abraham far off, and Lazarus at his bosom.
He cried and said,
'Father Abraham, have mercy on me,
and send Lazarus,
that he may dip the tip
of his finger
in water,
and cool my tongue!
For I am in anguish
in this flame.'"                                                                                16:19-24

"But Abraham said,
'Son, remember that you, in your lifetime, received your good things,
and Lazarus, in the same way, bad things.
But now here he is comforted and you are in anguish.
Besides all this,
between us and you
there is a great gulf fixed,
that those
who want to pass from here to you are not able,
and that none may cross over
from there to us.'"                                                                              16:25-26

"He said,
'I ask you therefore, father,
that you would send him to my father's house;
for I have five brothers,
that he may testify to them,
so they won't also come into this place of torment.'"                                            16:27-28

"But Abraham said to him,
'They have Moses and the prophets.
Let them listen to them.'"                                                                        16:29

"He said, 'No, father Abraham,
but if one goes to them from the dead, they will repent.'"                                        16:30

"He said to him, 'If they don't listen to Moses and the prophets,
neither will they be persuaded
if one rises from the dead.'"                                                                     16:31

**"It is impossible that no occasions of stumbling should come,**
but woe to him
through whom they come!
It would be better for him
if a millstone were hung around his neck,
and he were thrown into the sea,
rather than that he should cause one of these little ones to stumble.
Be careful.
If your brother sins against you, rebuke him.
If he repents,
forgive him.
If he sins against you seven times in the day,
and seven times returns,
saying, 'I repent,'
you shall forgive him."

17:1-4

"If you had faith like a grain of mustard seed,
you would tell this sycamore tree,
'Be uprooted, and be planted in the sea,'
and it would obey you.
But who is there among you, having a servant plowing
or keeping sheep,
that will say, when he comes in from the field,
'Come immediately and sit down at the table,'
and will not rather tell him,
'Prepare my supper, clothe yourself properly, and serve me,
while I eat and drink.
Afterward you shall eat and drink'?
Does he thank that servant
because he did the things that were commanded?
I think not.
Even so you also,
when you have done all the things that are commanded you, say,
'We are unworthy servants.
We have done our duty.'"

17:6-10

"Go and show yourselves to the priests."

17:14

"Weren't the ten cleansed?

But where are the nine?
Were there none found who returned to give glory to God,
except this stranger?"                                                                17:17-18

"Get up,
and go your way.
Your faith has healed you."                                                           17:19

"The Kingdom of God doesn't come with observation;
neither will they say,
'Look, here!'
or, 'Look, there!'
for behold,
the Kingdom of God is within you."                                                    17:20-21

"The days will come,
when you will desire to see one of the days
of the Son of Man,
and you will not see it.
They will tell you,
'Look, here!'
or 'Look, there!'
Don't go away, nor follow after them,
for as the lightning, when it flashes out of the one part under the sky,
shines to the other part under the sky;
so will the Son of Man be in his day.
But first, he must suffer many things
and be rejected by this generation.
As it happened in the days of Noah,
even so will it be also in the days
of the Son of Man.
They ate, they drank, they married, they were given in marriage,
until the day that Noah entered into the ship,
and the flood came, and destroyed them all.
Likewise, even as it happened in the days of Lot:
they ate, they drank, they bought, they sold,
they planted, they built;
but in the day that Lot went out from Sodom,
it rained fire and sulfur from the sky,
and destroyed them all.
It will be the same way

in the day
that the Son of Man
is revealed.
In that day,
he who will be on the housetop,
and his goods in the house,
let him not go down to take them away.
Let him who is in the field likewise
not turn back.
Remember Lot's wife!
Whoever seeks to save his life
loses it,
but whoever loses his life
preserves it.
I tell you,
in that night
there will be two people in one bed.
The one will be taken,
and the other will be left.
There will be two grinding grain together.
One will be taken,
and the other will be left."                                              17:22-36

"Where the body is,
there will the vultures also be gathered together."                        17:37

-------------------------------------------------------------------------------------
LUKE 18
-------------------------------------------------------------------------------------

## "There was a judge in a certain city

who didn't fear God, and didn't respect man.
A widow was in that city,
and she often came to him, saying,
'Defend me from my adversary!'
He wouldn't for a while,
but afterward he said to himself,
'Though I neither fear God, nor respect man,
yet because this widow bothers me,
I will defend her,
or else she will wear me out by her continual coming.'"                    18:2-5

"Listen to what the unrighteous judge says.

Won't God avenge
his chosen ones,
who are crying out to him day and night,
and yet he exercises patience with them?
I tell you
that he will avenge them quickly.
Nevertheless,
when the Son of Man comes,
will he find faith on the earth?"

18:6-8

"Two men went up into the temple to pray;
one was a Pharisee, and the other was a tax collector.
The Pharisee stood and prayed to himself like this:
'God, I thank you, that I am not like the rest of men,
extortioners, unrighteous, adulterers,
or even like this tax collector.
I fast twice a week. I give tithes of all that I get.'
But the tax collector, standing far away,
wouldn't even lift up his eyes to heaven,
but beat his breast, saying,
'God, be merciful to me, a sinner!'
I tell you,
this man went down to his house justified
rather than the other;
for everyone who exalts himself
will be humbled,
but he who humbles himself
will be exalted."

18:10-14

"Allow the little children to come to me,
and don't hinder them,
for the Kingdom of God
belongs to such as these.
Most certainly,
I tell you,
whoever doesn't receive the Kingdom of God
like a little child,
he will in no way enter into it."

18:16-17

"Why do you call me good?
No one is good, except one —
God.

You know the commandments:
'Don't commit adultery,'
'Don't murder,'
'Don't steal,'
'Don't give false testimony,'
'Honor your father and your mother.'"

18:19-20

"You still lack one thing.
Sell all that you have,
and distribute it to the poor.
You will have treasure in heaven.
Come,
follow me."

18:22

"How hard it is for those who have riches
to enter into the Kingdom of God!
For it is easier for a camel to enter in through a needle's eye,
than for a rich man to enter into the Kingdom of God."

18:24-25

"The things which are impossible with men
are possible with God."

18:27

"Most certainly
I tell you,
there is no one who has left house, or wife,
or brothers, or parents, or children,
for the Kingdom of God's sake,
who will not receive many times more in this time,
and in the world to come, eternal life."

18:29-30

"Behold,
we are going up to Jerusalem,
and all the things that are written through the prophets
concerning the Son of Man
will be completed.
For he will be delivered up to the Gentiles,
will be mocked, treated shamefully, and spit on.
They will scourge and kill him.
On the third day, he will rise again."

18:31-33

"What do you want me to do?"

18:41

"Receive your sight.
Your faith has healed you."                                                         18:42

---

---

**"Zacchaeus,**
hurry
and come down,
for today I must stay at your house."                                               19:5

"Today,
salvation has come to this house,
because he also is a son of Abraham.
For the Son of Man
came to seek and to save that which was lost."                                      19:9-10

"A certain nobleman went into a far country
to receive for himself a kingdom, and to return.
He called ten servants of his, and gave them ten mina coins,
and told them, 'Conduct business until I come.'
But his citizens hated him,
and sent an envoy after him, saying,
'We don't want this man to reign over us.'"                                          19:12-14

"It happened when he had come back again,
having received the kingdom,
that he commanded these servants, to whom he had given the money,
to be called to him,
that he might know what they had gained by conducting business.
The first came before him, saying,
'Lord, your mina has made ten more minas.'"                                          19:15-16

"He said to him, 'Well done, you good servant!
Because you were found faithful with very little,
you shall have authority over ten cities.'"                                          19:17

"The second came, saying,
'Your mina, Lord, has made five minas.'"                                             19:18

"So he said to him, 'And you are to be over five cities.'
Another came, saying,

'Lord, behold, your mina, which I kept laid away in a handkerchief,
for I feared you, because you are an exacting man.
You take up that which you didn't lay down,
and reap that which you didn't sow.'"                                      19:19-21

"He said to him,
'Out of your own mouth will I judge you, you wicked servant!
You knew that
I am an exacting man,
taking up that which I didn't lay down,
and reaping that which I didn't sow.
Then why didn't you deposit my money in the bank,
and at my coming,
I might have earned interest on it?'
He said to those who stood by,
'Take the mina away from him,
and give it to him who has the ten minas.'"                               19:22-24

"They said to him, 'Lord, he has ten minas!'
'For I tell you
that to everyone who has, will more be given;
but from him who doesn't have,
even that which he has will be taken away from him.
But bring those enemies of mine
who didn't want me to reign over them here,
and kill them before me.'"                                                19:25-27

"Go your way into the village on the other side,
in which, as you enter,
you will find a colt tied,
whereon no man ever yet sat.
Untie it, and bring it.
If anyone asks you, 'Why are you untying it?'
say to him: 'The Lord needs it.'"                                         19:30-31

"I tell you
that if these were silent, the stones would cry out."                     19:40

"If you, even you,
had known today
the things which belong to your peace!

But now, they are hidden from your eyes.
For the days will come on you,
when your enemies will throw up a barricade against you,
surround you, hem you in on every side,
and will dash you and your children within you
to the ground.
They will not leave in you one stone on another,
because you didn't know the time of your visitation."

19:41-44

"It is written,
'My house is a house of prayer,'
but you have made it a 'den of robbers'!"

19:46

---

LUKE 20

---

## "I also will ask you one question.
Tell me:
the baptism of John,
was it from heaven,
or from men?"

20:3-4

"Neither will I tell you
by what authority
I do these things."

20:8

"A man planted a vineyard,
and rented it out to some farmers,
and went into another country for a long time.
At the proper season,
he sent a servant to the farmers
to collect his share of the fruit of the vineyard.
But the farmers beat him, and sent him away empty.
He sent yet another servant,
and they also beat him, and treated him shamefully,
and sent him away empty.
He sent yet a third,
and they also wounded him, and threw him out.
The lord of the vineyard said, 'What shall I do?
I will send my beloved son.
It may be that seeing him, they will respect him.'"

20:9-13

"But when the farmers saw him, they reasoned among themselves, saying,
'This is the heir. Come, let's kill him,
that the inheritance may be ours.'
They threw him out of the vineyard, and killed him.
What therefore will the lord of the vineyard do to them?
He will come and destroy these farmers,
and will give the vineyard to others."                                  20:14-16

"Then what is this that is written,
'The stone which the builders rejected,
the same was made the chief cornerstone?'
Everyone who falls on that stone will be broken to pieces,
but it will crush whomever it falls on to dust."                        20:17-18

"Why do you test me?
Show me a denarius.
Whose image and inscription are on it?"                                  20:23-24

"Then give to Caesar the things that are Caesar's,
and to God the things that are God's."                                   20:25

"The children of this age marry, and are given in marriage.
But those who are considered worthy
to attain to that age and the resurrection from the dead,
neither marry, nor are given in marriage.
For they can't die any more,
for they are like the angels,
and are children of God,
being children of the resurrection.
But that the dead are raised,
even Moses showed at the bush,
when he called the Lord
'The God of Abraham, the God of Isaac, and the God of Jacob.'
Now he is not the God of the dead,
but of the living,
for all are alive to him."                                              20:34-38

"Why do they say that the Christ is David's son?
David himself says in the book of Psalms,
'The Lord said to my Lord,
"Sit at my right hand,

until I make your enemies the footstool of your feet"…
"David therefore calls him Lord, so how is he his son?"

20:41-44

"Beware of the scribes,
who like to walk in long robes,
and love greetings in the marketplaces,
the best seats in the synagogues,
and the best places at feasts;
who devour widows' houses,
and for a pretense make long prayers:
these will receive greater condemnation."

20:46-47

---

LUKE 21

---

**"Truly I tell you,**
this poor widow put in
more than all of them,
for all these put in gifts for God from their abundance,
but she,
out of her poverty,
put in all that she had to live on."

21:3-4

"As for these things which you see,
the days will come,
in which there will not be left here one stone on another
that will not be thrown down."

21:6

"Watch out that you don't get led astray,
for many will come in my name,
saying, 'I am he,'
and, 'The time is at hand.'
Therefore
don't
follow
them.
When you hear of wars and disturbances,
don't
be
terrified,
for these things must happen first,
but the end won't come immediately."

21:8-9

"Nation will rise against nation,
and kingdom against kingdom.
There will be great earthquakes, famines, and plagues
in various places.
There will be terrors and great signs from heaven.
But before all these things,
they will lay their hands on you and will persecute you,
delivering you up to synagogues and prisons,
bringing you before kings and governors for my name's sake.
It will turn out as a testimony for you.
Settle it therefore in your hearts
not to meditate beforehand how to answer,
for I will give you a mouth and wisdom
which all your adversaries
will not be able to withstand or to contradict.
You will be handed over even by parents,
brothers, relatives, and friends.
They will cause some of you to be put to death.
You will be hated by all men
for my name's sake.
And not a hair of your head will perish."                           21:10-18

"By your endurance you will win your lives."                        21:19

"But when you see Jerusalem surrounded by armies,
then know that its desolation is at hand.
Then let those who are in Judea
flee to the mountains.
Let those who are in the midst of her
depart.
Let those who are in the country
not enter therein.
For these are days of vengeance,
that
all things
which are written
may be
fulfilled.
Woe to those who are pregnant
and to those who nurse infants in those days!
For there will be great distress in the land,

and wrath to this people.
They will fall by the edge of the sword,
and will be led captive into all the nations.
Jerusalem will be trampled down by the Gentiles,
until the times of the Gentiles
are fulfilled.
There will be signs in the sun, moon, and stars;
and on the earth anxiety of nations,
in perplexity for the roaring of the sea and the waves;
men fainting for fear,
and for expectation of the things which are coming on the world:
for the powers of the heavens will be shaken.
Then they will see
the Son of Man
coming in a cloud with power and great glory.
But when these things begin to happen,
look up,
and lift up your heads,
because your redemption is near."                                          21:20-28


"See the fig tree, and all the trees.
When they are already budding,
you see it and know by your own selves
that the summer is already near.
Even so you also, when you see these things happening,
know that the Kingdom of God is near.
Most certainly
I tell you,
this generation will not pass away
until all things are accomplished.
Heaven and earth will pass away,
but
my
words
will
by
no
means
pass
away."                                                                              21:29-33

"So be careful,
or your hearts
will be loaded down
with carousing,
drunkenness,
and cares of this life,
and that day will come on you suddenly.
For it will come like a snare on all those
who dwell on the surface of all the earth.
Therefore be watchful all the time,
praying
that you may be counted worthy to escape
all these things that will happen,
and to stand before the Son of Man."

21:34-36

------------------------------------------------------------

LUKE 22

------------------------------------------------------------

**"Go and prepare the Passover for us,**
that we may eat."

22:8

"Behold,
when you have entered into the city,
a man carrying a pitcher of water will meet you.
Follow him into the house which he enters.
Tell the master of the house,
'The Teacher says to you,
"Where is the guest room,
where I may eat the Passover with my disciples?"'
He will show you a large, furnished upper room.
Make preparations there."

22:10-12

"I have earnestly desired
to eat this Passover with you
before I suffer,
for I tell you,
I will no longer by any means eat of it
until it is fulfilled in the Kingdom of God."

22:15-16

"Take this,
and share it among yourselves,
for I tell you,

I will not drink at all again from the fruit of the vine,
until the Kingdom of God comes."                                    22:17-18

"This is my body which is given for you.
Do this in memory of me."                                           22:19

"This cup is the new covenant in my blood,
which is poured out for you.
But behold,
the hand of him
who betrays me
is with me on the table.
The Son of Man indeed goes,
as it has been determined,
but woe to that man through whom he is betrayed!"                   22:20-22

"The kings of the nations lord it over them,
and those who have authority over them
are called 'benefactors.'
But not so with you.
But one who is the greater among you,
let him become as the younger,
and one who is governing,
as one who serves.
For who is greater,
one who sits at the table,
or one who serves?
Isn't it he who sits at the table?
But I am in the midst of you as one who serves.
But you are those
who have continued with me
in my trials.
I confer on you a kingdom,
even as my Father conferred on me,
that you may eat and drink
at my table in my Kingdom.
You will sit on thrones,
judging the twelve tribes of Israel."                               22:25-30

"Simon,
Simon,

behold,
Satan asked to have you,
that he might sift you as wheat,
but I prayed for you,
that your faith wouldn't fail.
You,
when once you have turned again,
establish your brothers."

22:31-32

"I tell you,
Peter,
the rooster will by no means crow today
until you deny that you know me three times."

22:34

"When I sent you out without purse, and wallet, and shoes,
did you lack anything?"

22:35

"But now,
whoever has a purse,
let him take it,
and likewise a wallet.
Whoever has none,
let him sell his cloak, and buy a sword.
For I tell you
that this which is written must still be fulfilled
in me:
'He was counted with transgressors.'
For that which concerns me has an end."

22:36-37

"That is enough."

22:38

"Pray
that you don't enter into temptation."

22:40

"Father,
if you are willing,
remove this cup from me.
Nevertheless,
not my will,
but yours, be done."

22:42

"Why do you sleep?

Rise
and pray
that you may not enter into temptation."                        22:46

"Judas,
do you betray the Son of Man with a kiss?"                      22:48

"Let me at least do this"                                       22:51

"Have you come out as against a robber,
with swords and clubs?
When I was with you in the temple daily,
you didn't stretch out your hands against me.
But this is your hour,
and the power of darkness."                                     22:52-53

"Before the rooster crows
you will deny me three times."                                  22:61

"If I tell you,
you won't believe,
and if I ask,
you will in no way answer me or let me go.
From now on,
the Son of Man
will be seated at the right hand of the power of God."         22:67-69

"You say it, because
I am."                                                          22:70

LUKE 23

**"So you say."**                                               23:3

"Daughters of Jerusalem,
don't weep for me,
but weep for yourselves and for your children.
For behold,
the days are coming in which they will say,
'Blessed are the barren,
the wombs that never bore,
and the breasts that never nursed.'

Then they will begin to tell the mountains,
'Fall on us!'
and tell the hills,
'Cover us.'
For if they do these things in the green tree,
what will be done in the dry?"

23:28-31

"Father,
forgive them,
for they don't know what they are doing."

23:34

"Assuredly I tell you,
today
you will be with me in Paradise."

23:43

"Father,
into your hands I commit my spirit!"

23:46

- - - - - - - - - - - - - - - - - - - - - - - - - - - - - - - - - - - - - - - - - - - - - -

## LUKE 24

- - - - - - - - - - - - - - - - - - - - - - - - - - - - - - - - - - - - - - - - - - - - - -

**"What are you talking about as you walk,**
and are sad?"

24:17

"What things?"

24:19

"Foolish men,
and slow of heart to believe
in all that the prophets have spoken!
Didn't the Christ have to suffer these things
and to enter into his glory?"

24:25-26

"Peace be to you."

24:36

"Why are you troubled?
Why do doubts arise in your hearts?
See my hands
and my feet,
that it is truly me.
Touch me and see,
for a spirit doesn't have flesh and bones,
as you see that I have."

24:38-39

"Do you have anything here to eat?"                                          24:41

"This is what I told you,
while I was still with you,
that all things which are written
in the law of Moses, the prophets, and the psalms,
concerning me
must be fulfilled."                                                          24:44

"Thus it is written,
and thus it was necessary
for the Christ to suffer
and to rise from the dead
the third day,
and that repentance and remission of sins should be preached
in his name
to all the nations,
beginning at Jerusalem.
You are witnesses of these things.
Behold,
I send forth the promise of my Father
on you.
But wait in the city of Jerusalem
until you are clothed
with power from on high."                                                    24:46-49

# THE GOOD NEWS ACCORDING TO *John*

## CHAPTER 1

### "What are you looking for?"

1:38

"Come,
and see."

1:39

"You are Simon the son of Jonah.
You shall be called Cephas"

1:42

"Follow me."

1:43

"Behold, an Israelite indeed,
in whom is no deceit!"

1:47

"Before Philip called you,
when you were under the fig tree,
I saw you."

1:48

"Because I told you,
'I saw you underneath the fig tree,'
do you believe?
You will see
greater things than these!"

1:50

"Most certainly,
I tell you,
hereafter
you will see
heaven opened,
and the angels of God
ascending and descending on the Son of Man."

1:51

## "Woman,
what does that have to do with you and me?
My hour has not yet come."

2:4

"Fill the water pots with water."

2:7

"Now draw some out,
and take it to the ruler of the feast."

2:8

"Take these things out of here!
Don't make my Father's house a marketplace!"

2:16

"Destroy this temple,
and in three days
I will raise it up."

2:19

JOHN 3

## "Most certainly,
I tell you,
unless one is born anew,
he can't see the Kingdom of God."

3:3

"Most certainly
I tell you,
unless one is born of water and spirit,
he can't enter into the Kingdom of God!
That which is born of the
flesh is flesh.
That which is born of the
Spirit is spirit.
Don't marvel that I said to you,
'You must be born anew.'
The wind blows
where it wants to,
and you hear its sound,
but don't know
where it comes from
and where it is going.

So is
everyone who is
born of the Spirit." 3:5-8

"Are you the teacher of Israel,
and don't understand these things?
Most certainly I tell you,
we speak that which we know,
and testify of that which we have seen,
and you don't receive our witness.
If I told you earthly things
and you don't believe,
how will you believe
if I tell you heavenly things?
No one has ascended into heaven,
but he
who descended out of heaven,
the Son of Man,
who is in heaven.
As Moses
lifted up the serpent
in the wilderness,
even so must the Son of Man
be lifted up,
that whoever believes
in him
should not perish,
but have eternal life." 3:10-15

"For God so loved the world,
that he gave
his one and only Son,
that whoever believes
in him
should not perish,
but have eternal life.
For God didn't send
his Son
into the world
to judge the world,
but that the world should be saved
through him." 3:16-17

"He who
believes
in him
is not judged.
He who
doesn't believe
has been judged already,
because he has not believed
in the name
of the one and only Son of God.
This is the judgment,
that the light
has come
into the world,
and men loved the darkness
rather than the light;
for their works were evil.
For everyone
who does evil
hates the light,
and doesn't come
to the light,
lest his works
would be exposed.
But he who
does the truth
comes to the light,
that his works may be revealed,
that they have been done in God."                3:18-21

------------------------------------------------------------

## JOHN 4

------------------------------------------------------------

### "Give me a drink."                                         4:7

"If you knew the gift of God,
and who it is
who says to you, 'Give me a drink,'
you would have asked him,
and he would have given you
living water."                                               4:10

"Everyone who drinks of this water will thirst again,
but whoever
drinks of the water
that I will give him
will never thirst again;
but the water that
I will give him
will become
in him
a well of water
springing up
to eternal life."                                          4:13-14

"Go,
call your husband,
and come here."                                            4:16

"You said well,
'I have no husband,'
for you have had five husbands;
and he whom you now have is not your husband.
This you have said truly."                                 4:17-18

"Woman,
believe me,
the hour comes,
when neither in this mountain, nor in Jerusalem,
will you worship the Father.
You worship that which you don't know.
We worship that which we know;
for salvation is from the Jews.
But the hour comes,
and now is,
when the true worshipers
will worship the Father
in spirit
and truth,
for the Father seeks
such to be his worshipers.
God
is

spirit,
and those who worship him
must worship
in spirit
and truth."                                                                          4:21-24

"I am he,
the one who speaks to you."                                                   4:26

"I have food to eat
that you don't know about."                                                  4:32

"My food
is to do the will of him
who sent me,
and to accomplish his work.
Don't you say, 'There are yet four months until the harvest?'
Behold, I tell you,
lift up your eyes,
and look at the fields, that
they are white for harvest already.
He who reaps receives wages,
and gathers fruit
to eternal life;
that both he who sows and he who reaps
may rejoice together.
For in this the saying is true,
'One sows, and another reaps.'
I sent you to reap
that for which you haven't labored.
Others have labored,
and you have entered into their labor."                                4:34-38

"Unless you see signs and wonders,
you will in no way believe."                                                4:48

"Go your way.
Your son lives."                                                                      4:50

"Your son lives."                                                                    4:53

JOHN 5

**"Do you want to be made well?"**                                      5:6

"Arise,
take up your mat, and walk."                                           5:8

" 'Take up your mat, and walk.' "                                      5:11

" 'Take up your mat, and walk' "                                      5:12

"Behold, you are made well.
Sin no more,
so that nothing worse happens to you."                                5:14

"My Father is
still working,
so I am
working, too."                                                        5:17

"Most certainly,
I tell you,
the Son can do nothing of himself,
but what he sees the Father doing.
For whatever things he does,
these the Son also does likewise.
For the Father has affection for the Son,
and shows him all things that he himself does.
He will show him greater works than these,
that you may marvel.
For as the Father raises the dead
and gives them life,
even so the Son also gives life
to whom he desires.
For the Father judges no one,
but he has given all judgment
to the Son,
that all may honor the Son,
even as they honor the Father.
He who doesn't honor the Son
doesn't honor the Father
who sent him."                                                        5:19-23

"Most certainly
I tell you,
he who hears my word,
and believes him
who sent me,
has eternal life,
and doesn't come into judgment,
but has passed
out of death into life.
Most certainly,
I tell you,
the hour comes,
and now is,
when the dead will hear
the Son of God's voice;
and those who hear
will live.
For as the Father has life in himself,
even so he gave to the Son also
to have life in himself.
He also gave him authority
to execute judgment,
because he is a son of man.
Don't marvel at this,
for the hour comes,
in which all that are in the tombs
will hear his voice,
and will come out;
those who have done good,
to the resurrection of life;
and those who have done evil,
to the resurrection of judgment.
I can of myself do nothing.
As I hear, I judge,
and my judgment is righteous;
because I don't seek
my own will,
but the will of my Father who sent me."                        5:24-30

"If I testify about myself,
my witness is not valid.

It is another
who testifies about me.
I know
that the testimony which he testifies about me is true.
You have sent to John,
and he has testified
to the truth.
But the testimony which I receive
is not from man.
However, I say these things
that you may be saved.
He was the burning
and shining lamp,
and you were willing
to rejoice for a while in his light.
But the testimony which I have is greater
than that of John,
for the works which the Father gave me to accomplish,
the very works that I do,
testify about me,
that the Father has sent me.
The Father himself, who sent me, has testified about me.
You have neither heard his voice at any time,
nor seen his form.
You don't have his word living in you;
because you don't believe him whom he sent."            5:31-38

"You search the Scriptures,
because you think that in them you have eternal life;
and these are they which testify about me.
Yet you will not come to me, that you may have life.
I don't receive glory from men.
But I know you,
that you don't have God's love in yourselves.
I have come in my Father's name,
and you don't receive me.
If another comes in his own name,
you will receive him.
How can you believe,
who receive glory from one another,
and you don't seek the glory
that comes from the only God?"                          5:39-44

"Don't think that I will accuse you to the Father.
There is one who accuses you, even Moses,
on whom you have set your hope.
For if you believed Moses,
you would believe me;
for he wrote about me.
But if you don't believe his writings,
how will you believe my words?"                              5:45-47

------------------------------------------------------------

JOHN 6

------------------------------------------------------------

**"Where**
are we to buy bread,
that these may eat?"                                          6:5

"Have the people sit down."                                   6:10

"Gather up the broken pieces
which are left over,
that nothing be lost."                                        6:12

"It is I.
Don't be afraid."                                             6:20

"Most certainly I tell you,
you seek me,
not because you saw signs,
but because you ate of the loaves,
and were filled.
Don't work for the food which perishes,
but for the food which remains to eternal life,
which the Son of Man will give to you.
For God the Father has sealed him."                           6:26-27

"This is the work of God,
that you believe
in him
whom he has sent."                                            6:29

"Most certainly,
I tell you,

it wasn't Moses
who gave you the bread out of heaven,
but my Father
gives you the true bread out of heaven.
For the bread of God
is that which comes down out of heaven,
and gives life to the world."                                    6:32-33

"I am the bread of life.
He who comes to me
will not be hungry,
and he who believes in me
will never be thirsty.
But I told you
that you have seen me,
and yet you don't believe.
All those whom the Father gives me
will come to me.
He who comes to me
I will in no way throw out.
For I have come down from heaven,
not to do my own will,
but the will of him who sent me.
This is the will of my Father who sent me,
that of all he has given to me
I should lose nothing,
but should raise him up at the last day.
This is the will of the one who sent me,
that everyone
who sees the Son,
and believes in him,
should have eternal life;
and I will raise him up
at the last day."                                                6:35-40

"I am the bread
which came down out of heaven."                                  6:41

'I have come down out of heaven.'"                               6:42

"Don't murmur

among yourselves.
No one can come to me
unless the Father who sent me
draws him,
and I will raise him up
in the last day.
It is written in the prophets,
'They will all be taught by God.'
Therefore everyone who hears from the Father,
and has learned,
comes to me.
Not that anyone has seen the Father,
except he
who is from God.
He has seen the Father.
Most certainly,
I tell you,
he who believes in me
has eternal life.
I am the bread of life.
Your fathers ate the manna
in the wilderness,
and they died.
This is the bread
which comes down out of heaven,
that anyone may eat of it
and not die.
I am the living bread
which came down out of heaven.
If anyone eats of this bread,
he will live forever.
Yes,
the bread which I will give
for the life of the world
is my flesh."                                                   6:43-51

"Most certainly I tell you,
unless you eat the flesh
of the Son of Man
and drink his blood,
you don't have life in yourselves.

He who eats my flesh
and drinks my blood
has eternal life,
and I will raise him up
at the last day.
For my flesh is food indeed,
and my blood is drink indeed.
He who eats my flesh
and drinks my blood
lives in me,
and I in him.
As the living Father sent me,
and I live because of the Father;
so he who feeds on me,
he will also live because of me.
This is the bread
which came down out of heaven —
not as our fathers ate the manna,
and died.
He who eats this bread
will live forever."                                                                  6:53-58

"Does this cause you to stumble?
Then what
if you would see the Son of Man ascending to where he was before?
It is the spirit who gives life.
The flesh profits nothing.
The words that I speak to you
are spirit,
and are life.
But there are some of you
who don't believe."                                                                6:61-64

"For this cause have I said to you
that no one can come to me,
unless it is given to him by my Father."                                      6:65

"You don't also want to go away, do you?"                             6:67

"Didn't I choose you,
the twelve,
and one of you is a devil?"                                                        6:70

---

---

**"My time**
has not yet come,
but your time
is always ready.
The world can't hate you,
but it hates me,
because I testify about it,
that its works are evil.
You go up to the feast.
I am not yet going up to this feast,
because my time
is not yet fulfilled."                                        7:6-8

"My teaching is not mine,
but his
who sent me.
If anyone desires to do his will,
he will know
about the teaching,
whether it is from God,
or if I am speaking from myself.
He who speaks from himself
seeks his own glory,
but he who seeks the glory of him who sent him
is true,
and no unrighteousness is in him.
Didn't Moses give you the law,
and yet none of you keeps the law?
Why do you seek to kill me?"                                7:16-19

"I did one work,
and you all marvel because of it.
Moses has given you circumcision
(not that it is of Moses,
but of the fathers),
and on the Sabbath you circumcise a boy.
If a boy receives circumcision on the Sabbath,
that the law of Moses may not be broken,
are you angry with me,

because I made a man completely healthy on the Sabbath?
Don't judge according to appearance,
but judge righteous judgment."                                                7:21-24

"You both know me,
and know where I am from.
I have not come of myself,
but he who sent me
is true,
whom you don't know.
I know him,
because I am from him,
and he sent me."                                                              7:28-29

"I will be with you
a little while longer,
then I go
to him who sent me.
You will seek me,
and won't find me;
and where I am,
you can't come."                                                              7:33-34

'You will seek me,
and won't find me;
and where I am,
you can't come.'"                                                             7:36

"If anyone is thirsty,
let him come to me
and drink!
He who believes in me,
as the Scripture has said,
from within him will flow
rivers of living water."                                                      7:37-38

## "He who is without sin
among you,
let him throw the first stone at her."                    8:7

"Woman,
where are your accusers?
Did no one condemn you?"                              8:10

"Neither do I condemn you.
Go your way.
From now on,
sin no more."                                       8:11

"I am the light of the world.
He who follows me
will not walk in the darkness,
but will have the light of life."                    8:12

"Even if I testify
about myself,
my testimony is true,
for I know where I came from,
and where I am going;
but you don't know
where I came from,
or where I am going.
You judge according to the flesh.
I judge no one.
Even if I do judge,
my judgment is true,
for I am not alone,
but I am with the Father
who sent me.
It's also written in your law
that the testimony of two people is valid.
I am one
who testifies about myself,
and the Father who sent me
testifies about me."                                8:14-18

"You know neither me,
nor my Father.
If you knew me,
you would know my Father also."

8:19

"I am going away,
and you will seek me,
and you will die
in your sins.
Where I go,
you can't come."

8:21

"'Where I am going,
you can't come.'"

8:22

"You are from beneath.
I am from above.
You are of this world.
I am not of this world.
I said therefore to you that
you will die in your sins;
for unless you believe
that I am he,
you will die in your sins."

8:23-24

"Just what I have been saying to you from the beginning.
I have many things to speak and to judge concerning you.
However he who sent me
is true;
and the things which I heard from him,
these I say to the world."

8:25-26

"When you have lifted up the Son of Man,
then you will know
that I am he,
and I do nothing
of myself,
but as my Father taught me,
I say these things.
He who sent me
is with me.

The Father hasn't left me alone,
for I always do
the things that are pleasing to him."                                8:28-29

"If you remain in my word,
then you are truly my disciples.
You will know the truth,
and the truth will make you free."                                   8:31-32

'You will be made free.'"                                            8:33

"Most certainly
I tell you,
everyone who commits sin
is the bondservant of sin.
A bondservant doesn't live in the house forever.
A son remains forever.
If therefore the Son makes you free,
you will be free indeed.
I know
that you are Abraham's seed,
yet you seek to kill me,
because my word
finds no place in you.
I say the things
which I have seen
with my Father;
and you also do the things
which you have seen
with your father."                                                   8:34-38

"If you were Abraham's children,
you would do the works of Abraham.
But now you seek to kill me,
a man who has told you the truth,
which I heard from God.
Abraham didn't do this.
You do the works
of your father."                                                     8:39-41

"If God were your father,
you would love me,

for I came out
and have come from God.
For I haven't come of myself,
but he sent me.
Why don't you understand my speech?
Because you can't hear
my word.
You are of your father,
the devil,
and you want to do
the desires of your father.
He was a murderer
from the beginning,
and doesn't stand in the truth,
because there is no truth in him.
When he speaks a lie,
he speaks on his own;
for he is a liar,
and its father.
But
because I tell the truth,
you don't believe me.
Which of you convicts me of sin?
If I tell the truth,
why do you not believe me?
He who is of God
hears the words of God.
For this cause you don't hear,
because you are not of God."

8:42-47

"I don't have a demon,
but I honor my Father,
and you dishonor me.
But I don't seek my own glory.
There is one who seeks
and judges.
Most certainly,
I tell you,
if a person keeps my word,
he will never see death."

8:49-51

"'If a man keeps my word,
he will never taste of death.'"                                                          8:52

"If I glorify myself,
my glory is nothing.
It is my Father
who glorifies me,
of whom you say that he is our God.
You have not known him,
but I know him.
If I said, 'I don't know him,'
I would be like you, a liar.
But I know him,
and keep his word.
Your father Abraham
rejoiced
to see my day.
He saw it,
and was glad."                                                                           8:54-56

"Most certainly,
I tell you,
before Abraham came into existence,
I AM."                                                                                   8:58

------------------------------------------------------------------------------------------
JOHN 9
------------------------------------------------------------------------------------------

**"Neither did this man sin,**
nor his parents;
but,
that the works of God
might be revealed
in him.
I must work the works
of him who sent me,
while it is day.
The night is coming,
when no one can work.
While I am in the world,
I am the light of the world."                                                            9:3-5

"Go,
wash in the pool of Siloam"                                                          9:7

"'Go
to the pool of Siloam,
and wash.'"                                                                             9:11

"Do you believe
in the Son of God?"                                                                 9:35

"You have
both
seen him,
and it is he
who speaks with you."                                                             9:37

"I came into this world for judgment,
that those who don't see
may see;
and that those who see
may become blind."                                                               9:39

"If you were blind,
you would have no sin;
but now you say,
'We see.'
Therefore your sin remains."                                                   9:41

-------------------------------------------------------------------------------------

JOHN 10
-------------------------------------------------------------------------------------

**"Most certainly,**
I tell you,
one who doesn't enter by the door into the sheep fold,
but climbs up some other way,
the same is a thief and a robber.
But one who enters in by the door
is the shepherd of the sheep.
The gatekeeper opens the gate for him,
and the sheep listen to his voice.
He calls his own sheep by name,
and leads them out.

Whenever he brings out
his own sheep,
he goes before them,
and the sheep follow him,
for they know his voice.
They will by no means
follow a stranger,
but will flee from him;
for they don't know
the voice of strangers." 10:1-5

"Most certainly,
I tell you,
I am the sheep's door.
All who came before me
are thieves and robbers,
but the sheep didn't listen to them.
I am the door.
If anyone enters in by me,
he will be saved,
and will go in and go out,
and will find pasture.
The thief only comes
to steal, kill, and destroy.
I came
that they may have life,
and may have it abundantly." 10:7-10

"I am the good shepherd.
The good shepherd
lays down his life
for the sheep.
He who is a hired hand,
and not a shepherd,
who doesn't own the sheep,
sees the wolf coming,
leaves the sheep,
and flees.
The wolf snatches the sheep,
and scatters them.
The hired hand flees

because he is a hired hand,
and doesn't care for the sheep."                                        10:11-13


"I am
the good shepherd.
I know
my own,
and I'm known
by my own;
even as the Father knows me,
and I know the Father.
I lay down my life
for the sheep.
I have other sheep,
which are not of this fold.
I must bring them also,
and they will
hear my voice.
They will become
one flock
with one shepherd.
Therefore the Father loves me,
because I lay down my life,
that I may take it again.
No one takes it away from me,
but I lay it down
by myself.
I have power
to lay it down,
and I have power
to take it again.
I received this commandment from my Father."              10:14-18


"I told you,
and you don't believe.
The works that I do
in my Father's name,
these testify about me.
But you don't believe,
because you are not of my sheep,
as I told you.

My sheep hear my voice,
and I know them,
and they follow me.
I give eternal life to them.
They will never perish,
and no one will snatch them out of my hand.
My Father,
who has given them to me,
is greater than all.
No one is able to snatch them out of my Father's hand.
I and the Father
are one."                                                                 10:25-30

"I have shown you
many good works
from my Father.
For which of those works do you stone me?"                              10:31

"Isn't it written in your law,
'I said, you are gods?'
If he called them gods,
to whom the word of God came
(and the Scripture can't be broken),
do you say of him
whom the Father sanctified
and sent into the world,
'You blaspheme,'
because I said,
'I am the Son of God'?
If I don't do the works of my Father,
don't believe me.
But if I do them,
though you don't believe me,
believe the works;
that you may know
and believe
that the Father is in me,
and I in the Father."                                                    10:34-38

---

---

**"This sickness**
is not to death,
but for the glory of God,
that God's Son
may be glorified by it."                                              11:4

"Let's go into Judea again."                                          11:7

"Aren't there twelve hours of daylight?
If a man walks in the day,
he doesn't stumble,
because he sees the light of this world.
But if a man walks in the night,
he stumbles,
because the light isn't in him."                                     11:9-10

"Our friend,
Lazarus,
has fallen asleep,
but I am going
so that I may awake him out of sleep."                               11:11

"Lazarus is dead.
I am glad for your sakes
that I was not there,
so that you may believe.
Nevertheless,
let's go to him."                                                     11:14-15

"Your brother will rise again."                                      11:23

"I am
the resurrection
and the life.
He who believes in me
will still live,
even if he dies.
Whoever lives
and believes in me

will never die.
Do you believe this?"                                          11:25-26

"Where have you laid him?"                                      11:34

"Take away the stone."                                          11:39

"Didn't I tell you that
if you believed,
you would see God's glory?"                                     11:40

"Father,
I thank you
that you listened to me.
I know
that you always listen to me,
but because of the multitude that stands around I said this,
that they may believe that
you sent me."                                                   11:41-42

"Lazarus,
come out!"                                                      11:43

"Free him,
and let him go."                                                11:44

- - - - - - - - - - - - - - - - - - - - - - - - - - - - - - - - - - - - - -
JOHN 12
- - - - - - - - - - - - - - - - - - - - - - - - - - - - - - - - - - - - - -

**"Leave her alone.**
She has kept this for the day of my burial.
For you always have the poor with you,
but you don't always have me."                                  12:7-8

"The time has come
for the Son of Man
to be glorified.
Most certainly I tell you,
unless a grain of wheat
falls into the earth
and dies,
it remains

by itself alone.
But if it dies,
it bears much fruit.
He who loves his life
will lose it.
He who hates his life
in this world
will keep it
to eternal life.
If anyone serves me,
let him follow me.
Where I am,
there will my servant also be.
If anyone serves me,
the Father
will honor him."

12:23-26

"Now my soul is troubled.
What shall I say?
'Father,
save me from this time?'
But for this cause
I came to this time.
Father,
glorify your name!"

12:27-28

"This voice
hasn't come for my sake,
but for your sakes.
Now
is the judgment of this world.
Now
the prince of this world
will be cast out.
And I, if I am lifted up from the earth,
will draw all people to myself."

12:30-32

"'The Son of Man must be lifted up?'"

12:34

"Yet a little while
the light is with you.

Walk while you have the light,
that darkness doesn't overtake you.
He who walks in the darkness
doesn't know where he is going.
While you have the light,
believe in the light,
that you may become children of light."

12:35-36

"Whoever believes in me,
believes not in me,
but in him who sent me.
He who sees me
sees him who sent me.
I have come as a light into the world,
that whoever believes in me
may not remain in the darkness.
If anyone listens to my sayings,
and doesn't believe,
I don't judge him.
For I came not to judge the world,
but to save the world.
He who rejects me,
and doesn't receive my sayings,
has one who judges him.
The word
that I spoke,
the same will judge him
in the last day.
For I spoke not from myself,
but the Father who sent me,
he gave me a commandment,
what I should say,
and what I should speak.
I know
that his commandment is
eternal life.
The things therefore which I speak,
even as the Father has said to me,
so I speak."

12:44-50

**"You don't know what**
I am doing now,
but you will understand later."

"If I don't wash you,
you have no part with me."

"Someone who has bathed
only needs to have his feet washed,
but is completely clean.
You are clean,
but not all of you."

"You are not all clean."

"Do you know
what I have done
to you?
You call me, 'Teacher' and 'Lord.'
You say so correctly,
for so I am.
If I then,
the Lord and the Teacher,
have washed your feet,
you also
ought to wash one another's feet.
For I have given you an example,
that you also should do
as I have done to you.
Most certainly I tell you,
a servant is not greater than his lord,
neither one who is sent greater than
he who sent him."

"If you know these things,
blessed are you
if you do them.
I don't speak concerning all of you.
I know whom
I have chosen.

But that the Scripture may be fulfilled,
'He who eats bread with me
has lifted up his heel against me.'
From now on,
I tell you
before it happens,
that when it happens,
you may believe that
I am he.
Most certainly I tell you,
he who receives whomever I send,
receives me;
and he who receives me,
receives him who sent me."

13:17-20

"Most certainly
I tell you
that one of you
will betray me."

13:21

"It is he
to whom I will give
this piece of bread
when I have dipped it."

13:26

"What you do,
do quickly."

13:27

"Now
the Son of Man has been
glorified,
and God has been
glorified
in him.
If God
has been glorified
in him,
God will also glorify
him
in himself,
and he will
glorify

him
immediately.
Little children,
I will be with you
a little while longer.
You will seek me,
and as I said to the Jews,
'Where I am going,
you can't come,'
so now I tell you.
A new commandment I give to you,
that you love one another,
just like I have loved you;
that you also love one another.
By this
everyone will know
that you are my disciples,
if you have
love for one another."

13:31-35

"Where I am going,
you can't follow
now,
but you will follow
afterwards."

13:36

"Will you
lay down your life
for me?
Most certainly I tell you,
the rooster won't crow
until you have denied me three times."

13:38

## JOHN 14

**"Don't let your heart be troubled.**
Believe in God.
Believe also in me.
In my Father's house
are many homes.
If it weren't so,

I would have told you.
I am going
to prepare a place for you.
If I go
and prepare a place for you,
I will come again,
and will receive you to myself;
that where I am,
you may be there also.
Where I go,
you know,
and you know the way."                                    14:1-4

"I am the way,
the truth,
and the life.
No one
comes to the Father,
except through me.
If you had known me,
you would have known my Father also.
From now on,
you know him,
and have seen him."                                      14:6-7

"Have I been with you
such a long time,
and do you not know me,
Philip?
He who has seen me
has seen the Father.
How do you say,
'Show us the Father?'
Don't you believe that
I am in the Father,
and the Father in me?
The words that I tell you,
I speak not from myself;
but the Father
who lives in me
does his works.

Believe me
that I am
in the Father,
and the Father in me;
or else
believe me
for the very works' sake.
Most certainly
I tell you,
he who believes in me,
the works that I do,
he will do also;
and he will do
greater works than these,
because I am going to my Father.
Whatever
you will ask in my name,
that will I do,
that the Father may be glorified in the Son.
If you will ask
anything
in my name,
I will do it."

14:9-14

"If you love me,
keep my commandments.
I will pray to the Father,
and he will give you
another Counselor,
that he may be with you forever,—
the Spirit of truth,
whom the world can't receive;
for it doesn't see him,
neither knows him.
You know him,
for he lives with you,
and will be in you.
I will not leave you orphans.
I will come to you.
Yet a little while,
and the world will see me no more;

but you will see me.
Because I live,
you will live also.
In that day
you will know
that I am in my Father,
and you in me,
and I in you.
One who has my commandments,
and keeps them,
that person is one who loves me.
One who loves me
will be loved by my Father,
and I will love him,
and will reveal myself to him."

14:15-21

"If a man loves me,
he will keep my word.
My Father will love him,
and we will come to him,
and make our home with him.
He who doesn't love me
doesn't keep my words.
The word which you hear
isn't mine,
but the Father's
who sent me.
I have said these things to you,
while still living with you.
But the Counselor,
the Holy Spirit,
whom the Father will send
in my name,
he will teach you all things,
and will remind you
of all that I said to you."

14:23-26

"Peace I leave with you.
My peace I give to you;
not as the world gives,
give I to you.

Don't let your heart be troubled, neither let it be fearful.
You heard how I told you,
'I go away,
and I come to you.'
If you loved me,
you would have rejoiced,
because I said
'I am going to my Father;'
for the Father is greater than I.
Now I have told you
before it happens
so that, when it happens,
you may believe.
I will no more speak much with you,
for the prince of the world comes,
and he has nothing in me.
But that the world may know
that I love the Father,
and as the Father commanded me, even so I do.
Arise,
let us go from here."                                    14:27-31

JOHN 15

**"I am the true vine,**
and my Father is the farmer.
Every branch in me
that doesn't bear fruit,
he takes away.
Every branch that bears fruit,
he prunes,
that it may bear more fruit.
You are already pruned clean
because of the word
which I have spoken to you.
Remain in me,
and I in you.
As the branch can't bear fruit by itself,
unless it remains in the vine,
so neither can you,
unless you remain in me."                                   15:1-4

"I am the vine.
You are the branches.
He who remains in me,
and I in him,
the same bears much fruit,
for apart from me
you can do nothing.
If a man doesn't remain in me,
he is thrown out as a branch,
and is withered;
and they gather them,
throw them into the fire,
and they are burned.
If you remain in me,
and my words remain in you,
you will ask whatever you desire,
and it will be done for you."

15:5-7

"In this is my Father glorified,
that you bear much fruit;
and so you will be my disciples.
Even as the Father has loved me,
I also have loved you.
Remain in my love.
If you keep my commandments,
you will remain in my love;
even as I have kept my Father's commandments,
and remain in his love.
I have spoken these things to you,
that my joy may remain in you,
and that your joy may be made full."

15:8-11

"This is my commandment,
that you love one another,
even as I have loved you.
Greater love has no one than this,
that someone lay down his life for his friends.
You are my friends,
if you do whatever I command you.
No longer do I call you servants,
for the servant doesn't know what his lord does.

But I have called you friends,
for everything that I heard from my Father,
I have made known to you.
You didn't choose me,
but I chose you,
and appointed you,
that you should go and bear fruit,
and that your fruit should remain;
that whatever you will ask of the Father in my name,
he may give it to you."

15:12-16

"I command these things to you,
that you may love one another.
If the world hates you,
you know that it has hated me before it hated you.
If you were of the world,
the world would love its own.
But because you are not of the world,
since I chose you out of the world,
therefore the world hates you.
Remember the word
that I said to you:
'A servant is not greater than his lord.'
If they persecuted me,
they will also persecute you.
If they kept my word,
they will keep yours also.
But all these things will they do to you
for my name's sake,
because they don't know
him who sent me.
If I had not come
and spoken to them,
they would not have had sin;
but now
they have no excuse for their sin.
He who hates me,
hates my Father also.
If I hadn't done among them
the works which no one else did,
they wouldn't have had sin.

But now
have they seen
and also hated both me and my Father.
But this happened
so that the word may be fulfilled
which was written in their law,
'They hated me without a cause.'"                                    15:17-25

"When the Counselor has come,
whom I will send to you
from the Father,
the Spirit of truth,
who proceeds from the Father,
he will testify about me.
You will also testify,
because you have been with me from the beginning."              15:26-27

--------------------------------------------------------------------------------
JOHN 16
--------------------------------------------------------------------------------

**"These things have I spoken to you,**
so that you wouldn't be caused to stumble.
They will put you out of the synagogues.
Yes,
the time comes
that whoever kills you
will think that he offers service to God.
They will do these things
because they have not known the Father, nor me.
But I have told you these things,
so that when the time comes,
you may remember that I told you about them.
I didn't tell you these things from the beginning,
because I was with you."                                            16:1-4

"But now I am going to him who sent me,
and none of you asks me,
'Where are you going?'
But because I have told you these things,
sorrow has filled your heart.
Nevertheless I tell you the truth:
It is to your advantage

that I go away,
for if I don't go away,
the Counselor won't come to you.
But if I go,
I will send him to you.
When he has come,
he will convict the world
about sin, about righteousness, and about judgment;
about sin,
because they don't believe in me;
about righteousness,
because I am going to my Father, and you won't see me any more;
about judgment,
because the prince of this world has been judged."

16:5-11

"I have yet many things to tell you,
but you can't bear them now.
However when he,
the Spirit of truth,
has come,
he will guide you into
all truth,
for he will not speak from himself;
but whatever he hears,
he will speak.
He will declare to you things that are coming.
He will glorify me,
for he will take from what is mine,
and will declare it to you.
All things whatever the Father has
are mine;
therefore I said
that he takes of mine,
and will declare it to you.
A little while,
and you will not see me.
Again a little while,
and you will see me."

16:12-16

"'A little while,
and you won't see me,

and again a little while,
and you will see me;'
'Because I go to the Father.'"

"'A little while.'"

"Do you inquire among yourselves
concerning this, that I said,
'A little while, and you won't see me,
and again a little while, and you will see me?'
Most certainly I tell you,
that you will weep and lament,
but the world will rejoice.
You will be sorrowful,
but your sorrow will be turned into joy.
A woman, when she gives birth, has sorrow,
because her time has come.
But when she has delivered the child,
she doesn't remember the anguish any more,
for the joy that a human being is born into the world.
Therefore you now have sorrow,
but I will see you again,
and your heart will rejoice,
and no one
will take your joy away from you."

"In that day
you will ask me no questions.
Most certainly
I tell you,
whatever you may ask of the Father in my name,
he will give it to you.
Until now,
you have asked nothing in my name.
Ask,
and you will receive,
that your joy may be made full.
I have spoken these things to you
in figures of speech.
But the time is coming
when I will no more speak to you in figures of speech,
but will tell you plainly

about the Father.
In that day
you will ask in my name;
and I don't say to you, that I will pray to the Father for you,
for the Father himself
loves you,
because you have loved me,
and have believed
that I came forth from God.
I came out from the Father,
and have come into the world.
Again, I leave the world, and go to the Father."                    16:23-28

"Do you now believe?
Behold, the time is coming,
yes,
and has now come,
that you will be scattered,
everyone to his own place,
and you will leave me alone.
Yet I am not alone,
because the Father is with me.
I have told you these things,
that in me
you may have peace.
In the world you have oppression;
but cheer up!
I have overcome the world."                                        16:31-33

- - - - - - - - - - - - - - - - - - - - - - - - - - - - - - - - - - - - - - - - - - - - -
JOHN 17
- - - - - - - - - - - - - - - - - - - - - - - - - - - - - - - - - - - - - - - - - - - - -

## "Father,
the time has come.
Glorify your Son,
that your Son may also glorify you;
even as you gave him authority over all flesh,
he will give eternal life to all whom you have given him.
This is eternal life,
that they should know you,
the only true God,
and him whom you sent,

Jesus Christ.
I glorified you on the earth.
I have accomplished the work which you have given me to do.
Now,
Father,
glorify me with your own self with the glory which I had with you
before the world existed."

17:1-5

"I revealed your name
to the people whom you have given me out of the world.
They were yours,
and you have given them to me.
They have kept your word.
Now they have known
that all things whatever you have given me
are from you,
for the words which you have given me
I have given to them,
and they received them,
and knew for sure
that I came forth from you,
and they have believed that you sent me.
I pray for them.
I don't pray for the world,
but for those whom you have given me,
for they are yours.
All things that are mine are yours,
and yours are mine,
and I am glorified in them.
I am no more in the world,
but these are in the world,
and I am coming to you.
Holy Father,
keep them
through your name
which you have given me,
that they may be one,
even as we are.
While I was with them in the world,
I kept them in your name.
Those whom you have given me I have kept.

None of them is lost,
except the son of destruction,
that the Scripture might be fulfilled.
But now
I come to you,
and I say
these things in the world,
that they may have
my joy made full in themselves.
I have given them your word.
The world hated them,
because they are not of the world,
even as I am not of the world.
I pray
not that you would take them from the world,
but that you would keep them
from the evil one.
They are not of the world
even as I am not of the world.
Sanctify them in your truth.
Your word is truth.
As you sent me into the world,
even so I have sent them into the world.
For their sakes I sanctify myself,
that they themselves also may be sanctified in truth."

17:6-19

"Not for these only do
I pray,
but for those also
who believe in me
through their word,
that they may all be one; even as you,
Father,
are in me,
and I in you,
that they also may be one in us;
that the world may believe
that you sent me.
The glory which you have given me,
I have given to them;
that they may be one,
even as we are one;

I in them,
and
you in me,
that they may be perfected into one;
that the world may know
that you sent me,
and loved them, even as you loved me.
Father,
I desire
that they also whom you have given me
be
with me
where I am,
that they may see my glory,
which you have given me,
for you loved me
before the foundation of the world.
Righteous Father,
the world hasn't known you,
but I knew you;
and these knew
that you sent me.
I made known to them your name,
and will make it known;
that the love with which you loved me
may be in them,
and I in them."

17:20-26

## JOHN 18

### "Who are you looking for?"

18:4

"I am he."

18:5

"I am he."

18:6

"Who are you looking for?"

18:7

"I told you
that I am he.
If therefore you seek me,
let these go their way,"

18:8

"Of those whom you have given me,
I have lost none."

18:9

"Put the sword into its sheath.
The cup which the Father has given me,
shall I not surely drink it?"

18:11

"I spoke openly to the world.
I always taught in synagogues, and in the temple,
where the Jews always meet.
I said nothing in secret.
Why do you ask me?
Ask those who have heard me
what I said to them.
Behold, these know the things which I said."

18:20-21

"If I have spoken evil,
testify of the evil;
but if well,
why do you beat me?"

18:23

"Do you say this by yourself,
or did others tell you about me?"

18:34

"My Kingdom is not of this world.
If my Kingdom were of this world,
then my servants would fight, that I wouldn't be delivered to the Jews.
But now my Kingdom is not from here."

18:36

"You say that I am a king.
For this reason
I have been born,
and for this reason I have come into the world,
that I should testify to the truth.
Everyone who is of the truth
listens to my voice."

18:37

## "You would have no power at all against me,
unless it were given to you from above.
Therefore he who delivered me to you
has greater sin."                                    19:11

"Woman, behold your son!"                             19:26

"Behold, your mother!"                               19:27

"I am thirsty."                                       19:28

"It
is
finished."                                           19:30

JOHN 20

## "Woman,
why are you weeping?
Who are you looking for?"                             20:15

"Mary."                                              20:16

"Don't hold me,
for I haven't yet ascended to my Father;
but go to my brothers,
and tell them,
'I am ascending
to my Father and your Father,
to my God and your God.'"                            20:17

"Peace be to you."                                   20:19

"Peace be to you.
As the Father has sent me,
even so I send you."                                 20:21

"Receive the Holy Spirit!
If you forgive anyone's sins,
they have been forgiven them.

If you retain anyone's sins,
they have been retained."

20:22-23

"Peace be to you."

20:26

"Reach here your finger,
and see my hands.
Reach here your hand,
and put it into my side.
Don't be unbelieving,
but believing."

20:27

"Because you have seen me,
you have believed.
Blessed are those who have not seen,
and have believed."

20:29

---

## JOHN 21

---

**"Children,**
have you anything to eat?"

21:5

"Cast the net on the right side of the boat,
and you will find some."

21:6

"Bring some of the fish which you have just caught."

21:10

"Come and eat breakfast."

21:12

"Simon,
son of Jonah,
do you love me
more than these?"...
"Feed my lambs."

21:15

"Simon,
son of Jonah,
do you love me?"...
"Tend my sheep."

21:16

"Simon,
son of Jonah,

do you have affection for me?"...
"Do you have affection for me?"...
"Feed my sheep."                                                           21:17

"Most certainly
I tell you,
when you were young,
you dressed yourself,
and walked where you wanted to.
But when you are old,
you will stretch out your hands,
and another will dress you,
and carry you where you don't want to go."                  21:18

"Follow me."                                                               21:19

"If I desire that he stay until I come,
what is that to you?
You follow me."                                                            21:22

"If I desire that he stay until I come,
what is that to you?"                                                      21:23

# *The Acts* OF THE APOSTLES

CHAPTER 1

**"Don't depart from Jerusalem,**
but wait
for the promise
of the Father,
which you heard from me.
For John indeed baptized in water,
but you will be baptized in the Holy Spirit
not many days from now."                                              1:4-5


"It isn't for you to know
times or seasons
which the Father has set
within his own authority.
But you will receive power when the Holy Spirit has come upon you.
You will be witnesses to me
in Jerusalem, in all Judea and Samaria,
and to the uttermost parts of the earth."                             1:7-8

---

ACTS 9

---

**"Saul,**
Saul,
why do you persecute me?"                                             9:4


"I am
Jesus,
whom you are persecuting.
But rise up,
and enter into the city,
and you will be told
what you must do."                                                    9:5-6


"Ananias!"                                                            9:10


"Arise,
and go

to the street which is called Straight,
and inquire in the house of Judah
for one named Saul, a man of Tarsus.
For behold,
he is praying,
and in a vision
he has seen a man
named Ananias coming in,
and laying his hands on him,
that he might receive his sight."                                    9:11-12

"Go your way,
for he is my chosen vessel
to bear my name
before the nations and kings,
and the children of Israel.
For I will show him
how many things
he must suffer
for my name's sake."                                                9:15-16

ACTS 10

**"Rise,**
Peter,
kill and eat!"                                                       10:13

"What God has cleansed,
you must not call unclean."                                          10:15

ACTS 11

**"'Rise,**
Peter,
kill and eat!'"                                                      11:7

"'What God has cleansed,
don't you call unclean.'"                                            11:9

"'John indeed baptized in water,
but you will be baptized
in the Holy Spirit.'"                                                11:16

---

ACTS 18

---

**"Don't be afraid,**
but speak
and don't be silent;
for I am with you,
and no one will attack you
to harm you,
for I have many people in this city."                                          18:9-10

---

ACTS 20

---

**'It is more blessed to give than to receive.'"**                             20:35

---

ACTS 22

---

**"'Saul,**
Saul,
why are you persecuting me?'"                                                   22:7

"'I am
Jesus
of Nazareth, whom you persecute.'"                                             22:8

"'Arise,
and go
into Damascus.
There you will be told about all things
which are appointed for you to do.'"                                           22:10

"'Hurry
and get out of Jerusalem quickly,
because they will not receive testimony concerning me from you.'"              22:18

"'Depart,
for I will send you out
far from here to the Gentiles.'"                                               22:21

---

---

## "Cheer up,

Paul,
for as you have testified about me at Jerusalem,
so you must testify also at Rome."                        23:11

---

---

## "'Saul,

Saul,
why are you persecuting me?
It is hard for you to kick against the goads.'"            26:14

"'I am
Jesus,
whom you are persecuting.
But arise,
and stand
on your feet,
for I have appeared to you
for this purpose:
to appoint you
a servant
and a witness
both of the things which you have seen,
and of the things which I will reveal to you;
delivering you from the people,
and from the Gentiles,
to whom I send you,
to open their eyes,
that they may turn from darkness to light
and from the power of Satan to God,
that they may receive remission of sins
and an inheritance among those
who are sanctified
by faith in me.'"                                          26:15-18

## PAUL'S SECOND LETTER TO THE *Corinthians*

CHAPTER 12

**"My grace is sufficient for you,**
for my power is made perfect in weakness."

12:9

# *The Revelation* TO JOHN

**"I am**
the Alpha
and
the Omega,"...
"who is
and
who was
and
who is to come,
the Almighty."

1:8

"What you see,
write in a book
and send to the seven assemblies:
to Ephesus,
Smyrna,
Pergamum,
Thyatira,
Sardis,
Philadelphia,
and to Laodicea."

1:11

"Don't be afraid.
I am the first and the last,

and the Living one.
I was dead,
and behold,
I am alive
forevermore. Amen.
I have the keys of Death and of Hades.
Write therefore the things which you have seen,
and the things which are,
and the things which will happen hereafter;
the mystery of the seven stars
which you saw in my right hand,
and the seven golden lampstands.
The seven stars
are the angels of the seven assemblies.
The seven lampstands
are seven assemblies."                                                  1:17-20

----------------------------------------------------------------------

REVELATION 2

----------------------------------------------------------------------

## "To the angel of the assembly in Ephesus write:

'He who holds the seven stars in his right hand,
he who walks among the seven golden lampstands
says these things:'"                                                    2:1

"I know your works,
and your toil and perseverance,
and that you can't tolerate evil men,
and have tested those who call themselves apostles,
and they are not, and found them false.
You have perseverance
and have endured
for my name's sake,
and have not grown weary.
But I have this against you,
that you left your first love.
Remember therefore from where you have fallen,
and repent
and do the first works;
or else I am coming to you swiftly,
and will move your lampstand out of its place,
unless you repent.

But this you have,
that you hate the works of the Nicolaitans,
which I also hate.
He who has an ear,
let him hear what the Spirit says to the assemblies.
To him who overcomes
I will give to eat of the tree of life,
which is in the Paradise of my God."

2:2-7

"To the angel of the assembly in Smyrna write:
'The first and the last,
who was dead,
and has come to life
says these things:'"

2:8

"I know
your works,
oppression,
and your poverty (but you are rich),
and the blasphemy of those who say they are Jews,
and they are not,
but are a synagogue of Satan.
Don't be afraid of the things which you are about to suffer.
Behold,
the devil is about to throw some of you into prison,
that you may be tested;
and you will have oppression for ten days.
Be faithful to death,
and I will give you the crown of life.
He who has an ear,
let him hear what the Spirit says to the assemblies.
He who overcomes
won't be harmed by the second death."

2:9-11

"To the angel of the assembly in Pergamum write:
'He who has the sharp two-edged sword
says these things:'"

2:12

"I know
your works
and where you dwell,

where Satan's throne is.
You hold firmly to my name,
and didn't deny my faith
in the days of Antipas my witness,
my faithful one,
who was killed among you,
where Satan dwells.
But I have a few things against you,
because you have there some who hold the teaching of Balaam,
who taught Balak to throw
a stumbling block before the children of Israel,
to eat things sacrificed to idols,
and to commit sexual immorality.
So you also have some who hold to
the teaching of the Nicolaitans likewise.
Repent therefore,
or else I am coming to you quickly,
and I will make war against them
with the sword of my mouth.
He who has an ear,
let him hear what the Spirit says to the assemblies.
To him who overcomes,
to him I will give of the hidden manna,
and I will give him a white stone,
and on the stone a new name written,
which no one knows but he who receives it."                          2:13-17

"To the angel of the assembly in Thyatira write:
'The Son of God,
who has his eyes like a flame of fire,
and his feet are like burnished brass,
says these things:'"                                                 2:18

"I know
your works,
your love,
faith,
service,
patient endurance,
and that your last works are more than the first.
But I have this against you,

that you tolerate your woman, Jezebel,
who calls herself a prophetess.
She teaches and seduces my servants
to commit sexual immorality,
and to eat things sacrificed to idols.
I gave her time to repent,
but she refuses to repent
of her sexual immorality.
Behold,
I will throw her into a bed,
and those who commit adultery with her into great oppression,
unless they
repent of her works.
I will kill her children with Death,
and all the assemblies will know that
I am he who searches the minds and hearts.
I will give to each one of you
according to your deeds.
But to you I say,
to the rest who are in Thyatira,
as many as don't have this teaching,
who don't know what some call 'the deep things of Satan,'
to you I say, I am not putting any other burden on you.
Nevertheless, hold that which you have firmly until I come.
He who overcomes,
and he who keeps my works to the end,
to him I will give authority over the nations.
He will rule them with a rod of iron,
shattering them like clay pots;
as I also have received of my Father:
and I will give him the morning star.
He who has an ear,
let him hear what the Spirit says to the assemblies."

                                                              2:19-29

---

---

**"And to the angel of the assembly in Sardis write:**
'He who has the seven Spirits of God,
and the seven stars
says these things:
I know
your works,
that you have a reputation of being alive,
but you are dead.'"                                    3:1

"Wake up,
and keep the things that remain,
which you were about to throw away,
for I have found no works of yours perfected before my God.
Remember therefore how you have received and heard.
Keep it, and
repent.
If therefore you won't watch, I will come as a thief,
and you won't know what hour I will come upon you.
Nevertheless
you have a few names in Sardis
that did not defile their garments.
They will walk with me in white,
for they are worthy.
He who overcomes
will be arrayed in white garments,
and I will in no way blot his name
out of the book of life,
and I will confess his name before my Father,
and before his angels.
He who has an ear,
let him hear what the Spirit says to the assemblies."                    3:2-6

"To the angel of the assembly in Philadelphia write:
'He who is holy,
he who is true,
he who has the key of David,
he who opens and no one can shut,
and who shuts and no one opens,
says these things:'"                                    3:7

"I know
your works
(behold,
I have set before you an open door,
which no one can shut),
that you have a little power,
and kept my word,
and didn't deny my name.
Behold,
I give of the synagogue of Satan,
of those who say they are Jews,
and they are not, but lie.
Behold,
I will make them to come
and worship before your feet,
and to know that I have loved you.
Because you kept my command to endure,
I also will keep you from the hour of testing,
which is to come on the whole world,
to test those who dwell on the earth.
I am coming quickly!
Hold firmly that which you have,
so that no one takes your crown.
He who overcomes,
I will make him a pillar in the temple of my God,
and he will go out from there no more.
I will write on him the name of my God,
and the name of the city of my God,
the new Jerusalem,
which comes down out of heaven from my God,
and my own new name.
He who has an ear,
let him hear what the Spirit says to the assemblies."

3:8-13

"To the angel of the assembly in Laodicea write:
'The Amen,
the Faithful and True Witness,
the Head of God's creation,
says these things:'"

3:14

"I know
your works,
that you are neither cold nor hot.
I wish you were cold or hot.
So, because you are lukewarm,
and neither hot nor cold,
I will vomit you out of my mouth.
Because you say,
'I am rich, and have gotten riches,
and have need of nothing;'
and don't know that you are the wretched one,
miserable, poor, blind, and naked;
I counsel you to buy from me gold refined by fire,
that you may become rich;
and white garments, that you may clothe yourself,
and that the shame of your nakedness
may not be revealed;
and eye salve to anoint your eyes, that you may see.
As many as I love, I reprove and chasten.
Be zealous therefore, and
repent.
Behold,
I stand at the door and knock.
If anyone hears my voice and opens the door,
then I will come in to him,
and will dine with him,
and he with me.
He who overcomes,
I will give to him to sit down with me on my throne,
as I also overcame,
and sat down with my Father on his throne.
He who has an ear,
let him hear what the Spirit says to the assemblies."                    3:15-22

**"Behold,**
I come like a thief.
Blessed is he who watches,
and keeps his clothes,
so that he doesn't walk naked,
and they see his shame."

16:15

**"Behold,**
I am making all things new."

"Write,
for these words of God are faithful and true."

21:5

"It is done!
I am
the Alpha
and
the Omega,
the Beginning
and
the End.
I will give freely to him
who is thirsty
from the spring of the water of life.
He who overcomes,
I will give him these things.
I will be his God, and
he will be my son.
But for the cowardly, unbelieving, sinners,
abominable, murderers, sexually immoral,
sorcerers, idolaters, and all liars,
their part is in the lake that burns with fire and sulfur,
which is the second death."

21:6-8

**"Behold,**
I come quickly.
Blessed is he
who keeps the words
of the prophecy of this book."

22:7

"Behold,
I come quickly.
My reward is with me,
to repay to each man according to his work.
I am the Alpha and the Omega,
the First and the Last,
the Beginning and the End.
Blessed are those
who do his commandments,
that they may have the right to the tree of life,
and may enter in by the gates into the city.
Outside are the dogs,
the sorcerers, the sexually immoral,
the murderers, the idolaters,
and everyone who loves and practices falsehood.
I,
Jesus,
have sent my angel
to testify these things to you for the assemblies.
I am
the root
and
the offspring of David;
the Bright and Morning Star."

22:12-16

"Yes,
I come quickly."

22:20

# HOW TO KNOW Jesus

God loves you and created you to know him personally. He expresses this love in his Word:

> For God so loved the world that he gave his only begotten Son, that whoever believes in him should not perish, but have eternal life … Now this is eternal life: that they may know you, the only true God, and Jesus Christ, whom you have sent.
>
> —JOHN 3:16; 17:3

He knows you and wants you to know him!

Sin separates you from God, preventing you from knowing him. "All have sinned and fall short of the glory of God" (ROMANS 3:23). Sin has created the natural, willful desire you have to do your own thing. This causes spiritual separation from a Holy God that leads to death. "The wages of sin is death" (ROMANS 6:23). Sin also created the "God-void" in your soul which can be filled only by Jesus. People try all sorts of things to satisfy the longing in their hearts, but Jesus is the only answer.

Jesus Christ is God's only provision for our sin. He is the only Way to God.

> But God commends his own love toward us, in that while we were yet sinners, Christ died for us. For I delivered to you first of all that which I also received: that Christ died for our sins according to the Scriptures, that he was buried, that he was raised on the third day according to the Scriptures, and that he appeared to Cephas, then to the twelve. Then he appeared to over five hundred brothers at once, most of whom remain until now… "I am the way, the truth, and the life. No one comes to the Father, except through me."
>
> —ROMANS 5:8; 1 CORINTHIANS 15:3-6; JOHN 14:6

We must individually receive Jesus Christ as Savior and Lord. Then we can know God personally and experience his love.

- We receive Jesus by faith. Receiving him means experiencing a new birth!

> But as many as received him, to them he gave the right to become God's children, to those who believe in his name. For by grace you have been saved through faith, and that not of yourselves; it is the

gift of God, not of works, that no one would boast. Jesus answered, "Most certainly I tell you, unless one is born of water and spirit, he can't enter into the Kingdom of God! That which is born of the flesh is flesh. That which is born of the Spirit is spirit. Don't marvel that I said to you, 'You must be born anew.'"

—JOHN 1:12; EPHESIANS 2:8-9; JOHN 3:5-7

- We receive Jesus by personally inviting him into our lives!

  Behold, I stand at the door and knock. If anyone hears my voice and opens thedoor, then I will come in to him, and will dine with him, and he with me.

  —REVELATION 3:20

Receiving Jesus into our hearts means turning from self and trusting him to come into our lives forgiving us of our sins and making us what he wants us to be.

- We receive Jesus by faith as an act of our will. Ephesians 2:8 discusses the gift of salvation:

  "For by grace you have been saved through faith, and that not of yourselves; it is the gift of God."

The only act of your will needed is to believe and receive.

Pray the following to ask Jesus into your heart:

> *Jesus, I want to know you personally. Thank you for dying on the cross for my sins. Please come into my heart as my Savior and my Lord. Thank you for forgiving me of my sins and giving me eternal life. I turn my will over to you. Make me the person you want me to be. Praise you! Thank you. Help me trust in you. Amen.*

Do not follow feelings. Depending on feelings can be deceptive. Put your faith in the fact of God's Word and his promises for you. As you fill up with his Word, your feelings will follow your faith in what he says. Pray to God regularly and ask to be lead by the Holy Spirit. Read the Bible so you can become more intimately acquainted with God's ways. Surround yourself with good friends who know Jesus. Look for a friend whose life is producing the fruits of the Holy Spirit. Ask them to help disciple you in godly growth.

Tell someone about your decision to follow Jesus! It will strengthen your faith.

ANSWERS FOR *Life*

"What would Jesus do?" was a trendy saying for a few years. Bracelets and t-shirts promoted this slogan and encouraged everyone to consider Jesus' thought process before they acted. It was a movement that changed a lot of lives.

But, how exactly did Jesus decide what to do? How did he go about evaluating his options and discerning the right choices? He listened to his Father and did what his Father said. And, we can learn to how to follow in his footsteps by listening to him speak to our hearts through his Word. Follow Jesus by engaging in an intimate conversation with Him—about anything.

You may be surprised to learn the diverse topics that Jesus talks about in the Bible. Is there an issue in your life that is overwhelming or needs resolution? It is likely that Jesus has something to say about it. He understands more than you realize.

Every time Jesus spoke, what he said was loaded with meaning on many levels. His words are collected here under topical headings so that he may speak to your heart right now.

These are his personal promises to you. What will you do with them?

What does Jesus say about...

## Abandonment

"Eli, Eli, lima sabachthani?" ... "My God, my God, why have you forsaken me?" ~ "Behold, I am with you always, even to the end of the age." ~ "The foxes have holes, and the birds of the sky have nests, but the Son of Man has no place to lay his head." ~ "The time has come for the Son of Man to be glorified. Most certainly I tell you, unless a grain of wheat falls into the earth and dies, it remains by itself alone. But if it dies, it bears much fruit. He who loves his life will lose it. He who hates his life in this world will keep it to eternal life. If anyone serves me, let him follow me. Where I am, there will my servant also be. If anyone serves me, the Father will honor him." ~ "I am the true vine, and my Father is the farmer. Every branch in me that doesn't bear fruit, he takes away. Every branch that bears fruit, he prunes, that it may bear more fruit. You are already pruned clean because of the word which I have spoken to you. Remain in me, and I in you. As the branch can't bear fruit by itself, unless it remains in the vine, so neither can you, unless you remain in me. I am the vine. You are the branches. He who remains in me, and I in him, the same bears much fruit, for apart from me you can do nothing. If a man doesn't remain in me, he is thrown out as a branch, and is withered; and they gather them, throw them into the fire, and they are burned. If you remain in me, and my words remain in you, you will ask whatever you desire, and it will be done for you." ~ "I pray for them. I don't pray for the world, but for those whom you have given me, for they are yours. All things that are mine are yours, and yours are mine, and I am glorified in them."

MATT. 27:46, MATT. 28:20; LUKE 9:58; JOHN 12:23-26, 15:1-7, 17:9-10

## *Adultery*

"You have heard that it was said, 'You shall not commit adultery' but I tell you that everyone who gazes at a woman to lust after her has committed adultery with her already in his heart. If your right eye causes you to stumble, pluck it out and throw it away from you. For it is more profitable for you that one of your members should perish, than for your whole body to be cast into Gehenna. If your right hand causes you to stumble, cut it off, and throw it away from you. For it is more profitable for you that one of your members should perish, than for your whole body to be cast into Gehenna." ~ "It was also said, 'Whoever shall put away his wife, let him give her a writing of divorce' but I tell you that whoever puts away his wife, except for the cause of sexual immorality, makes her an adulteress; and whoever marries her when she is put away commits adultery." ~ "You said well, 'I have no husband,' for you have had five husbands; and he whom you now have is not your husband. This you have said truly." ~ "Woman, believe me, the hour comes, when neither in this mountain, nor in Jerusalem, will you worship the Father. You worship that which you don't know. We worship that which we know; for salvation is from the Jews. But the hour comes, and now is, when the true worshipers will worship the Father in spirit and truth, for the Father seeks such to be his worshipers." ~ "Peace be to you."

MATT. 5:27-30, 31-32; JOHN 4:18, 21-23, 20:26

## Anointing

"The Spirit of the Lord is on me, because he has anointed me to preach good news to the poor. He has sent me to heal the brokenhearted, to proclaim release to the captives, recovering of sight to the blind, to deliver those who are crushed, and to proclaim the acceptable year of the Lord." ~ "This is my commandment, that you love one another, even as I have loved you. Greater love has no one than this that someone lay down his life for his friends. You are my friends, if you do whatever I command you. No longer do I call you servants, for the servant doesn't know what his lord does. But I have called you friends, for everything that I heard from my Father, I have made known to you. You didn't choose me, but I chose you, and appointed you, that you should go and bear fruit, and that your fruit should remain; that whatever you will ask of the Father in my name, he may give it to you." ~ "I am Jesus, whom you are persecuting. But arise, and stand on your feet, for I have appeared to you for this purpose: to appoint you a servant and a witness both of the things which you have seen, and of the things which I will reveal to you; delivering you from the people, and from the Gentiles, to whom I send you, to open their eyes, that they may turn from darkness to light and from the power of Satan to God, that they may receive remission of sins and an inheritance among those who are sanctified by faith in me."

LUKE 4:18-19; JOHN 15:12-16; ACTS 26:15-18

## Anxiety

"No one can serve two masters, for either he will hate the one and love the other; or else he will be devoted to one and despise the other. You can't serve both God and Mammon. Therefore, I tell you, don't be anxious for your life: what you will eat, or what you will drink; nor yet for your body, what you will wear. Isn't life more than food, and the body more than clothing? See the birds of the sky, that they don't sow, neither do they reap, nor gather into barns. Your heavenly Father feeds them. Aren't you of much more value than they?" ~ "Which of you, by being anxious, can add one moment to his lifespan? Why are you anxious about clothing? Consider the lilies of the field, how they grow. They don't toil, neither do they spin, yet I tell you that even Solomon in all his glory was not dressed like one of these. But if God so clothes the grass of the field, which today exists, and tomorrow is thrown into the oven, won't he much more clothe you, you of little faith?" ~ "Therefore don't be anxious, saying, 'What will we eat?', 'What will we drink?' or, 'With what will we be clothed?' For the Gentiles seek after all these things; for your heavenly Father knows that you need all these things. But seek first God's Kingdom, and his righteousness; and all these things will be given to you as well. Therefore don't be anxious for tomorrow, for tomorrow will be anxious for itself. Each day's own evil is sufficient." ~ "What do you want me to do for you?" ~ "Martha, Martha, you are anxious and troubled about many things, but one thing is needed. Mary has chosen the good part, which will not be taken away from her." ~ "Peace I leave with you. My peace I give to you; not as the world gives, give I to you. Don't let your heart be troubled, neither let it be fearful."

MATT. 6:24-26, 27-30, 31-34; MARK 10:36; LUKE 10:41-42; JOHN 14:27

# Appearance

"Moreover when you fast, don't be like the hypocrites, with sad faces. For they disfigure their faces, that they may be seen by men to be fasting. Most certainly I tell you, they have received their reward. But you, when you fast, anoint your head, and wash your face; so that you are not seen by men to be fasting, but by your Father who is in secret, and your Father, who sees in secret, will reward you." ~ "Woe to you, scribes and Pharisees, hypocrites! For you clean the outside of the cup and of the platter, but within they are full of extortion and unrighteousness. You blind Pharisee, first clean the inside of the cup and of the platter, that its outside may become clean also." ~ "Beware of the scribes, who like to walk in long robes, and to get greetings in the marketplaces, and the best seats in the synagogues, and the best places at feasts: those who devour widows' houses, and for a pretense make long prayers. These will receive greater condemnation." ~ "Beware of the yeast of the Pharisees, which is hypocrisy. But there is nothing covered up, that will not be revealed, nor hidden, that will not be known. Therefore whatever you have said in the darkness will be heard in the light. What you have spoken in the ear in the inner rooms will be proclaimed on the housetops." ~ "I did one work, and you all marvel because of it. Moses has given you circumcision (not that it is of Moses, but of the fathers), and on the Sabbath you circumcise a boy. If a boy receives circumcision on the Sabbath, that the law of Moses may not be broken, are you angry with me, because I made a man completely healthy on the Sabbath? Don't judge according to appearance, but judge righteous judgment."

MATT. 6:16-18, 23:25-26; MARK 12:38-40; LUKE 12:1-3; JOHN 7:21-24

# Approval

"Most certainly I tell you that the tax collectors and the prostitutes are entering into the Kingdom of God before you. For John came to you in the way of righteousness, and you didn't believe him, but the tax collectors and the prostitutes believed him. When you saw it, you didn't even repent afterward, that you might believe him." ~ "His lord said to him, 'Well done, good and faithful servant. You have been faithful over a few things, I will set you over many things. Enter into the joy of your lord.'" ~ "You are those who justify yourselves in the sight of men, but God knows your hearts. For that which is exalted among men is an abomination in the sight of God." ~ "If you know these things, blessed are you if you do them." ~ "I don't speak concerning all of you. I know whom I have chosen. But that the Scripture may be fulfilled, 'He who eats bread with me has lifted up his heel against me.' From now on, I tell you before it happens, that when it happens, you may believe that I am he. Most certainly I tell you, he who receives whomever I send, receives me; and he who receives me, receives him who sent me." ~ "Nevertheless you have a few names in Sardis that did not defile their garments. They will walk with me in white, for they are worthy. He who overcomes will be arrayed in white garments, and I will in no way blot his name out of the book of life, and I will confess his name before my Father, and before his angels. He who has an ear, let him hear what the Spirit says to the assemblies."

MATT. 21:31-32, 25:21; LUKE 16:15; JOHN 13:17, 18-20, 13:17; REV. 3:4-6

# *Authenticity*

"For you set aside the commandment of God, and hold tightly to the tradition of men —the washing of pitchers and cups, and you do many other such things"... "Full well do you reject the commandment of God, that you may keep your tradition. For Moses said, 'Honor your father and your mother;' and, 'He who speaks evil of father or mother, let him be put to death.' But you say, 'If a man tells his father or his mother, "Whatever profit you might have received from me is Corban, that is to say, given to God;" then you no longer allow him to do anything for his father or his mother, making void the word of God by your tradition, which you have handed down. You do many things like this." ~ "For there is no good tree that brings forth rotten fruit; nor again a rotten tree that brings forth good fruit. For each tree is known by its own fruit. For people don't gather figs from thorns, nor do they gather grapes from a bramble bush. The good man out of the good treasure of his heart brings out that which is good, and the evil man out of the evil treasure of his heart brings out that which is evil, for out of the abundance of the heart, his mouth speaks." ~ "If I tell you, you won't believe, and if I ask, you will in no way answer me or let me go. From now on, the Son of Man will be seated at the right hand of the power of God." ~ "You say it, because I am." ~ "Behold, an Israelite indeed, in whom is no deceit!" ~ "If I testify about myself, my witness is not valid. It is another who testifies about me. I know that the testimony which he testifies about me is true. You have sent to John, and he has testified to the truth. But the testimony which I receive is not from man. However, I say these things that you may be saved. He was the burning and shining lamp, and you were willing to rejoice for a while in his light. But the testimony which I have is greater than that of John, for the works which the Father gave me to accomplish, the very works that I do, testify about me, that the Father has sent me. The Father himself, who sent me, has testified about me. You have neither heard his voice at any time, nor seen his form. You don't have his word living in you; because you don't believe him whom he sent."

MARK 7:8-13; LUKE 6:43-45, 22:67-69, 22:70; JOHN 1:47, 5:31-38

# Authority

"Why do you think evil in your hearts? For which is easier, to say, 'Your sins are forgiven;' or to say, 'Get up, and walk?' But that you may know that the Son of Man has authority on earth to forgive sins" . . . "Get up, and take up your mat, and go up to your house." ~ "Blessed are you, Simon Bar Jonah, for flesh and blood has not revealed this to you, but my Father who is in heaven. I also tell you that you are Peter, and on this rock I will build my assembly, and the gates of Hades will not prevail against it. I will give to you the keys of the Kingdom of Heaven, and whatever you bind on earth will have been bound in heaven; and whatever you release on earth will have been released in heaven." ~ "The Sabbath was made for man, not man for the Sabbath. Therefore the Son of Man is lord even of the Sabbath." ~ "Why are you reasoning so in your hearts? Which is easier to say, 'Your sins are forgiven you;' or to say, 'Arise and walk?' But that you may know that the Son of Man has authority on earth to forgive sins" ~ "I tell you, I have not found such great faith, no, not in Israel." ~ "You say that I am a king. For this reason I have been born, and for this reason I have come into the world, that I should testify to the truth. Everyone who is of the truth listens to my voice." ~ "You would have no power at all against me, unless it were given to you from above. Therefore he who delivered me to you has greater sin." ~ "It is finished." ~ "I am the Alpha and the Omega," ... "who is and who was and who is to come, the Almighty."

MATT. 9:4-6, 16:17-19; MARK 2:27-28; LUKE 5:22-24, 7:9; JOHN 18:37, 19:11, 19: 30; REV. 1:8

# Belief

"Son, cheer up! Your sins are forgiven you." ~ "Daughter, cheer up! Your faith has made you well." ~ "Make room, because the girl isn't dead, but sleeping." ~ "Do you believe that I am able to do this?" ~ "According to your faith be it done to you." ~ "See that no one knows about this." ~ "Why does this generation seek a sign? Most certainly I tell you, no sign will be given to this generation." ~ "Unbelieving generation, how long shall I be with you? How long shall I bear with you? Bring him to me." ~ "How long has it been since this has come to him?" ~ "If you can believe, all things are possible to him who believes." ~ "You mute and deaf spirit, I command you, come out of him, and never enter him again!" ~

"This kind can come out by nothing, except by prayer and fasting." ~ "With men it is impossible, but not with God, for all things are possible with God." ~ "I tell you, I have not found such great faith, no, not in Israel." ~ "What do you want me to do?" ~ "Receive your sight. Your faith has healed you." ~ "He who believes in him is not judged. He who doesn't believe has been judged already, because he has not believed in the name of the one and only Son of God." ~ "This is the work of God, that you believe in him whom he has sent." ~ "Do you believe in the Son of God?"

MATT. 9:2, 9:22, 9:24, 9:28, 9:29, 9:30; MARK 8:12, 9:19, 9:21, 9:23, 9:25, 9:29, 10:27; LUKE 7:9, 18:41, 18:42; JOHN 3:18, 6:29, 9:35

# Betrayal

"Most certainly I tell you that one of you will betray me." ~ "He who dipped his hand with me in the dish, the same will betray me. The Son of Man goes, even as it is written of him, but woe to that man through whom the Son of Man is betrayed! It would be better for that man if he had not been born." ~ "Most certainly I tell you that tonight, before the rooster crows, you will deny me three times." ~ "Sleep on now, and take your rest. Behold, the hour is at hand, and the Son of Man is betrayed into the hands of sinners. Arise, let's be going. Behold, he who betrays me is at hand." ~ "Most certainly I tell you, one of you will betray me—he who eats with me." ~ "It is one of the twelve, he who dips with me in the dish. For the Son of Man goes, even as it is written about him, but woe to that man by whom the Son of Man is betrayed! It would be better for that man if he had not been born." ~ "Beware of the scribes, who like to walk in long robes, and love greetings in the marketplaces, the best seats in the synagogues, and the best places at feasts; who devour widows' houses, and for a pretense make long prayers: these will receive greater condemnation." ~ "This cup is the new covenant in my blood, which is poured out for you. But behold, the hand of him who betrays me is with me on the table. The Son of Man indeed goes, as it has been determined, but woe to that man through whom he is betrayed!" ~ "Someone who has bathed only needs to have his feet washed, but is completely clean. You are clean, but not all of you."

MATT. 26:21, 26:23-24, 26:34, 26:45-46; MARK 14:18, 14:20-21; LUKE 20:46-47, 22:20-22; JOHN 13:10

# Business

"No one can serve two masters, for either he will hate the one and love the other; or else he will be devoted to one and despise the other. You can't serve both God and Mammon. Therefore, I tell you, don't be anxious for your life: what you will eat, or what you will drink; nor yet for your body, what you will wear. Isn't life more than food, and the body more than clothing? See the birds of the sky, that they don't sow, neither do they reap, nor gather into barns. Your heavenly Father feeds them. Aren't you of much more value than they?" ~ "There was a certain rich man who had a manager. An accusation was made to him that this man was wasting his possessions. He called him, and said to him, 'What is this that I hear about you? Give an accounting of your management, for you can no longer be manager.'" ~ "The manager said within himself, 'What will I do, seeing that my lord is taking away the management position from me? I don't have strength to dig. I am ashamed to beg. I know what I will do, so that when I am removed from management, they may receive me into their houses.' Calling each one of his lord's debtors to him, he said to the first, 'How much do you owe to my lord?' He said, 'A hundred batos of oil.' He said to him, 'Take your bill, and sit down quickly and write fifty.' Then he said to another, 'How much do you owe?' He said, 'A hundred cors of wheat.' He said to him, 'Take your bill, and write eighty.'" ~ "His lord commended the dishonest manager because he had done wisely, for the children of this world are, in their own generation, wiser than the children of the light. I tell you, make for yourselves friends by means of unrighteous mammon, so that when you fail, they may receive you into the eternal tents. He who is faithful in a very little is faithful also in much. He who is dishonest in a very little is also dishonest in much. If therefore you have not been faithful in the unrighteous mammon, who will commit to your trust the true riches? If you have not been faithful in that which is another's, who will give you that which is your own? No servant can serve two masters, for either he will hate the one, and love the other; or else he will hold to one, and despise the other. You aren't able to serve God and mammon." ~ "A certain nobleman went into a far country to receive for himself a kingdom, and to return. He called ten servants of his, and gave them ten mina coins, and told them, 'Conduct business until I come.' But his citizens hated him, and sent an envoy after him, saying, 'We don't want this man to reign over us.'"

~ "It happened when he had come back again, having received the kingdom, that he commanded these servants, to whom he had given the money, to be called to him, that he might know what they had gained by conducting business. The first came before him, saying, 'Lord, your mina has made ten more minas.'" ~ "He said to him, 'Well done, you good servant! Because you were found faithful with very little, you shall have authority over ten cities.'" ~ "The second came, saying, 'Your mina, Lord, has made five minas.'" ~ "So he said to him, 'And you are to be over five cities.' Another came, saying, 'Lord, behold, your mina, which I kept laid away in a handkerchief, for I feared you, because you are an exacting man. You take up that which you didn't lay down, and reap that which you didn't sow.'" ~ "He said to him, 'Out of your own mouth will I judge you, you wicked servant! You knew that I am an exacting man, taking up that which I didn't lay down, and reaping that which I didn't sow. Then why didn't you deposit my money in the bank, and at my coming, I might have earned interest on it?' He said to those who stood by, 'Take the mina away from him, and give it to him who has the ten minas.'" ~ "They said to him, 'Lord, he has ten minas!' 'For I tell you that to everyone who has, will more be given; but from him who doesn't have, even that which he has will be taken away from him. But bring those enemies of mine who didn't want me to reign over them here, and kill them before me.'"

MATT. 6:24-26; LUKE 16:1-2, 16:3-7, 16:8-13, 19:12-14, 19:15-16, 19:17, 19:18, 19:19-21, 19:22-24, 19:25-27

## Character

"Either make the tree good, and its fruit good, or make the tree corrupt, and its fruit corrupt; for the tree is known by its fruit. You offspring of vipers, how can you, being evil, speak good things? For out of the abundance of the heart, the mouth speaks. The good man out of his good treasure brings out good things, and the evil man out of his evil treasure brings out evil things. I tell you that every idle word that men speak, they will give account of it in the day of judgment. For by your words you will be justified, and by your words you will be condemned." ~ "The Kingdom of God doesn't come with observation; neither will they say, 'Look, here!' or, 'Look, there!' for behold, the Kingdom of God is within you." ~ "Nevertheless you have a few names in Sardis that did not defile their garments. They will walk with me in white, for they are worthy. He who overcomes will be arrayed in white garments, and I will in no way blot his name out of the book of life, and I will confess his name before my Father, and before his angels. He who has an ear, let him hear what the Spirit says to the assemblies."

MATT. 12: 33-37; LUKE 17:20-21; REV. 3:4-6·

# Children

"Most certainly I tell you, unless you turn, and become as little children, you will in no way enter into the Kingdom of Heaven. Whoever therefore humbles himself as this little child, the same is the greatest in the Kingdom of Heaven. Whoever receives one such little child in my name receives me, but whoever causes one of these little ones who believe in me to stumble, it would be better for him that a huge millstone should be hung around his neck, and that he should be sunk in the depths of the sea." ~ "Allow the little children, and don't forbid them to come to me; for the Kingdom of Heaven belongs to ones like these." ~ "Whoever receives one such little child in my name, receives me, and whoever receives me, doesn't receive me, but him who sent me." ~ "Allow the little children to come to me, and don't hinder them, for the Kingdom of God belongs to such as these. Most certainly, I tell you, whoever doesn't receive the Kingdom of God like a little child, he will in no way enter into it."

MATT. 18:3-6, 19:14; MARK 9:37; LUKE 18:16-17

# Comfort

"Blessed are the poor in spirit, for theirs is the Kingdom of Heaven. Blessed are those who mourn, for they shall be comforted. Blessed are the gentle, for they shall inherit the earth. Blessed are those who hunger and thirst after righteousness, for they shall be filled. Blessed are the merciful, for they shall obtain mercy. Blessed are the pure in heart, for they shall see God. Blessed are the peacemakers, for they shall be called children of God. Blessed are those who have been persecuted for righteousness' sake, for theirs is the Kingdom of Heaven." ~ "Blessed are you when people reproach you, persecute you, and say all kinds of evil against you falsely, for my sake. Rejoice, and be exceedingly glad, for great is your reward in heaven. For that is how they persecuted the prophets who were before you." ~ "Come to me, all you who labor and are heavily burdened, and I will give you rest. Take my yoke upon you, and learn from me, for I am gentle and lowly in heart; and you will find rest for your souls. For my yoke is easy, and my burden is light." ~ "Aren't five sparrows sold for two assaria coins? Not one of them is forgotten by God. But the very hairs of your head are all numbered. Therefore don't be afraid. You are of more value than many sparrows." ~ "Why are you troubled? Why do doubts arise in your hearts? See my hands and my feet, that it is truly me. Touch me and see, for a spirit doesn't have flesh and bones, as you see that I have." ~ "Do you have anything here to eat?" ~ "I am he, the one who speaks to you." ~ "Most certainly, I tell you, I am the sheep's door. All who came before me are thieves and robbers, but the sheep didn't listen to them. I am the door. If anyone enters in by me, he will be saved, and will go in and go out, and will find pasture. The thief only comes to steal, kill, and destroy. I came that they may have life, and may have it abundantly." ~ "Woman, why are you weeping? Who are you looking for?"

MATT. 5:3-10, 5:11-12, 11:28-29; LUKE 12:6-7, 24:38-39, 24:41; JOHN 4:26, 10:7-10, 20:15

# *Control*

"Allow it now, for this is the fitting way for us to fulfill all righteousness." ~ "Come to me, all you who labor and are heavily burdened, and I will give you rest. Take my yoke upon you, and learn from me, for I am gentle and lowly in heart; and you will find rest for your souls. For my yoke is easy, and my burden is light." ~ "Most certainly I tell you, unless you turn, and become as little children, you will in no way enter into the Kingdom of Heaven. Whoever therefore humbles himself as this little child, the same is the greatest in the Kingdom of Heaven." ~ "When they lead you away and deliver you up, don't be anxious beforehand, or premeditate what you will say, but say whatever will be given you in that hour. For it is not you who speak, but the Holy Spirit." ~ "When the strong man, fully armed, guards his own dwelling, his goods are safe. But when someone stronger attacks him and overcomes him, he takes from him his whole armor in which he trusted, and divides his plunder." ~ "Because I told you, 'I saw you underneath the fig tree,' do you believe? You will see greater things than these!"

MATT. 3:15, 11:28-29, 18:3-4; MARK 13:11; LUKE 11:21-22; JOHN 1:50

# *Courage*

"Behold, I send you out as sheep in the midst of wolves. Therefore be wise as serpents, and harmless as doves. But beware of men: for they will deliver you up to councils, and in their synagogues they will scourge you. Yes, and you will be brought before governors and kings for my sake, for a testimony to them and to the nations. But when they deliver you up, don't be anxious how or what you will say, for it will be given you in that hour what you will say. For it is not you who speak, but the Spirit of your Father who speaks in you." ~ "Aren't two sparrows sold for an assarion coin? Not one of them falls on the ground apart from your Father's will, but the very hairs of your head are all numbered. Therefore don't be afraid. You are of more value than many sparrows. Everyone therefore who confesses me before men, him I will also confess before my Father who is in heaven. But whoever denies me before men, him I will also deny before my Father who is in heaven." ~ "I tell you, arise, take up your mat, and go to your house." ~ "Follow me!" ~ "It is I. Don't be afraid." ~ "Don't let your heart be troubled. Believe in God. Believe also in me. In my Father's house are many homes. If it weren't so, I would have told you. I am going to prepare a place for you. If I go and prepare a place for you, I will come again, and will receive you to myself; that where I am, you may be there also. Where I go, you know, and you know the way." ~ "Rise, Peter, kill and eat!" ~ "Don't be afraid, but speak and don't be silent; for I am with you, and no one will attack you to harm you, for I have many people in this city."

MATT. 10:16-20, 10:29-33; MARK 2:11; LUKE 9:59; JOHN 6:20, 14:1-4; ACTS 10:13, 18:9-10

# *Death*

"Don't be afraid, only believe." ~ "Why do you make an uproar and weep? The child is not dead, but is asleep." ~ "Talitha cumi!" . . . "Girl, I tell you, get up!" ~ "Most certainly I tell you, there are some standing here who will in no way taste death until they see the Kingdom of God come with power." ~ "Don't be afraid. Only believe, and she will be healed." ~ "Don't weep. She isn't dead, but sleeping." ~ "Child, arise!" ~ "If anyone desires to come after me, let him deny himself, take up his cross, and follow me. For whoever desires to save his life will lose it, but whoever will lose his life for my sake, the same will save it. For what does it profit a man if he gains the whole world, and loses or forfeits his own self? For whoever will be ashamed of me and of my words, of him will the Son of Man be ashamed, when he comes in his glory, and the glory of the Father, and of the holy angels. But I tell you the truth: There are some of those who stand here, who will in no way taste of death, until they see the Kingdom of God." ~ "I tell you, my friends, don't be afraid of those who kill the body, and after that have no more that they can do. But I will warn you whom you should fear. Fear him, who after he has killed, has power to cast into Gehenna. Yes, I tell you, fear him." ~ " Most certainly, I tell you, if a person keeps my word, he will never see death." ~ "Our friend, Lazarus, has fallen asleep, but I am going so that I may awake him out of sleep." ~ "Lazarus is dead. I am glad for your sakes that I was not there, so that you may believe. Nevertheless, let's go to him." ~ "Your brother will rise again." ~ "I am the resurrection and the life. He who believes in me will still live, even if he dies. Whoever lives and believes in me will never die. Do you believe this?" ~ "Most certainly I tell you, unless a grain of wheat falls into the earth and dies, it remains by itself alone. But if it dies, it bears much fruit. He who loves his life will lose it. He who hates his life in this world will keep it to eternal life. If anyone serves me, let him follow me. Where I am, there will my servant also be. If anyone serves me, the Father will honor him."

MARK 5:36, 5:39, 5:41, 9:1; LUKE 8:50, 8:52, 8:54, 9:23-27, 12:4-5; JOHN 8:51, 11:11, 11:14-15, 11:23, 11:25-26, 12:24-26

# Deliverance

"Heal the sick, cleanse the lepers, and cast out demons. Freely you received, so freely give." ~ "This kind can come out by nothing, except by prayer and fasting." ~ "What do you want me to do for you?" ~ "Follow me!" ~ "Leave the dead to bury their own dead, but you go and announce the Kingdom of God." ~ "Listen to what the unrighteous judge says. Won't God avenge his chosen ones, who are crying out to him day and night, and yet he exercises patience with them? I tell you that he will avenge them quickly. Nevertheless, when the Son of Man comes, will he find faith on the earth?" ~ "Are you the teacher of Israel, and don't understand these things? Most certainly I tell you, we speak that which we know, and testify of that which we have seen, and you don't receive our witness. If I told you earthly things and you don't believe, how will you believe if I tell you heavenly things? No one has ascended into heaven, but he who descended out of heaven, the Son of Man, who is in heaven. As Moses lifted up the serpent in the wilderness, even so must the Son of Man be lifted up, that whoever believes in him should not perish, but have eternal life." ~ "Who are you looking for?" ~ "I am the Alpha and the Omega" . . . "who is and who was and who is to come, the Almighty."

MATT.10:8; MARK 9:29, 10:36; LUKE 9:59, 9:60, 18:6-8; JOHN 3:10-15, 18:4; REV. 1:8

## Depression

"What do you want me to do for you?" ~ "Have faith in God. For most certainly I tell you, whoever may tell this mountain, 'Be taken up and cast into the sea,' and doesn't doubt in his heart, but believes that what he says is happening; he shall have whatever he says. Therefore I tell you, all things whatever you pray and ask for, believe that you have received them, and you shall have them. Whenever you stand praying, forgive, if you have anything against anyone; so that your Father, who is in heaven, may also forgive you your transgressions. But if you do not forgive, neither will your Father in heaven forgive your transgressions." ~ "Follow me!" ~ "I tell you, keep asking, and it will be given you. Keep seeking, and you will find. Keep knocking, and it will be opened to you. For everyone who asks receives. He who seeks finds. To him who knocks it will be opened." ~ "What are you talking about as you walk, and are sad?" ~ "You will know the truth, and the truth will make you free." ~ "If you love me, keep my commandments. I will pray to the Father, and he will give you another Counselor, that he may be with you forever,— the Spirit of truth, whom the world can't receive; for it doesn't see him, neither knows him. You know him, for he lives with you, and will be in you. I will not leave you orphans. I will come to you. Yet a little while, and the world will see me no more; but you will see me. Because I live, you will live also. In that day you will know that I am in my Father, and you in me, and I in you. One who has my commandments, and keeps them, that person is one who loves me. One who loves me will be loved by my Father, and I will love him, and will reveal myself to him." ~ "My grace is sufficient for you, for my power is made perfect in weakness."

MARK 10:36, 11:22-26; LUKE 9:59, 11:9-10, 24:17; JOHN 8:32, 14:15-21, 2 COR. 12:9

# Destiny

"The Son of Man is being handed over to the hands of men, and they will kill him; and when he is killed, on the third day he will rise again." ~ "Behold, we are going up to Jerusalem. The Son of Man will be delivered to the chief priests and the scribes. They will condemn him to death, and will deliver him to the Gentiles. They will mock him, spit on him, scourge him, and kill him. On the third day he will rise again." ~ "Have you come out, as against a robber, with swords and clubs to seize me? I was daily with you in the temple teaching, and you didn't arrest me. But this is so that the Scriptures might be fulfilled." ~ "Today, this Scripture has been fulfilled in your hearing." ~ "Behold, we are going up to Jerusalem, and all the things that are written through the prophets concerning the Son of Man will be completed. For he will be delivered up to the Gentiles, will be mocked, treated shamefully, and spit on. They will scourge and kill him. On the third day, he will rise again." ~ "This is what I told you, while I was still with you, that all things which are written in the law of Moses, the prophets, and the psalms, concerning me must be fulfilled." ~ "It is finished." ~ "Peace be to you." ~ "He who has an ear, let him hear what the Spirit says to the assemblies. To him who overcomes, to him I will give of the hidden manna, and I will give him a white stone, and on the stone a new name written, which no one knows but he who receives it."

MARK 9:31, 10:33-34, 14:48-49; LUKE 4:21, 18:31-33, 24:44; JOHN 19:30, 20:19; REV. 2:17

# Devotion

"Follow me." ~ "Whoever gives one of these little ones just a cup of cold water to drink in the name of a disciple, most certainly I tell you he will in no way lose his reward." ~ "The greatest is, 'Hear, Israel, the Lord our God, the Lord is one: you shall love the Lord your God with all your heart, and with all your soul, and with all your mind, and with all your strength.' This is the first commandment. The second is like this, 'You shall love your neighbor as yourself.' There is no other commandment greater than these." ~ "You are not far from the Kingdom of God." ~ "Leave her alone. Why do you trouble her? She has done a good work for me. For you always have the poor with you, and whenever you want to, you can do them good; but you will not always have me. She has done what she could.

She has anointed my body beforehand for the burying. Most certainly I tell you, wherever this Good News may be preached throughout the whole world, that which this woman has done will also be spoken of for a memorial of her." ~ "A certain man was going down from Jerusalem to Jericho, and he fell among robbers, who both stripped him and beat him, and departed, leaving him half dead. By chance a certain priest was going down that way. When he saw him, he passed by on the other side. In the same way a Levite also, when he came to the place, and saw him, passed by on the other side. But a certain Samaritan, as he traveled, came where he was. When he saw him, he was moved with compassion, came to him, and bound up his wounds, pouring on oil and wine. He set him on his own animal, and brought him to an inn, and took care of him. On the next day, when he departed, he took out two denarii, and gave them to the host, and said to him, 'Take care of him. Whatever you spend beyond that, I will repay you when I return.' Now which of these three do you think seemed to be a neighbor to him who fell among the robbers?" ~ "Truly I tell you, this poor widow put in more than all of them, for all these put in gifts for God from their abundance, but she, out of her poverty, put in all that she had to live on."

MATT 9:9, 10:42; MARK 12:29-31, 12:34, 14:6-9; LUKE 10:30-36, 21:3-4

## *Direction and Guidance*

"Come after me, and I will make you fishers for men." ~ "Follow me." ~ "Let's go over to the other side." ~ "No one, having put his hand to the plow, and looking back, is fit for the Kingdom of God." ~ "I tell you, keep asking, and it will be given you. Keep seeking, and you will find. Keep knocking, and it will be opened to you. For everyone who asks receives. He who seeks finds. To him who knocks it will be opened." ~ "What do you want me to do?" ~ "Arise, take up your mat, and walk." ~ "Most certainly, I tell you, one who doesn't enter by the door into the sheep fold, but climbs up some other way, the same is a thief and a robber. But one who enters in by the door is the shepherd of the sheep. The gatekeeper opens the gate for him, and the sheep listen to his voice. He calls his own sheep by name, and leads them out. Whenever he brings out his own sheep, he goes before them, and the sheep follow him, for they know his voice. They will by no means follow a stranger, but will flee from him; for they don't know the voice of strangers." ~ "Yet a little while the light is with you. Walk while you have the light, that darkness doesn't overtake you. He who walks in the darkness doesn't know where he is going. While you have the light, believe in the light, that you may become children of light." ~ "Arise, and go into Damascus. There you will be told about all things which are appointed for you to do.'"

MATT. 4:19; MARK 2:14, 4:35; LUKE 9:62, 11:9-10, 18:41; JOHN 5:8, 10:1-5, 12:35-36; ACTS 22:10

# Discernment

"Beware of false prophets, who come to you in sheep's clothing, but inwardly are ravening wolves. By their fruits you will know them. Do you gather grapes from thorns, or figs from thistles? Even so, every good tree produces good fruit; but the corrupt tree produces evil fruit. A good tree can't produce evil fruit, neither can a corrupt tree produce good fruit. Every tree that doesn't grow good fruit is cut down, and thrown into the fire. Therefore, by their fruits you will know them. Not everyone who says to me, 'Lord, Lord,' will enter into the Kingdom of Heaven; but he who does the will of my Father who is in heaven. Many will tell me in that day, 'Lord, Lord, didn't we prophesy in your name, in your name cast out demons, and in your name do many mighty works?' Then I will tell them, 'I never knew you. Depart from me, you who work iniquity.'" ~ "'By hearing you will hear, and will in no way understand; Seeing you will see, and will in no way perceive: for this people's heart has grown callous, their ears are dull of hearing, they have closed their eyes; or else perhaps they might perceive with their eyes, hear with their ears, understand with their heart, and should turn again; and I would heal them.'" ~ "Then if any man tells you, 'Behold, here is the Christ,' or, 'There,' don't believe it. For there will arise false christs, and false prophets, and they will show great signs and wonders, so as to lead astray, if possible, even the chosen ones." ~ "Behold, I have told you beforehand. If therefore they tell you, 'Behold, he is in the wilderness,' don't go out; 'Behold, he is in the inner rooms,' don't believe it." ~ "Follow me." ~ "Watch out that you don't get led astray, for many will come in my name, saying, 'I am he,' and, 'The time is at hand.' Therefore don't follow them. When you hear of wars and disturbances, don't be terrified, for these things must happen first, but the end won't come immediately." ~ "Behold, I come like a thief. Blessed is he who watches, and keeps his clothes, so that he doesn't walk naked, and they see his shame."

MATT. 7:15-23, 13:14-15, 24:23-24, 24:25-26; LUKE 5:27, 21:8-9; REV. 16:15

# Division

"Don't think that I came to send peace on the earth. I didn't come to send peace, but a sword. For I came to set a man at odds against his father, and a daughter against her mother, and a daughter-in-law against her mother-in-law. A man's foes will be those of his own household. He who loves father or mother more than me is not worthy of me; and he who loves son or daughter more than me isn't worthy of me. He who doesn't take his cross and follow after me, isn't worthy of me." ~ "Don't forbid him, for there is no one who will do a mighty work in my name, and be able quickly to speak evil of me. For whoever is not against us is on our side. For whoever will give you a cup of water to drink in my name, because you are Christ's, most certainly I tell you, he will in no way lose his reward." ~ "The greatest is, 'Hear, Israel, the Lord our God, the Lord is one: you shall love the Lord your God with all your heart, and with all your soul, and with all your mind, and with all your strength.' This is the first commandment. The second is like this, 'You shall love your neighbor as yourself.' There is no other commandment greater than these." ~ "Every kingdom divided against itself is brought to desolation. A house divided against itself falls. If Satan also is divided against himself, how will his kingdom stand? For you say that I cast out demons by Beelzebul. But if I cast out demons by Beelzebul, by whom do your children cast them out? Therefore will they be your judges. But if I by the finger of God cast out demons, then the Kingdom of God has come to you." ~ "I came to throw fire on the earth. I wish it were already kindled. But I have a baptism to be baptized with, and how distressed I am until it is accomplished! Do you think that I have come to give peace in the earth? I tell you, no, but rather division. For from now on, there will be five in one house divided, three against two, and two against three. They will be divided, father against son, and son against father; mother against daughter, and daughter against her mother; mother-in-law against her daughter-in-law, and daughter-in-law against her mother-in-law." ~ "Peace be to you."

MATT. 10:34-38; MARK 9:39-41, 12:29-31; LUKE 11:17-20, 12:49-53; JOHN 20:26

# Divorce

"It was also said, 'Whoever shall put away his wife, let him give her a writing of divorce' but I tell you that whoever puts away his wife, except for the cause of sexual immorality,  makes her an adulteress; and whoever marries her when she is put away commits adultery." ~ "Moses, because of the hardness of your hearts, allowed you to divorce your wives, but from the beginning it has not been so. I tell you that whoever divorces his wife, except for sexual immorality, and marries another, commits adultery; and he who marries her when she is divorced commits adultery." ~ "Everyone who divorces his wife, and marries another, commits adultery. He who marries one who is divorced from a husband commits adultery." ~ "Why do you call me good? No one is good, except one—God. You know the commandments: 'Don't commit adultery,' 'Don't murder,' 'Don't steal,' 'Don't give false testimony,' 'Honor your father and your mother.'" ~ "He who is without sin among you, let him throw the first stone at her."…"Woman, where are your accusers? Did no one condemn you?"…"Neither do I condemn you. Go your way. From now on, sin no more." ~ "Peace be to you."

MATT 5:31-32; 19:8-9; LUKE 16:18; 18:19-20; JOHN 8:7-11, 20:19

# Dominion

"Every kingdom divided against itself is brought to desolation, and every city or house divided against itself will not stand. If Satan casts out Satan, he is divided against himself. How then will his kingdom stand? If I by Beelzebul cast out demons, by whom do your children cast them out? Therefore they will be your judges. But if I by the Spirit of God cast out demons, then the Kingdom of God has come upon you. Or how can one enter into the house of the strong man, and plunder his goods, unless he first bind the strong man? Then he will plunder his house." ~ "Did you never read what David did, when he had need, and was hungry—he, and those who were with him? How he entered into God's house when Abiathar was high priest, and ate the show bread, which is not lawful to eat except for the priests, and gave also to those who were with him?" ~ "The Sabbath was made for man, not man for the Sabbath. Therefore the Son of Man is lord even of the Sabbath." ~ "Peace! Be still!" ~ "Is it lawful to heal on the Sabbath?" ~ "Which of you, if your son or an ox fell into a well, wouldn't immediately pull him out on a Sabbath day?" ~ "I am the Alpha and the Omega" ... "who is and who was and who is to come, the Almighty."

MATT. 12:25-29; MARK 2:25-26, 2:27-28, 4:39; LUKE 14:3, 14:5 REV 1:8

# Eating Disorders

"It is written, 'Man shall not live by bread alone, but by every word that proceeds out of the mouth of God.'" ~ "Hear, and understand. That which enters into the mouth doesn't defile the man; but that which proceeds out of the mouth, this defiles the man." ~ "Do you also still not understand? Don't you understand that whatever goes into the mouth passes into the belly, and then out of the body? But the things which proceed out of the mouth come out of the heart, and they defile the man. For out of the heart come forth evil thoughts, murders, adulteries, sexual sins, thefts, false testimony, and blasphemies. These are the things which defile the man; but to eat with unwashed hands doesn't defile the man." ~ "'You shall love the Lord your God with all your heart, with all your soul, and with all your mind.' This is the first and great commandment." ~ "Cheer up! It is I! Don't be afraid." ~ "With men it is impossible, but not with God, for all things are possible with God." ~ "What do you want me to do for you?" ~ "Beware of the yeast of the Pharisees, which is hypocrisy. But there is nothing covered up, that will not be revealed, nor hidden, that will not be known. Therefore whatever you have said in the darkness will be heard in the light. What you have spoken in the ear in the inner rooms will be proclaimed on the housetops." ~ "Give me a drink." ~ "If you knew the gift of God, and who it is who says to you, 'Give me a drink,' you would have asked him, and he would have given you living water." ~ "I have food to eat that you don't know about." ~ "My food is to do the will of him who sent me, and to accomplish his work." ~ "Do you want to be made well?" ~ "Arise, take up your mat, and walk." ~ "Most certainly I tell you, you seek me, not because you saw signs, but because you ate of the loaves, and were filled. Don't work for the food which perishes, but for the food which remains to eternal life, which the Son of Man will give to you. For God the Father has sealed him." ~ "Don't murmur among yourselves. No one can come to me unless the Father who sent him draws him, and I will raise him up in the last day. It is written in the prophets, 'They will all be taught by God.' Therefore everyone who hears from the Father, and has learned, comes to me. Not that anyone has seen the Father, except he who is from God. He has seen the Father. Most certainly, I tell you, he who believes in me has eternal life. I am the bread of life. Your fathers ate the manna in the wilderness, and they died. This is the bread which comes down out of heaven, that anyone may eat of it and not die. I am the living bread which came down out of heaven. If anyone eats of this bread, he will live forever. Yes, the bread which I will give for the life of the world is my flesh."

MATT. 4:4, 15:10-11, 15:16-20, 22:37-38; MARK 6:50, 10:27, 10:36; LUKE 12:1-3; JOHN 4:7, 4:10, 4:32, 4:34, 5:6, 5:8, 6:26-27, 6:43-51

## Encouragement

"Cheer up! It is I. Don't be afraid." ~ "Blessed are you who are poor, for yours is the Kingdom of God. Blessed are you who hunger now, for you will be filled. Blessed are you who weep now, for you will laugh." ~ "Don't let your heart be troubled. Believe in God. Believe also in me. In my Father's house are many homes. If it weren't so, I would have told you. I am going to prepare a place for you. If I go and prepare a place for you, I will come again, and will receive you to myself; that where I am, you may be there also. Where I go, you know, and you know the way." ~ "Do you now believe? Behold, the time is coming, yes, and has now come, that you will be scattered, everyone to his own place, and you will leave me alone. Yet I am not alone, because the Father is with me. I have told you these things, that in me you may have peace. In the world you have oppression; but cheer up! I have overcome the world." ~ "Woman, why are you weeping? Who are you looking for?" ~ "Mary." ~ "Don't hold me, for I haven't yet ascended to my Father; but go to my brothers, and tell them, 'I am ascending to my Father and your Father, to my God and your God.'" ~ "Cheer up, Paul, for as you have testified about me at Jerusalem, so you must testify also at Rome."

MATT. 14:27; LUKE 6:20-21, JOHN 14:1-4, 16:31-33, 20:15, 20:16, 20:17; ACTS 23:11

## Enemies

"You have heard that it was said, 'You shall love your neighbor and hate your enemy.' But I tell you, love your enemies, bless those who curse you, do good to those who hate you, and pray for those who mistreat you and persecute you, that you may be children of your Father who is in heaven. For he makes his sun to rise on the evil and the good, and sends rain on the just and the unjust. For if you love those who love you, what reward do you have? Don't even the tax collectors do the same? If you only greet your friends, what more do you do than others? Don't even the tax collectors do the same? Therefore you shall be perfect, just as your Father in heaven is perfect." ~ "Every plant which my heavenly Father didn't plant will be uprooted. Leave them alone. They are blind guides of the blind. If the blind guide the blind, both will fall into a pit." ~ "When you hear of wars and rumors of wars, don't be troubled. For those must happen, but the end is not yet. For nation will rise against nation, and kingdom against kingdom. There will be earthquakes in various places. There will be famines and troubles. These things are the beginning of birth pains. But watch yourselves, for they will deliver you up to councils. You will be beaten in synagogues. You will stand before rulers and kings for my sake, for a testimony to them. The Good News must first be preached to all the nations. When they lead you away and deliver you up, don't be anxious beforehand, or premeditate what you will say, but say whatever will be given you in that hour. For it is not you who speak, but the Holy Spirit. " ~ "Woe to you lawyers also! For you load men with burdens that are difficult to carry, and you yourselves won't even lift one finger to help carry those burdens. Woe to you! For you build the tombs of the prophets, and your fathers killed them. So you testify and consent to the works of your fathers. For they killed them, and you build their tombs. Therefore also the wisdom of God said, 'I will send to them prophets and apostles; and some of them they will kill and persecute, that the blood of all the prophets, which was shed from the foundation of the world, may be required of this generation; from the blood of Abel to the blood of Zachariah, who perished between the altar and the sanctuary.' Yes, I tell you, it will be required of this generation. Woe to you lawyers! For you took away the key of knowledge. You didn't enter in yourselves, and those who were entering in, you hindered." ~ "If you, even you, had known today the things which belong to your peace! But now, they are hidden from your eyes. For the days will come on you, when your enemies will throw up a barricade against you, surround you, hem you in on every side, and will dash you and your children within you to the ground. They will not leave in you one stone on another, because you didn't know the time of your visitation." ~ "Father, forgive them. For they don't know what they are doing." ~ "Most certainly

I tell you that one of you will betray me." ~ "It is he to whom I will give this piece of bread when I have dipped it." ~ "What you do, do quickly." ~ "Saul, Saul, why are you persecuting me?" ~ "I am Jesus of Nazareth, whom you persecute."

MATT. 5:43-48, 15:13-14; MARK 13:7-11; LUKE 11:46-52, 19:41-44, 23:24; JOHN 13:21, 13:26, 13:27; ACTS 22:7, 22:8

## *Energy*

"You are witnesses of these things. Behold, I send forth the promise of my Father on you. But wait in the city of Jerusalem until you are clothed with power from on high." ~ "The wind blows where it wants to, and you hear its sound, but don't know where it comes from and where it is going. So is everyone who is born of the Spirit." ~ "Everyone who drinks of this water will thirst again, but whoever drinks of the water that I will give him will never thirst again; but the water that I will give him will become in him a well of water springing up to eternal life." ~ "Most certainly I tell you, he who hears my word, and believes him who sent me, has eternal life, and doesn't come into judgment, but has passed out of death into life. Most certainly, I tell you, the hour comes, and now is, when the dead will hear the Son of God's voice; and those who hear will live. For as the Father has life in himself, even so he gave to the Son also to have life in himself. He also gave him authority to execute judgment, because he is a son of man. Don't marvel at this, for the hour comes, in which all that are in the tombs will hear his voice, and will come out; those who have done good, to the resurrection of life; and those who have done evil, to the resurrection of judgment. I can of myself do nothing. As I hear, I judge, and my judgment is righteous; because I don't seek my own will, but the will of my Father who sent me." ~ "If you were Abraham's children, you would do the works of Abraham. But now you seek to kill me, a man who has told you the truth, which I heard from God. Abraham didn't do this. You do the works of your father." ~ "Most certainly, I tell you, before Abraham came into existence, I AM." ~ "I told you, and you don't believe. The works that I do in my Father's name, these testify about me." ~ "Don't you believe that I am in the Father, and the Father in me? The words that I tell you, I speak not from myself; but the Father who lives in me does his works." ~ "I have yet many things to tell you, but you can't bear them now. However when he, the Spirit of truth, has come, he will guide you into all truth, for he will not speak from himself; but whatever he hears, he will speak. He will declare to you things that are coming." ~ "It isn't for you to know times or seasons which the Father has set within his own authority. But you will receive power when the Holy Spirit has come upon you. You will be witnesses to me in Jerusalem, in all Judea and Samaria, and to the uttermost parts of the earth." ~ "'It is more blessed to give than to receive.'" ~ "My grace is sufficient for you, for my power is made perfect in weakness."

LUKE 24:48-49; JOHN 3:8, 4:13-14, 5:24-30, 8:39-41, 8:58, 10:25, 14:10, 16:12-13; ACTS 1:7-8, 20:35; 2 COR. 12:9

## Failure

"Blessed are the poor in spirit, for theirs is the Kingdom of Heaven. Blessed are those who mourn, for they shall be comforted." ~ "Before the rooster crows twice, you will deny me three times." ~ "Don't cry." ~ "Young man, I tell you, arise!" ~ "You give them something to eat." ~ "Make them sit down in groups of about fifty each." ~ "If anyone desires to come after me, let him deny himself, take up his cross, and follow me. For whoever desires to save his life will lose it, but whoever will lose his life for my sake, the same will save it. For what does it profit a man if he gains the whole world, and loses or forfeits his own self? For whoever will be ashamed of me and of my words, of him will the Son of Man be ashamed, when he comes in his glory, and the glory of the Father, and of the holy angels. But I tell you the truth: There are some of those who stand here, who will in no way taste of death, until they see the Kingdom of God." ~ "Don't forbid him, for he who is not against us is for us." ~ "You don't know of what kind of spirit you are. For the Son of Man didn't come to destroy men's lives, but to save them." ~ "Arise, take up your mat, and walk." ~ "Lazarus, come out!" ~ "Free him, and let him go." ~ "Peace be to you."

MATT. 5:3-4; MARK 14:72; LUKE 7:13, 7:14. 9:13, 9:14. 9:23-27, 9:50, 9:55-56; JOHN 5:8, 11:43, 11:44, 20:26

## Faith

"Go your way. Let it be done for you as you have believed." ~ "Why are you fearful, O you of little faith?" ~ "Go!" ~ "Cheer up! It is I! Don't be afraid." ~ "Come!" ~ "You of little faith, why did you doubt?" ~ "Woman, great is your faith! Be it done to you even as you desire." ~ "For this saying, go your way. The demon has gone out of your daughter." ~ "Unbelieving generation, how long shall I be with you? How long shall I bear with you? Bring him to me." ~ "Allow the little children to come to me! Don't forbid them, for the Kingdom of God belongs to such as these. Most certainly I tell you, whoever will not receive the Kingdom of God like a little child, he will in no way enter into it." ~ "Call him." ~ "What do you want me to do for you?" ~ "Go your way. Your faith has made you well." ~ "I tell you, I have not found such great faith, no, not in Israel." ~ "Who touched me?" ~ "Someone did touch me, for I perceived that power has gone out of me." ~ "Daughter, cheer up. Your faith has made you well. Go in peace." ~ " But if this is how God clothes the grass in the field, which today exists, and tomorrow is cast into the oven, how much more will he clothe you, O you of little faith?" ~ "Go and show yourselves to the priests." ~ "Weren't the ten cleansed? But where are the nine? Were there none found who returned to give glory to God, except this stranger?" ~ "Get up, and go your way. Your faith has healed you." ~ "Unless you see signs and wonders, you will in no way believe." ~ "Didn't I tell you that if you believed, you would see God's glory?" ~ "Because you have seen me, you have believed. Blessed are those who have not seen, and have believed."

MATT. 8:13, 8;26, 8:32, 14:27, 14:29, 14:31, 15:28; MARK 7:29, 9:19, 10:14-15, 10:49, 10:51, 10:52; LUKE 7:9, 8:45, 8:46, 8:48, 12:28, 17:14, 17:17-18, 17:19; JOHN 4:48, 11:40, 20:29

# *Faithfulness*

"His lord said to him, 'Well done, good and faithful servant. You have been faithful over a few things, I will set you over many things. Enter into the joy of your lord.'" ~ "You know that they who are recognized as rulers over the nations lord it over them, and their great ones exercise authority over them. But it shall not be so among you, but whoever wants to become great among you shall be your servant. Whoever of you wants to become first among you, shall be bondservant of all. For the Son of Man also came not to be served, but to serve, and to give his life as a ransom for many." ~ "Return to your house, and declare what great things God has done for you." ~ "Don't be afraid. Only believe, and she will be healed." ~ "Don't weep. She isn't dead, but sleeping." ~ "Child, arise!" ~ "I am the true vine, and my Father is the farmer. Every branch in me that doesn't bear fruit, he takes away. Every branch that bears fruit, he prunes, that it may bear more fruit. You are already pruned clean because of the word which I have spoken to you.

Remain in me, and I in you. As the branch can't bear fruit by itself, unless it remains in the vine, so neither can you, unless you remain in me. I am the vine. You are the branches. He who remains in me, and I in him, the same bears much fruit, for apart from me you can do nothing. If a man doesn't remain in me, he is thrown out as a branch, and is withered; and they gather them, throw them into the fire, and they are burned. If you remain in me, and my words remain in you, you will ask whatever you desire, and it will be done for you." ~ "To the angel of the assembly in Philadelphia write: "He who is holy, he who is true, he who has the key of David, he who opens and no one can shut, and who shuts and no one opens, says these things" ~ "I know your works (behold, I have set before you an open door, which no one can shut), that you have a little power, and kept my word, and didn't deny my name. Behold, I give of the synagogue of Satan, of those who say they are Jews, and they are not, but lie. Behold, I will make them to come and worship before your feet, and to know that I have loved you. Because you kept my command to endure, I also will keep you from the hour of testing, which is to come on the whole world, to test those who dwell on the earth. I am coming quickly! Hold firmly that which you have, so that no one takes your crown. He who overcomes, I will make him a pillar in the temple of my God, and he will go out from there no more. I will write on him the name of my God, and the name of the city of my God, the new Jerusalem, which comes down out of heaven from my God, and my own new name. He who has an ear, let him hear what the Spirit says to the assemblies."

MATT. 25:23; MARK 10:42-45; LUKE 8:39, 8:50, 8:52, 8:54; JOHN 15:1-7; REV. 3:7, 3:8-13

## *Family*

"Brother will deliver up brother to death, and the father his child. Children will rise up against parents, and cause them to be put to death. You will be hated by all men for my name's sake, but he who endures to the end will be saved. But when they persecute you in this city, flee into the next, for most certainly I tell you, you will not have gone through the cities of Israel, until the Son of Man has come." ~ "Who is my mother? Who are my brothers?" ... "Behold, my mother and my brothers! For whoever does the will of my Father who is in heaven, he is my brother, and sister, and mother." ~ "A prophet is not without honor, except in his own country, and in his own house." ~ "Allow the little children, and don't forbid them to come to me; for the Kingdom of Heaven belongs to ones like these." ~ "Most certainly I tell you, there is no one who has left house, or brothers, or sisters, or father, or mother, or wife, or children, or land, for my sake, and for the sake of the Good News, but he will receive one hundred times more now in this time, houses, brothers, sisters, mothers, children, and land, with persecutions; and in the age to come eternal life. But many who are first will be last and the last first." ~ "My mother and my brothers are these who hear the word of God, and do it." ~ "Faithless and perverse generation, how long shall I be with you and bear with you? Bring your son here." ~ "Woman, behold your son!" ~ "Behold, your mother!" ~ "Peace be to you."

MATT. 10:21-23, 12:48-50, 13:57, 19:14; MARK 10:29-31; LUKE 8:21, 9:41; JOHN 19:26, 19:27, 20:19

# Fear

"Get up, and don't be afraid." ~ "Peace! Be still!" ~ "Why are you so afraid? How is it that you have no faith?" ~ "Cheer up! It is I! Don't be afraid." ~ "Which of you fathers, if your son asks for bread, will give him a stone? Or if he asks for a fish, he won't give him a snake instead of a fish, will he? Or if he asks for an egg, he won't give him a scorpion, will he? If you then, being evil, know how to give good gifts to your children, how much more will your heavenly Father give the Holy Spirit to those who ask him?" ~ "I tell you, my friends, don't be afraid of those who kill the body, and after that have no more that they can do. But I will warn you whom you should fear. Fear him, who after he has killed, has power to cast into Gehenna. Yes, I tell you, fear him." ~ "The things which are impossible with men are possible with God." ~ "Peace be to you." ~ "I am the light of the world. He who follows me will not walk in the darkness, but will have the light of life." ~ "Of those whom you have given me, I have lost none." ~ "Don't be afraid. I am the first and the last, and the Living one. I was dead, and behold, I am alive forevermore. Amen. I have the keys of Death and of Hades."

MATT. 17:7; MARK 4:39, 4:40, 6:50; LUKE 11:11-13, 12:4-5, 18:27, 24:36; JOHN 8:12, 18:9; REV. 1:17-18

# Fighting

"Don't forbid him, for he who is not against us is for us." ~ "You don't know of what kind of spirit you are. For the Son of Man didn't come to destroy men's lives, but to save them." ~ "Every kingdom divided against itself is brought to desolation. A house divided against itself falls. If Satan also is divided against himself, how will his kingdom stand? For you say that I cast out demons by Beelzebul. But if I cast out demons by Beelzebul, by whom do your children cast them out? Therefore will they be your judges. But if I by the finger of God cast out demons, then the Kingdom of God has come to you."

LUKE 9:50, 9:55-56, 11:17-20

# Filling the God Void

"An evil and adulterous generation seeks after a sign, but no sign will be given it but the sign of Jonah the prophet. For as Jonah was three days and three nights in the belly of the whale, so will the Son of Man be three days and three nights in the heart of the earth. The men of Nineveh will stand up in the judgment with this generation, and will condemn it, for they repented at the preaching of Jonah; and behold, someone greater than Jonah is here. The queen of the south will rise up in the judgment with this generation, and will condemn it, for she came from the ends of the earth to hear the wisdom of Solomon; and behold, someone greater than Solomon is here. But the unclean spirit, when he is gone out of the man, passes through waterless places, seeking rest, and doesn't find it. Then he says, 'I will return into my house from which I came out,' and when he has come back, he finds it empty, swept, and put in order. Then he goes, and takes with himself seven other spirits more evil than he is, and they enter in and dwell there. The last state of that man becomes worse than the first. Even so will it be also to this evil generation." ~ "Why do you reason among yourselves, you of little faith, 'because you have brought no bread?' Don't you yet perceive, neither remember the five loaves for the five thousand, and how many baskets you took up? Nor the seven loaves for the four thousand, and how many baskets you took up? How is it that you don't perceive that I didn't speak to you concerning bread? But beware of the yeast of the Pharisees and Sadducees." ~ "Most certainly I tell you, unless one is born of water and spirit, he can't enter into the Kingdom of God! That which is born of the flesh is flesh. That which is born of the Spirit is spirit. Don't marvel that I said to you, 'You must be born anew.' The wind blows where it wants to, and you hear its sound, but don't know where it comes from and where it is going. So is everyone who is born of the Spirit." ~ "If you knew the gift of God, and who it is who says to you, 'Give me a drink,' you would have asked him, and he would have given you living water." ~ "Most certainly I tell you, you seek me, not because you saw signs, but because you ate of the loaves, and were filled. Don't work for the food which perishes, but for the food which remains to eternal life, which the Son of Man will give to you. For God the Father has sealed him." ~ "I am the bread of life. Your fathers ate the manna in the wilderness, and they died. This is the bread which comes down out of heaven, that anyone may eat of it and not die. I am the living bread which came down out of heaven. If anyone eats of this bread, he will live forever. Yes, the bread which I will give for the life of the world is my flesh."

MATT. 12:39-45, 16:8-11; JOHN 3:5-8, 4:10, 6:26-27, 6:48-51

# *Forgiveness*

"If therefore you are offering your gift at the altar, and there remember that your brother has anything against you, leave your gift there before the altar, and go your way. First be reconciled to your brother, and then come and offer your gift. Agree with your adversary quickly, while you are with him in the way; lest perhaps the prosecutor deliver you to the judge, and the judge deliver you to the officer, and you be cast into prison. Most certainly I tell you, you shall by no means get out of there, until you have paid the last penny." ~ "For if you forgive men their trespasses, your heavenly Father will also forgive you. But if you don't forgive men their trespasses, neither will your Father forgive your trespasses." ~ "I don't tell you until seven times, but, until seventy times seven. Therefore the Kingdom of Heaven is like a certain king, who wanted to reconcile accounts with his servants. When he had begun to reconcile, one was brought to him who owed him ten thousand talents. But because he couldn't pay, his lord commanded him to be sold, with his wife, his children, and all that he had, and payment to be made. The servant therefore fell down and kneeled before him, saying, 'Lord, have patience with me, and I will repay you all!' The lord of that servant, being moved with compassion, released him, and forgave him the debt." ~ "But that servant went out, and found one of his fellow servants, who owed him one hundred denarii, and he grabbed him, and took him by the throat, saying, 'Pay me what you owe!'" ~ "So his fellow servant fell down at his feet and begged him, saying, 'Have patience with me, and I will repay you!' He would not, but went and cast him into prison, until he should pay back that which was due. So when his fellow servants saw what was done, they were exceedingly sorry, and came and told to their lord all that was done. Then his lord called him in, and said to him, 'You wicked servant! I forgave you all that debt, because you begged me. Shouldn't you also have had mercy on your fellow servant, even as I had mercy on you?' His lord was angry, and delivered him to the tormentors, until he should pay all that was due to him. So my heavenly Father will also do to you, if you don't each forgive your brother from your hearts for his misdeeds." ~ "Son, your sins are forgiven you." ~ "Did you never read what David did, when he had need, and was hungry —he, and those who were with him? How he entered into the house of God when Abiathar was high priest, and ate the show bread, which is not lawful to eat except for the priests, and gave also to those who were with him?" ~ "A certain lender had two debtors. The one owed five hundred denarii, and the other fifty. When they couldn't pay, he forgave them both. Which of them therefore will love him most?" ~ "You have judged correctly." ~ "Do you see this woman? I entered into your house, and you gave me no water for my feet, but she has wet my feet with her tears, and wiped them with the hair of her head. You gave me no kiss, but she, since the time I came in, has not ceased to kiss my feet. You didn't anoint my head with oil, but she has anointed my feet with ointment. Therefore I tell you, her sins, which are many, are forgiven, for she loved much. But to whom little is forgiven, the same loves little." ~ "Your sins are forgiven." ~ "It is impossible that no occasions of stumbling should come, but woe to him through whom they come! It would be better for him if a millstone were hung around his neck, and he were thrown into the sea, rather than that he should cause one of these little ones to stumble. Be careful. If your brother sins against you, rebuke him. If he repents, forgive him. If he sins against you seven times in the day, and seven times returns, saying, 'I repent,' you shall forgive him." ~ "Peace be to you."

MATT. 5:23-26, 6:14-15, 18:22-27, 18:28, 18:29-35; MARK 2:5, 2:25-26; LUKE 7:41-42, 7:43, 7:44-47, 7:48, 17:1-4; JOHN 20:26

## Freedom

"Is it lawful on the Sabbath day to do good, or to do harm? To save a life, or to kill?" ~ "Haven't you read what David did when he was hungry, he, and those who were with him; how he entered into God's house, and took and ate the show bread, and gave also to those who were with him, which is not lawful to eat except for the priests alone?" ~ "The Son of Man is lord of the Sabbath." ~ "Therefore be merciful, even as your Father is also merciful. Don't judge, and you won't be judged. Don't condemn, and you won't be condemned. Set free, and you will be set free." ~ "Woman, you are freed from your infirmity." ~ "You hypocrites! Doesn't each one of you free his ox or his donkey from the stall on the Sabbath, and lead him away to water? Ought not this woman, being a daughter of Abraham, whom Satan had bound eighteen long years, be freed from this bondage on the Sabbath day?" ~ "If you remain in my word, then you are truly my disciples. You will know the truth, and the truth will make you free." ~ "Most certainly I tell you, everyone who commits sin is the bondservant of sin. A bondservant doesn't live in the house forever. A son remains forever. If therefore the Son makes you free, you will be free indeed. I know that you are Abraham's seed, yet you seek to kill me, because my word finds no place in you. I say the things which I have seen with my Father; and you also do the things which you have seen with your father."

MARK 3:4; LUKE 6:3-4, 6:5. 6:36-37, 13:12, 13:15-16; JOHN 8:31-32, 8:34-38

## Friendship

"Don't judge, so that you won't be judged. For with whatever judgment you judge, you will be judged; and with whatever measure you measure, it will be measured to you. Why do you see the speck that is in your brother's eye, but don't consider the beam that is in your own eye? Or how will you tell your brother, 'Let me remove the speck from your eye;' and behold, the beam is in your own eye? You hypocrite! First remove the beam out of your own eye, and then you can see clearly to remove the speck out of your brother's eye." ~ "Sit here, while I go there and pray." ~ "My soul is exceedingly sorrowful, even to death. Stay here, and watch with me." ~ "Which of you, if you go to a friend at midnight, and tell him, 'Friend, lend me three loaves of bread, for a friend of mine has come to me from a journey, and I have nothing to set before him,' and he from within will answer and say, 'Don't bother me. The door is now shut, and my children are with me in bed. I can't get up and give it to you'? I tell you, although he will not rise and give it to him because he is his friend, yet because of his persistence, he will get up and give him as many as he needs." ~ "Simon, Simon, behold, Satan asked to have you, that he might sift you as wheat, but I prayed for you, that your faith wouldn't fail. You, when once you have turned again, establish your brothers." ~ "I tell you, Peter, the rooster will by no means crow today until you deny that you know me three times." ~ "Will you lay down your life for me? Most certainly I tell you, the rooster won't crow until you have denied me three times." ~ "This is my commandment, that you love one another, even as I have loved you. Greater love has no one than this, that someone lay down his life for his friends. You are my friends, if you do whatever I command you. No longer do I call you servants, for the servant doesn't know what his lord does. But I have called you friends, for everything that I heard from my Father, I have made known to you. You didn't choose me, but I chose you, and appointed you, that you should go and bear fruit, and that your fruit should remain; that whatever you will ask of the Father in my name, he may give it to you." ~ "Peace be to you. As the Father has sent me, even so I send you." ~ "Come and eat breakfast."

MATT. 7:1-5, 26:36, 26:38; LUKE 11:5-8; 22:31-32, 22:34; JOHN 13:38, 15:12-16, 20:21, 21:12

## *Future*

"Therefore don't be anxious, saying, 'What will we eat?', 'What will we drink?' or, 'With what will we be clothed?' For the Gentiles seek after all these things; for your heavenly Father knows that you need all these things. But seek first God's Kingdom, and his righteousness; and all these things will be given to you as well. Therefore don't be anxious for tomorrow, for tomorrow will be anxious for itself. Each day's own evil is sufficient." ~ "When it is evening, you say, 'It will be fair weather, for the sky is red.' In the morning, 'It will be foul weather today, for the sky is red and threatening.' Hypocrites! You know how to discern the appearance of the sky, but you can't discern the signs of the times! An evil and adulterous generation seeks after a sign, and there will be no sign given to it, except the sign of the prophet Jonah." ~ "Now from the fig tree learn this parable. When its branch has now become tender, and puts forth its leaves, you know that the summer is near. Even so you also, when you see all these things, know that it is near, even at the doors. Most certainly I tell you, this generation will not pass away, until all these things are accomplished. Heaven and earth will pass away, but my words will not pass away. But no one knows of that day and hour, not even the angels of heaven, but my Father only." ~ "Behold, I am with you always, even to the end of the age." ~ "Do you see these great buildings? There will not be left here one stone on another, which will not be thrown down." ~ "Behold, I have told you all things beforehand. But in those days, after that oppression, the sun will be darkened, the moon will not give its light, the stars will be falling from the sky, and the powers that are in the heavens will be shaken. Then they will see the Son of Man coming in clouds with great power and glory. Then he will send out his angels, and will gather together his chosen ones from the four winds, from the ends of the earth to the ends of the sky." ~ "Let your waist be dressed and your lamps burning. Be like men watching for their lord, when he returns from the marriage feast; that, when he comes and knocks, they may immediately open to him. Blessed are those servants, whom the lord will find watching when he comes. Most certainly I tell you, that he will dress himself, and make them recline, and will come and serve them. They will be blessed if he comes in the second or third watch, and finds them so. But know this, that if the master of the house had known in what hour the thief was coming, he would have watched, and not allowed his house to be broken into. Therefore be ready also, for the Son of Man is coming in an hour that you don't expect him." ~ "Nation will rise against nation, and kingdom against kingdom. There will be great earthquakes, famines, and plagues in various places. There will be terrors and great signs from heaven. But before all these things, they will lay their hands on you and will persecute you, delivering you up to synagogues and prisons, bringing you before kings and governors for my name's sake. It will turn out as a testimony for you. Settle it therefore in your hearts not to meditate beforehand how to answer, for I will give you a mouth and wisdom which all your adversaries will not be able to withstand or to contradict. You will be handed over even by parents, brothers, relatives, and friends. They will cause some of you to be put to death. You will be hated by all men for my name's sake. And not a hair of your head will perish."

MATT. 6:31-34, 16:2-4, 24:32-36, 28:20; MARK 13:2, 13:23-27; LUKE 12:35-40, 21:10-18

# Gentleness

"Come to me, all you who labor and are heavily burdened, and I will give you rest. Take my yoke upon you, and learn from me, for I am gentle and lowly in heart; and you will find rest for your souls. For my yoke is easy, and my burden is light." ~ "Allow the little children to come to me, and don't hinder them, for the Kingdom of God belongs to such as these. Most certainly, I tell you, whoever doesn't receive the Kingdom of God like a little child, he will in no way enter into it." ~ "It is I. Don't be afraid." ~ "Don't let your heart be troubled. Believe in God. Believe also in me. In my Father's house are many homes. If it weren't so, I would have told you. I am going to prepare a place for you. If I go and prepare a place for you, I will come again, and will receive you to myself; that where I am, you may be there also. Where I go, you know, and you know the way." ~ "But the Counselor, the Holy Spirit, whom the Father will send in my name, he will teach you all things, and will remind you of all that I said to you." ~ "Peace I leave with you. My peace I give to you; not as the world gives, give I to you. Don't let your heart be troubled, neither let it be fearful."

MATT. 11:28-29; LUKE 18:16-17; JOHN 6:20, 14:1-4, 14:26, 14:27

# Giving

"Be careful that you don't do your charitable giving before men, to be seen by them, or else you have no reward from your Father who is in heaven. Therefore when you do merciful deeds, don't sound a trumpet before yourself, as the hypocrites do in the synagogues and in the streets, that they may get glory from men. Most certainly I tell you, they have received their reward. But when you do merciful deeds, don't let your left hand know what your right hand does, so that your merciful deeds may be in secret, then your Father who sees in secret will reward you openly." ~ "Heal the sick, cleanse the lepers, and cast out demons. Freely you received, so freely give." ~ "If you want to be perfect, go, sell what you have, and give to the poor, and you will have treasure in heaven; and come, follow me." ~ "Most certainly I say to you, a rich man will enter into the Kingdom of Heaven with difficulty. Again I tell you, it is easier for a camel to go through a needle's eye, than for a rich man to enter into the Kingdom of God." ~ "How many loaves do you have?"  ~  "Most certainly I tell you, this poor widow gave more than all those who are giving into the treasury, for they all gave out of their abundance, but she, out of her poverty, gave all that she had to live on."  ~  "Give, and it will be given to you: good measure, pressed down, shaken together, and running over, will be given to you. For with the same measure you measure it will be measured back to you."  ~  "This is my body which is given for you. Do this in memory of me."  ~  "For God so loved the world, that he gave his one and only Son, that whoever believes in him should not perish, but have eternal life."  ~  "I revealed your name to the people whom you have given me out of the world. They were yours, and you have given them to me. They have kept your word. Now they have known that all things whatever you have given me are from you, the words which you have given me I have given to them, and they received them, and knew for sure that I came forth from you, and they have believed that you sent me."  ~ "It is more blessed to give than to receive."

MATT. 6:1-4, 10:8, 19:21, 19:23-24; MARK 8:5, 12:43-44; LUKE 6:38, 22:19; JOHN 3:16, 17:6-8; ACTS 20:35

# Goals in Life

"Get up, and take up your mat, and go up to your house."  ~  "Most certainly I tell you, there is no one who has left house, or wife, or brothers, or parents, or children, for the Kingdom of God's sake, who will not receive many times more in this time, and in the world to come, eternal life."  ~  "Most certainly, I tell you, the Son can do nothing of himself, but what he sees the Father doing. For whatever things he does, these the Son also does likewise. For the Father has affection for the Son, and shows him all things that he himself does. He will show him greater works than these, that you may marvel. For as the Father raises the dead and gives them life, even so the Son also gives life to whom he desires. For the Father judges no one, but he has given all judgment to the Son, that all may honor the Son, even as they honor the Father. He who doesn't honor the Son doesn't honor the Father who sent him."  ~  "Arise, and go into Damascus. There you will be told about all things which are appointed for you to do."

MATT. 9:6; LUKE 18:29-30; JOHN 5:19-23; ACTS 22:10

# Goodness

"Leave her alone. Why do you trouble her? She has done a good work for me. For you always have the poor with you, and whenever you want to, you can do them good; but you will not always have me. She has done what she could. She has anointed my body beforehand for the burying. Most certainly I tell you, wherever this Good News may be preached throughout the whole world, that which this woman has done will also be spoken of for a memorial of her." ~ "Rise up, and stand in the middle." ~ "I will ask you something: Is it lawful on the Sabbath to do good, or to do harm? To save a life, or to kill?" ~ "Stretch out your hand." ~ "It is I. Don't be afraid." ~ "Neither did this man sin, nor his parents; but, that the works of God might be revealed in him. I must work the works of him who sent me, while it is day. The night is coming, when no one can work. While I am in the world, I am the light of the world."

MARK 14:6-9; LUKE 6:8, 6:9, 6:10; JOHN 6:20, 9:3-5

# Government

"Why do you test me, you hypocrites? Show me the tax money." ~ "Whose is this image and inscription?" ~ "Give therefore to Caesar the things that are Caesar's, and to God the things that are God's." ~ "You shall love the Lord your God with all your heart, with all your soul, and with all your mind." ~ "This is the first and great commandment." ~ "Why do you test me? Show me a denarius. Whose image and inscription are on it?" ~ "Then give to Caesar the things that are Caesar's, and to God the things that are God's." ~ "Follow me."

MATT. 22:18-19, 22:20, 22:21; 22:37, 22:38; LUKE 20:23-24, 20:25; JOHN 1:43

# Greatness

"What did you go out into the wilderness to see? A reed shaken by the wind? But what did you go out to see? A man in soft clothing? Behold, those who wear soft clothing are in king's houses. But why did you go out? To see a prophet? Yes, I tell you, and much more than a prophet. For this is he, of whom it is written, 'Behold, I send my messenger before your face, who will prepare your way before you.' Most certainly I tell you, among those who are born of women there has not arisen anyone greater than John the Baptizer; yet he who is least in the Kingdom of

Heaven is greater than he." ~ "You know that the rulers of the nations lord it over them, and their great ones exercise authority over them. It shall not be so among you, but whoever desires to become great among you shall be your servant. Whoever desires to be first among you shall be your bondservant, even as the Son of Man came not to be served, but to serve, and to give his life as a ransom for many." ~ "What were you arguing among yourselves on the way?" ~ "If any man wants to be first, he shall be last of all, and servant of all." ~ "You shall indeed drink the cup that I drink, and you shall be baptized with the baptism that I am baptized with; but to sit at my right hand and at my left hand is not mine to give, but for whom it has been prepared." ~ "The kings of the nations lord it over them, and those who have authority over them are called 'benefactors.' But not so with you. But one who is the greater among you, let him become as the younger, and one who is governing, as one who serves. For who is greater, one who sits at the table, or one who serves? Isn't it he who sits at the table? But I am in the midst of you as one who serves. But you are those who have continued with me in my trials. I confer on you a kingdom, even as my Father conferred on me, that you may eat and drink at my table in my Kingdom. You will sit on thrones, judging the twelve tribes of Israel." ~ "Father, the time has come. Glorify your Son, that your Son may also glorify you; even as you gave him authority over all flesh, he will give eternal life to all whom you have given him. This is eternal life, that they should know you, the only true God, and him whom you sent, Jesus Christ. I glorified you on the earth. I have accomplished the work which you have given me to do. Now, Father, glorify me with your own self with the glory which I had with you before the world existed."

MATT. 11:7-11, 20:25-28; MARK 9:33, 9:35, 10:39-40; LUKE 22:25-30; JOHN 17:1-5

# Guard Your Heart

"Enter in by the narrow gate; for wide is the gate and broad is the way that leads to destruction, and many are those who enter in by it. How narrow is the gate, and restricted is the way that leads to life! Few are those who find it." ~ "Beware of false prophets, who come to you in sheep's clothing, but inwardly are ravening wolves. By their fruits you will know them. Do you gather grapes from thorns, or figs from thistles? Even so, every good tree produces good fruit; but the corrupt tree produces evil fruit. A good tree can't produce evil fruit, neither can a corrupt tree produce good fruit. Every tree that doesn't grow good fruit is cut down, and thrown into the fire. Therefore, by their fruits you will know them. Not everyone who says to me, 'Lord, Lord,' will enter into the Kingdom of Heaven; but he who does the will of my Father who is in heaven. Many will tell me in that day, 'Lord, Lord, didn't we prophesy in your name, in your name cast out demons, and in your name do many mighty works?' Then I will tell them, 'I never knew you. Depart from me, you who work iniquity." ~ "Take heed; beware of the yeast of the Pharisees and the yeast of Herod." ~ "It is like a man, traveling to another country, having left his house, and given authority to his servants, and to each one his work, and also commanded the doorkeeper to keep watch. Watch therefore, for you don't know when the lord of the house is coming, whether at evening, or at midnight, or when the rooster crows, or in the morning; lest coming suddenly he might find you sleeping. What I tell you, I tell all: Watch." ~ "So be careful, or your hearts will be loaded down with carousing, drunkenness, and cares of this life, and that day will come on you suddenly. For it will come like a snare on all those who dwell on the surface of all the earth. Therefore be watchful all the time, praying that you may be counted worthy to escape all these things that will happen, and to stand before the Son of Man." ~ "I have given them your word. The world hated them, because they are not of the world, even as I am not of the world. I pray not that you would take them from the world, but that you would keep them from the evil one. They are not of the world even as I am not of the world. Sanctify them in your truth. Your word is truth. As you sent me into the world, even so I have sent them into the world. For their sakes I sanctify myself, that they themselves also may be sanctified in truth." ~ "I will kill her children with Death, and all the assemblies will know that I am he who searches the minds and hearts. I will give to each one of you according to your deeds." ~ "Behold, I come like a thief. Blessed is he who watches, and keeps his clothes, so that he doesn't walk naked, and they see his shame."

MATT. 7:13-14, 7:15-23; MARK 8:15, 13:34-37; LUKE 21:34-36; JOHN 17:14-19; REV. 2:23; 16:15

# Healing

"I want to. Be made clean." ~ "I will come and heal him." ~ "Go and tell John the things which you hear and see: the blind receive their sight, the lame walk, the lepers are cleansed, the deaf hear, the dead are raised up, and the poor have good news preached to them. Blessed is he who finds no occasion for stumbling in me." ~ "Stretch out your hand." ~ "Who touched my clothes?" ~ "Daughter, your faith has made you well. Go in peace, and be cured of your disease." ~ "For this saying, go your way. The demon has gone out of your daughter." ~ "Ephphatha!" . . . "Be opened!" ~ "But go your way, and show yourself to the priest, and offer for your cleansing according to what Moses commanded, for a testimony to them." ~ "Why are you reasoning so in your hearts? Which is easier to say, 'Your sins are forgiven you;' or to say, 'Arise and walk?' But that you may know that the Son of Man has authority on earth to forgive sins" . . . "I tell you, arise, and take up your cot, and go to your house." ~ "Who touched me?" ~ "Someone did touch me, for I perceived that power has gone out of me." ~ "Daughter, cheer up. Your faith has made you well. Go in peace." ~ "Don't be afraid. Only believe, and she will be healed." ~ "Don't weep. She isn't dead, but sleeping." ~ "Child, arise!" ~ "Go your way. Your son lives." ~ "Do you want to be made well?" ~ "Arise, take up your mat, and walk." ~ "This sickness is not to death, but for the glory of God, that God's Son may be glorified by it."

MATT 8:3, 8:7, 11:4-6; MARK 3:5, 5:30, 5:34, 7:29, 7:34; LUKE 5:14, 5:22-24, 8:45, 8:46, 8:48, 8:50, 8:52, 8:54; JOHN 4:50, 5:6, 5:8, 11:4

# Hell

"You have heard that it was said to the ancient ones, 'You shall not murder' and 'Whoever shall murder shall be in danger of the judgment.' But I tell you, that everyone who is angry with his brother without a cause shall be in danger of the judgment; and whoever shall say to his brother, 'Raca!' [You good-for-nothing] shall be in danger of the council; and whoever shall say, 'You fool!' shall be in danger of the fire of Gehenna." ~ "Again, the Kingdom of Heaven is like a dragnet, that was cast into the sea, and gathered some fish of every kind, which, when it was filled, they drew up on the beach. They sat down, and gathered the good into containers, but the bad they threw away. So will it be in the end of the world. The angels will come forth, and separate the wicked from among the righteous, and will cast them into the furnace of fire. There will be the weeping and the gnashing of teeth." ~ "Have you understood all these things?" ~ "Now there was a certain rich man, and he was clothed in purple and fine linen, living in luxury every day. A certain beggar, named Lazarus, was laid at his gate, full of sores, and desiring to be fed with the crumbs that fell from the rich man's table. Yes, even the dogs came and licked his sores. It happened that the beggar died, and that he was carried away by the angels to Abraham's bosom. The rich man also died, and was buried. In Hades, he lifted up his eyes, being in torment, and saw Abraham far off, and Lazarus at his bosom. He cried and said, 'Father Abraham, have mercy on me, and send Lazarus, that he may dip the tip of his finger in water, and cool my tongue! For I am in anguish in this flame.'" ~ "But Abraham said, 'Son, remember that you, in your lifetime, received your good things, and Lazarus, in the same way, bad things. But now here he is comforted and you are in anguish. Besides all this, between us and you there is a great gulf fixed, that those who want to pass from here to you are not able, and that none may cross over from there to us.'" ~ "He said, 'I ask you therefore, father, that you would send him to my father's house; for I have five brothers, that he may testify to them, so they won't also come into this place of torment.'" ~ "But Abraham said to him, 'They have Moses and the prophets. Let them listen to them.'" ~ "He said, 'No, father Abraham, but if one goes to them from the dead, they will repent.'" ~ "He said to him, 'If they don't listen to Moses and the prophets, neither will they be persuaded if one rises from the dead.'" ~ "It is done! I am the Alpha and the Omega, the Beginning and the End. I will give freely to him who is thirsty from the spring of the water of life. He who overcomes, I will give him these things. I will be his God, and he will be my son. But for the cowardly, unbelieving, sinners, abominable, murderers, sexually immoral, sorcerers, idolaters, and all liars, part is in the lake that burns with fire and sulfur, which is the second death."

MATT. 5:21-23, 13:47-50, 13:51; LUKE 16:19-24, 16:25-26, 16:27-28, 16:29, 16:30, 16:31; REV. 21:6-8

# Help in Need

"Ask, and it will be given you. Seek, and you will find. Knock, and it will be opened for you. For everyone who asks receives. He who seeks finds. To him who knocks it will be opened. Or who is there among you, who, if his son asks him for bread, will give him a stone? Or if he asks for a fish, who will give him a serpent? If you then, being evil, know how to give good gifts to your children, how much more will your Father who is in heaven give good things to those who ask him! Therefore whatever you desire for men to do to you, you shall also do to them; for this is the Torah and the Prophets." ~ "I have compassion on the multitude, because they have stayed with me now three days, and have nothing to eat. If I send them away fasting to their home, they will faint on the way, for some of them have come a long way." ~ "Call him." ~ "What do you want me to do for you?" ~ "Go your way. Your faith has made you well." ~ "A certain man was going down from Jerusalem to Jericho, and he fell among robbers, who both stripped him and beat him, and departed, leaving him half dead. By chance a certain priest was going down that way. When he saw him, he passed by on the other side. In the same way a Levite also, when he came to the place, and saw him, passed by on the other side. But a certain Samaritan, as he traveled, came where he was. When he saw him, he was moved with compassion, came to him, and bound up his wounds, pouring on oil and wine. He set him on his own animal, and brought him to an inn, and took care of him. On the next day, when he departed, he took out two denarii, and gave them to the host, and said to him, 'Take care of him. Whatever you spend beyond that, I will repay you when I return.' Now which of these three do you think seemed to be a neighbor to him who fell among the robbers?" ~ "Which of you fathers, if your son asks for bread, will give him a stone? Or if he asks for a fish, he won't give him a snake instead of a fish, will he? Or if he asks for an egg, he won't give him a scorpion, will he? If you then, being evil, know how to give good gifts to your children, how much more will your heavenly Father give the Holy Spirit to those who ask him?" ~ "There was a judge in a certain city who didn't fear God, and didn't respect man. A widow was in that city, and she often came to him, saying, 'Defend me from my adversary!' He wouldn't for a while, but afterward he said to himself, 'Though I neither fear God, nor respect man, yet because this widow bothers me, I will defend her, or else she will wear me out by her continual coming.'" ~ "What do you want me to do?" ~ "I am the good shepherd. The good shepherd lays down his life for the sheep. He who is a hired hand, and not a shepherd, who doesn't own the sheep, sees the wolf coming, leaves the sheep, and flees. The wolf snatches the sheep, and scatters them. The hired hand flees because he is a hired hand, and doesn't care for the sheep." ~ "Have I been with you such a long time, and do you not know me, Philip? He who has seen me has seen the Father. How do you say, 'Show us the Father?' Don't you believe that I am in the Father, and the Father in me? The words that I tell you, I speak not from myself; but the Father who lives in me does his works. Believe me that I am in the Father, and the Father in me; or else believe me for the very works' sake. Most certainly I tell you, he who believes in me, the works that I do, he will do also; and he will do greater works than these, because I am going to my Father. Whatever you will ask in my name, that will I do, that the Father may be glorified in the Son. If you will ask anything in my name, I will do it." ~ "I am thirsty." ~ "My grace is sufficient for you, for my power is made perfect in weakness."

MATT 7: 7-12; MARK 8:2-3, 10:49, 10:51, 10:52; LUKE 10:30-36, 11:11-13, 18:2-5, 18:41; JOHN 10:11-13, 14:9-14, 19:28; 2 COR. 12:9

## Helping Others

"Be careful that you don't do your charitable giving before men, to be seen by them, or else you have no reward from your Father who is in heaven. Therefore when you do merciful deeds, don't sound a trumpet before yourself, as the hypocrites do in the synagogues and in the streets, that they may get glory from me. Most certainly I tell you, they have received their reward. But when you do merciful deeds, don't let your left hand know what your right hand does, so that your merciful deeds may be in secret, then your Father who sees in secret will reward you openly." ~ "The harvest indeed is plentiful, but the laborers are few. Pray therefore that the Lord of the harvest will send out laborers into his harvest." ~ "What man is there among you, who has one sheep, and if this one falls into a pit on the Sabbath day, won't he grab on to it, and lift it out? Of how much more value then is a man than a sheep! Therefore it is lawful to do good on the Sabbath day." ~ "Stretch out your hand." ~ "They don't need to go away. You give them something to eat." ~ "I have compassion on the multitude, because they continue with me now three days and have nothing to eat. I don't want to send them away fasting, or they might faint on the way." ~ "You give them something to eat." ~ "How many loaves do you have? Go see." ~ "As you would like people to do to you, do exactly so to them. If you love those who love you, what credit is that to you? For even sinners love those who love them. If you do good to those who do good to you, what credit is that to you? For even sinners do the same. If you lend to those from whom you hope to receive, what credit is that to you? Even sinners lend to sinners, to receive back as much. But love your enemies, and do good, and lend, expecting nothing back; sand your reward will be great, and you will be children of the Most High; for he is kind toward the unthankful and evil." ~ "Fill the water pots with water." ~ "I am thirsty."

MATT. 6:1-4, 9:37-38, 12:11-12, 12:13, 14:16, 15:32-34; MARK 6:37, 6:38; LUKE 6:31-35; JOHN 2:7, 19:28

# Hope

"The Kingdom of Heaven is like a grain of mustard seed, which a man took, and sowed in his field; which indeed is smaller than all seeds. But when it is grown, it is greater than the herbs, and becomes a tree, so that the birds of the air come and lodge in its branches." ~ "The Kingdom of Heaven is like yeast, which a woman took, and hid in three measures of meal, until it was all leavened." ~ "But go your way, and show yourself to the priest, and offer for your cleansing according to what Moses commanded, for a testimony to them." ~ "Your son lives." ~ "Just what I have been saying to you from the beginning. I have many things to speak and to judge concerning you. However he who sent me is true; and the things which I heard from him, these I say to the world." ~ "You will be made free." ~ "Don't let your heart be troubled. Believe in God. Believe also in me. In my Father's house are many homes. If it weren't so, I would have told you. I am going to prepare a place for you. If I go and prepare a place for you, I will come again, and will receive you to myself; that where I am, you may be there also. Where I go, you know, and you know the way." ~ "I have told you these things, that in me you may have peace. In the world you have oppression; but cheer up! I have overcome the world." ~ "Yes, I come quickly."

MATT. 13:31-32, 13:33; LUKE 5:14; JOHN 4:53, 8:25-26, 8:33, 14:1-4, 16:33; REV. 22:20

# How to Know God

"Who do men say that I, the Son of Man, am?" ~ "But who do you say that I am?" ~ "The Kingdom of God is as if a man should cast seed on the earth, and should sleep and rise night and day, and the seed should spring up and grow, he doesn't know how. For the earth bears fruit: first the blade, then the ear, then the full grain in the ear. But when the fruit is ripe, immediately he puts forth the sickle, because the harvest has come." ~ "How will we liken the Kingdom of God? Or with what parable will we illustrate it? It's like a grain of mustard seed, which, when it is sown in the earth, though it is less than all the seeds that are on the earth, yet when it is sown, grows up, and becomes greater than all the herbs, and puts out great branches, so that the birds of the sky can lodge under its shadow." ~ "Allow the little children to come to me! Don't forbid them, for the Kingdom of God belongs to such as these. Most certainly I tell you, whoever will not receive the Kingdom of God a little child, he will in no way enter into it." ~ "The greatest is, 'Hear, Israel, the Lord our God, the Lord is one: you shall love the Lord your God with all your heart, and with all your soul, and with all your mind, and with all your strength.' This is the first commandment. The second is like this, 'You shall love your neighbor as yourself.' There is no other commandment greater than these." ~ "You are not far from the Kingdom of God." ~ "For I tell you, among those who are born of women there is not a greater prophet than John the Baptizer, yet he who is least in the Kingdom of God is greater than he." ~ "To what shall I compare the Kingdom of God? It is like yeast, which a woman took and hid in three measures of flour, until it was all leavened." ~ "For God so loved the world, that he gave his one and only Son, that whoever believes in him should not perish, but have eternal life. For God didn't send his Son into the world to judge the world, but that the world should be saved through him." ~ "My Kingdom is not of this world. If my Kingdom were of this world, then my servants would fight, that I wouldn't be delivered to the Jews. But now my Kingdom is not from here."

MATT. 16:13, 16:15; MARK 4:26-27, 4:30-32, 10:14-15, 12:29-31,12:34; LUKE 7:28, 13:20-21; JOHN 3:16-17, 18:36

# Humility

"But don't you be called 'Rabbi,' for one is your teacher, the Christ, and all of you are brothers. Call no man on the earth your father, for one is your Father, he who is in heaven. Neither be called masters, for one is your master, the Christ. But he who is greatest among you will be your servant. Whoever exalts himself will be humbled, and whoever humbles himself will be exalted." ~ "A prophet is not without honor, except in his own country, and among his own relatives, and in his own house." ~ "If any man wants to be first, he shall be last of all, and servant of all." ~ "You know that they who are recognized as rulers over the nations lord it over them, and their great ones exercise authority over them. But it shall not be so among you, but whoever wants to become great among you shall be your servant. Whoever of you wants to become first among you, shall be bondservant of all. For the Son of Man also came not to be served, but to serve, and to give his life as a ransom for many." ~ "When you are invited by anyone to a marriage feast, don't sit in the best seat, since perhaps someone more honorable than you might be invited by him, and he who invited both of you would come and tell you, 'Make room for this person.' Then you would begin, with shame, to take the lowest place. But when you are invited, go and sit in the lowest place, so that when he who invited you comes, he may tell you, 'Friend, move up higher.' Then you will be honored in the presence of all who sit at the table with you. For everyone who exalts himself will be humbled, and whoever humbles himself will be exalted." ~ "Two men went up into the temple to pray; one was a Pharisee, and the other was a tax collector. The Pharisee stood and prayed to himself like this: 'God, I thank you, that I am not like the rest of men, extortioners, unrighteous, adulterers, or even like this tax collector. I fast twice a week. I give tithes of all that I get.' But the tax collector, standing far away, wouldn't even lift up his eyes to heaven, but beat his breast, saying, 'God, be merciful to me, a sinner!' I tell you, this man went down to his house justified rather than the other; for everyone who exalts himself will be humbled, but he who humbles himself will be exalted." ~ "I command these things to you, that you may love one another. If the world hates you, you know that it has hated me before it hated you. If you were of the world, the world would love its own. But because you are not of the world, since I chose you out of the world, therefore the world hates you. Remember the word that I said to you: 'A servant is not greater than his lord.' If they persecuted me, they will also persecute you. If they kept my word, they will keep yours also. But all these things will they do to you for my name's sake, because they don't know him who sent me. If I had not come and spoken to them, they would not have had sin; but now they have no excuse for their sin. He who hates me, hates my Father also. If I hadn't done among them the works which no one else did, they wouldn't have had sin. But now have they seen and also hated both me and my Father. But this happened so that the word may be fulfilled which was written in their law, 'They hated me without a cause.'"

MATT. 23:8-12; MARK 6:4, 9:35, 10:42-45; LUKE 14:8-11, 18:10-14; JOHN 15:17-25

## *Hunger*

"Blessed are you who are poor, for yours is the Kingdom of God. Blessed are you who hunger now, for you will be filled. Blessed are you who weep now, for you will laugh. Blessed are you when men shall hate you, and when they shall exclude and mock you, and throw out your name as evil, for the Son of Man's sake. Rejoice in that day, and leap for joy, for behold, your reward is great in heaven, for their fathers did the same thing to the prophets. But woe to you who are rich! For you have received your consolation. Woe to you, you who are full now, for you will be hungry. Woe to you who laugh now, for you will mourn and weep. Woe when men speak well of you, for their fathers did the same thing to the false prophets." ~ "Give me a drink." ~ "I have food to eat that you don't know about." ~ "My food is to do the will of him who sent me, and to accomplish his work." ~ "Most certainly I tell you, you seek me, not because you saw signs, but because you ate of the loaves, and were filled. Don't work for the food which perishes, but for the food which remains to eternal life, which the Son of Man will give to you. For God the Father has sealed him." ~ "I am the bread of life. He who comes to me will not be hungry, and he who believes in me will never be thirsty." ~ "Don't murmur among yourselves. No one can come to me unless the Father who sent me draws him, and I will raise him up in the last day. It is written in the prophets, 'They will all be taught by God.' Therefore everyone who hears from the Father, and has learned, comes to me. Not that anyone has seen the Father, except he who is from God. He has seen the Father. Most certainly, I tell you, he who believes in me has eternal life. I am the bread of life. Your fathers ate the manna in the wilderness, and they died. This is the bread which comes down out of heaven, that anyone may eat of it and not die. I am the living bread which came down out of heaven. If anyone eats of this bread, he will live forever. Yes, the bread which I will give for the life of the world is my flesh." ~ "I am thirsty." ·

LUKE 6:20-26; JOHN 4:7, 4:32, 4:34, 6:26-27, 6:35, 6:43-51, 19:28

## Hypocrisy

"Be careful that you don't do your charitable giving before men, to be seen by them, or else you have no reward from your Father who is in heaven. Therefore when you do merciful deeds, don't sound a trumpet before yourself, as the hypocrites do in the synagogues and in the streets, that they may get glory from me. Most certainly I tell you, they have received their reward. But when you do merciful deeds, don't let your left hand know what your right hand does, so that your merciful deeds may be in secret, then your Father who sees in secret will reward you openly." ~ "These people draw near to me with their mouth, and honor me with their lips; but their heart is far from me. And in vain do they worship me, teaching as doctrine rules made by men." ~ "Woe to you, scribes and Pharisees, Hypocrites! For you devour widows' houses, And as a pretense you make long prayers. Therefore you will receive greater condemnation." ~ "Woe to you, scribes and Pharisees, hypocrites! For you tithe mint, dill, and cumin, and have left undone the weightier matters of the law: justice, mercy, and faith. But you ought to have done these, and not to have left the other undone. You blind guides, who strain out a gnat, and swallow a camel!" ~ "Woe to you, scribes and Pharisees, hypocrites! For you clean the outside of the cup and of the platter, but within they are full of extortion and unrighteousness. You blind Pharisee, first clean the inside of the cup and of the platter, that its outside may become clean also." ~ "Woe to you, scribes and Pharisees, hypocrites! For you are like whitened tombs, which outwardly appear beautiful, but inwardly are full of dead men's bones, and of all uncleanness. Even so you also outwardly appear righteous to men, but inwardly you are full of hypocrisy and iniquity." ~ "It is written, 'My house is a house of prayer,' but you have made it a 'den of robbers'!"

MATT 6:1-4, 15:8-9, 23:13, 23:23-24, 23:25-26, 23:27-28; LUKE 19:46

# Identity

"You are the salt of the earth, but if the salt has lost its flavor, with what will it be salted? It is then good for nothing, but to be cast out and trodden under the feet of men. You are the light of the world. A city located on a hill can't be hidden. Neither do you light a lamp, and put it under a measuring basket, but on a stand; and it shines to all who are in the house. Even so, let your light shine before men; that they may see your good works, and glorify your Father who is in heaven." ~ "For I tell you, among those who are born of women there is not a greater prophet than John the Baptizer, yet he who is least in the Kingdom of God is greater than he." ~ "Now the parable is this: The seed is the word of God. Those along the road are those who hear, then the devil comes, and takes away the word from their heart, that they may not believe and be saved. Those on the rock are they who, when they hear, receive the word with joy; but these have no root, who believe for a while, then fall away in time of temptation. That which fell among the thorns, these are those who have heard, and as they go on their way they are choked with cares, riches, and pleasures of life, bring no fruit to maturity. That in the good ground, these are such as in an honest and good heart, having heard the word, hold it tightly, and bring forth fruit with patience." ~ "Who do the multitudes say that I am?" ~ "But who do you say that I am?" ~ "I am the good shepherd. I know my own, and I'm known by my own; even as the Father knows me, and I know the Father. I lay down my life for the sheep. I have other sheep, which are not of this fold. I must bring them also, and they will hear my voice. They will become one flock with one shepherd. Therefore the Father loves me, because I lay down my life, that I may take it again. No one takes it away from me, but I lay it down by myself. I have power to lay it down, and I have power to take it again. I received this commandment from my Father." ~ "I am the vine. You are the branches. He who remains in me, and I in him, the same bears much fruit, for apart from me you can do nothing." ~ "Who are you looking for?" ~ "I am he."

MATT. 5:13-16; LUKE 7:28, 8:11-15, 9:18, 9:20; JOHN 10:14-18, 15:5, 18:4, 18:5

## Impurity

"Do you also still not understand? Don't you understand that whatever goes into the mouth passes into the belly, and then out of the body? But the things which proceed out of the mouth come out of the heart, and they defile the man. For out of the heart come forth evil thoughts, murders, adulteries, sexual sins, thefts, false testimony, and blasphemies. These are the things which defile the man; but to eat with unwashed hands doesn't defile the man." ~ "Whoever divorces his wife, and marries another, commits adultery against her. If a woman herself divorces her husband, and marries another, she commits adultery." ~ "No one, when he has lit a lamp, puts it in a cellar or under a basket, but on a stand, that those who come in may see the light. The lamp of the body is the eye. Therefore when your eye is good, your whole body is also full of light; but when it is evil, your body also is full of darkness. Therefore see whether the light that is in you isn't darkness. If therefore your whole body is full of light, having no part dark, it will be wholly full of light, as when the lamp with its bright shining gives you light." ~ "It is written, 'My house is a house of prayer,' but you have made it a 'den of robbers'!" ~ "To the angel of the assembly in Pergamum write: 'He who has the sharp two-edged sword says these things.'" ~ "I know your works and where you dwell, where Satan's throne is. You hold firmly to my name, and didn't deny my faith in the days of Antipas my witness, my faithful one, who was killed among you, where Satan dwells. But I have a few things against you, because you have there some who hold the teaching of Balaam, who taught Balak to throw a stumbling block before the children of Israel, to eat things sacrificed to idols, and to commit sexual immorality."

MATT. 15:16-20; MARK 10:11-12; LUKE 11:33-36, 19:46; REV. 2:12, 2:13-14

## Intimacy

"I thank you, Father, Lord of heaven and earth, that you hid these things from the wise and understanding, and revealed them to infants. Yes, Father, for so it was well-pleasing in your sight. All things have been delivered to me by my Father. No one knows the Son, except the Father; neither does anyone know the Father, except the Son, and he to whom the Son desires to reveal him." ~ "All things have been delivered to me by my Father. No one knows who the Son is, except the

Father, and who the Father is, except the Son, and he to whomever the Son desires to reveal him." ~ "Blessed are the eyes which see the things that you see, for I tell you that many prophets and kings desired to see the things which you see, and didn't see them, and to hear the things which you hear, and didn't hear them." ~ "You know neither me, nor my Father. If you knew me, you would know my Father also." ~ "When you have lifted up the Son of Man, then you will know that I am he, and I do nothing of myself, but as my Father taught me, I say these things. He who sent me is with me. The Father hasn't left me alone, for I always do the things that are pleasing to him." ~ "If I glorify myself, my glory is nothing. It is my Father who glorifies me, of whom you say that he is our God. You have not known him, but I know him. If I said, 'I don't know him,' I would be like you, a liar. But I know him, and keep his word. Your father Abraham rejoiced to see my day. He saw it, and was glad." ~ "Who are you looking for?" ~ "I am he." ~ "Behold, I stand at the door and knock. If anyone hears my voice and opens the door, then I will come in to him, and will dine with him, and he with me." ~ "Come and eat breakfast."

MATT. 11:25-27; LUKE 10:22, 10:23-24; JOHN 8:19, 8:28-29, 8:54-56, 18:4, 18:5; REV. 3:20; JOHN 21:12

# Joy

"Again, the Kingdom of Heaven is like a treasure hidden in the field, which a man found, and hid. In his joy, he goes and sells all that he has, and buys that field." ~ "His lord said to him, 'Well done, good and faithful servant. You have been faithful over a few things, I will set you over many things. Enter into the joy of your lord.'" ~ "Rejoice!" ~ "I thank you, O Father, Lord of heaven and earth, that you have hidden these things from the wise and understanding, and revealed them to little children. Yes, Father, for so it was well-pleasing in your sight." ~ "If anyone is thirsty, let him come to me and drink! He who believes in me, as the Scripture has said, from within him will flow rivers of living water." ~ "In this is my Father glorified, that you bear much fruit; and so you will be my disciples. Even as the Father has loved me, I also have loved you. Remain in my love. If you keep my commandments, you will remain in my love; even as I have kept my Father's commandments, and remain in his love. I have spoken these things to you, that my joy may remain in you, and that your joy may be made full."

MATT. 13:44, 25:23, 28:9; LUKE 10:21; JOHN 7:37-38, 15:8-11

# Kindness

" Whoever gives one of these little ones just a cup of cold water to drink in the name of a disciple, most certainly I tell you he will in no way lose his reward." ~ "They don't need to go away. You give them something to eat." ~ "Bring them here to me." ~ "See that you don't despise one of these little ones, for I tell you that in heaven their angels always see the face of my Father who is in heaven. For the Son of Man came to save that which was lost." ~ "You give them something to eat." ~ "But when the Son of Man comes in his glory, and all the holy angels with him, then he will sit on the throne of his glory. Before him all the nations will be gathered, and he will separate them one from another, as a shepherd separates the sheep from the goats. He will set the sheep on his right hand, but the goats on the left. Then the King will tell those on his right hand, 'Come, blessed of my Father, inherit the Kingdom prepared for you from the foundation of the world; for I was hungry, and you gave me food to eat. I was thirsty, and you gave me drink. I was a stranger, and you took me in. I was naked, and you clothed me. I was sick, and you visited me. I was in prison, and you came to me.'" ~ "Then the righteous will answer him, saying, 'Lord, when did we see you hungry, and feed you; or thirsty, and give you a drink? When did we see you as a stranger, and take you in; or naked, and clothe you? When did we see you sick, or in prison, and come to you?'" ~ "The King will answer them, 'Most certainly I tell you, inasmuch as you did it to one of the least of these my brothers, you did it to me.' Then he will say also to those on the left hand, 'Depart from me, you cursed, into the eternal fire which is prepared for the devil and his angels; for I was hungry, and you didn't give me food to eat; I was thirsty, and you gave me no drink; I was a stranger, and you didn't take me in; naked, and you didn't clothe me; sick, and in prison, and you didn't visit me.'" ~ "Then they will also answer, saying, 'Lord, when did we see you hungry, or thirsty, or a stranger, or naked, or sick, or in prison, and didn't help you?'" ~ "Then he will answer them, saying, 'Most certainly I tell you, inasmuch as you didn't do it to one of the least of these, you didn't do it to me.' These will go away into eternal punishment, but the righteous into eternal life." ~ "But I tell you who hear: love your enemies, do good to those who hate you, bless those who curse you, and pray for those who mistreat you. To him who strikes you on the cheek, offer also the other; and from him who takes away your cloak, don't withhold your coat also. Give to everyone who asks you, and don't ask him who takes away your goods to give them back again." ~ "Peace be to you."

MATT. 10:42, 14:16, 14:18, 18:10-11; 25:31-36, 25:37-39, 25:40-43, 25:44, 25:45-46; MARK 6:37; LUKE 6:27-30; JOHN 20:19

# Kingdom of Heaven

"Most certainly I tell you, I haven't found so great a faith, not even in Israel. I tell you that many will come from the east and the west, and will sit down with Abraham, Isaac, and Jacob in the Kingdom of Heaven, but the children of the Kingdom will be thrown out into the outer darkness. There will be weeping and gnashing of teeth." ~ "The Kingdom of Heaven is like a man who sowed good seed in his field, but while people slept, his enemy came and sowed darnel weeds also among the wheat, and went away. But when the blade sprang up and brought forth fruit, then the darnel weeds appeared also. The servants of the householder came and said to him, 'Sir, didn't you sow good seed in your field? Where did this darnel come from?'" ~ "He said to them, 'An enemy has done this.' "The servants asked him, 'Do you want us to go and gather them up?'" ~ "But he said, 'No, lest perhaps while you gather up the darnel weeds, you root up the wheat with them. Let both grow together until the harvest, and in the harvest time I will tell the reapers, "First, gather up the darnel weeds, and bind them in bundles to burn them; but gather the wheat into my barn."'" ~ "The Kingdom of Heaven is like a grain of mustard seed, which a man took, and sowed in his field; which indeed is smaller than all seeds. But when it is grown, it is greater than the herbs, and becomes a tree, so that the birds of the air come and lodge in its branches." ~ "The Kingdom of Heaven is like yeast, which a woman took, and hid in three measures of meal, until it was all leavened." ~ "But concerning the resurrection of the dead, haven't you read that which was spoken to you by God, saying, 'I am the God of Abraham, and the God of Isaac, and the God of Jacob? God is not the God of the dead, but of the living." ~ "Take, eat; this is my body."…"All of you drink it, for this is my blood of the new covenant, which is poured out for many for the remission of sins. But I tell you that I will not drink of this fruit of the vine from now on, until that day when I drink it anew with you in my Father's

Kingdom." ~ "The time is fulfilled, and the Kingdom of God is at hand! Repent, and believe in the Good News." ~ "The Kingdom of God doesn't come with observation; neither will they say, 'Look, here!' or, 'Look, there!' for behold, the Kingdom of God is within you." ~ "I am the bread which came down out of heaven."

MATT. 8:10-12, 13:24-27, 13:28, 13:29-30, 13:31-32, 13:33, 22:31-32, 26:26-29; MARK 1:15; LUKE 17:20-21; JOHN 6:41

## Knowing Jesus

"Follow me, and leave the dead to bury their own dead." ~ "How then does David in the Spirit call him Lord, saying, 'The Lord said to my Lord, sit on my right hand, until I make your enemies a footstool for your feet?'" "If then David calls him Lord, how is he his son?" ~ "Who touched my clothes?" ~ "Who do men say that I am?" ~ "But who do you say that I am?" ~ "Why are you reasoning so in your hearts? Which is easier to say, 'Your sins are forgiven you;' or to say, 'Arise and walk?' But that you may know that the Son of Man has authority on earth to forgive sins" . . . "I tell you, arise, and take up your cot, and go to your house." ~ "What did you go out into the wilderness to see? A reed shaken by the wind? But what did you go out to see? A man clothed in soft clothing? Behold, those who are gorgeously dressed, and live delicately, are in kings' courts. But what did you go out to see? A prophet? Yes, I tell you, and much more than a prophet. This is he of whom it is written, 'Behold, I send my messenger before your face, who will prepare your way before you.'" ~ "Who touched me?" ~ "Someone did touch me, for I perceived that power has gone out of me." ~ "I am the bread which came down out of heaven." ~ "You both know me, and know where I am from. I have not come of myself, but he who sent me is true, whom you don't know. I know him, because I am from him, and he sent me." ~ "Most certainly, I tell you, before Abraham came into existence, I AM." ~ "You have both seen him, and it is he who speaks with you."

MATT. 8:22, 22:42-45; MARK 5:30, 8:27, 8:29; LUKE 5:22-24, 7:24-27, 8:45, 8:46; JOHN 6:41, 7:28-29, 8:58, 9:37

# Leadership

"Put out into the deep, and let down your nets for a catch." ~ "Don't be afraid. From now on you will be catching people alive." ~ "No one puts a piece from a new garment on an old garment, or else he will tear the new, and also the piece from the new will not match the old. No one puts new wine into old wineskins, or else the new wine will burst the skins, and it will be spilled, and the skins will be destroyed. But new wine must be put into fresh wineskins, and both are preserved. No man having drunk old wine immediately desires new, for he says, 'The old is better.'" ~ "Can the blind guide the blind? Won't they both fall into a pit? A disciple is not above his teacher, but everyone when he is fully trained will be like his teacher. Why do you see the speck of chaff that is in your brother's eye, but don't consider the beam that is in your own eye? Or how can you tell your brother, 'Brother, let me remove the speck of chaff that is in your eye,' when you yourself don't see the beam that is in your own eye? You hypocrite! First remove the beam from your own eye, and then you can see clearly to remove the speck of chaff that is in your brother's eye." ~ "The farmer went out to sow his seed. As he sowed, some fell along the road, and it was trampled under foot, and the birds of the sky devoured it. Other seed fell on the rock, and as soon as it grew, it withered away, because it had no moisture. Other fell amid the thorns, and the thorns grew with it, and choked it. Other fell into the good ground, and grew, and brought forth fruit one hundred times." ~ "Let's go over to the other side of the lake." ~ "Where is your faith?" ~ "Return to your house, and declare what great things God has done for you." ~ "No one, having put his hand to the plow, and looking back, is fit for the Kingdom of God." ~ "Yet a little while the light is with you. Walk while you have the light, that darkness doesn't overtake you. He who walks in the darkness doesn't know where he is going. While you have the light, believe in the light, that you may become children of light." ~ "Peace be to you." ~ "Rise, Peter, kill and eat!" ~ "Don't be afraid, but speak and don't be silent; for I am with you, and no one will attack you to harm you, for I have many people in this city."

LUKE 5:4, 5:10, 5:36-39, 6:39-42, 8:5-8, 8:22, 8:25, 8:39, 9:62; JOHN 12:35-36, 20:26; ACTS 11:7, 18:9-10

# Letting Go

"Allow it now, for this is the fitting way for us to fulfill all righteousness." ~ "You have heard that it was said, 'An eye for an eye, and a tooth for a tooth.' But I tell you, don't resist him who is evil; but whoever strikes you on your right cheek, turn to him the other also. If anyone sues you to take away your coat, let him have your cloak also. Whoever compels you to go one mile, go with him two. Give to him who asks you, and don't turn away him who desires to borrow from you." ~ "Haven't you read what David did, when he was hungry, and those who were with him; how he entered into the house of God, and ate the show bread, which was not lawful for him to eat, neither for those who were with him, but only for the priests? Or have you not read in the law, that on the Sabbath day, the priests in the temple profane the Sabbath, and are guiltless? But I tell you that one greater than the temple is here. But if you had known what this means, 'I desire mercy, and not sacrifice,' you would not have condemned the guiltless. For the Son of Man is Lord of the Sabbath." ~ "Wherever you enter into a house, stay there until you depart from there. Whoever will not receive you nor hear you, as you depart from there, shake off the dust that is under your feet for a testimony against them. Assuredly, I tell you, it will be more tolerable for Sodom and Gomorrah in the day of judgment than for that city!" ~ "So you say." ~ "You still lack one thing. Sell all that you have, and distribute it to the poor. You will have treasure in heaven. Come, follow me." ~ "How hard it is for those who have riches to enter into the Kingdom of God! For it is easier for a camel to enter in through a needle's eye, than for a rich man to enter into the Kingdom of God." ~ "Father, into your hands I commit my spirit!" ~ "The time has come for the Son of Man to be glorified. Most certainly I tell you, unless a grain of wheat falls into the earth and dies, it remains by itself alone. But if it dies, it bears much fruit. He who loves his life will lose it. He who hates his life in this world will keep it to eternal life. If anyone serves me, let him follow me. Where I am, there will my servant also be. If anyone serves me, the Father will honor him." ~ "Don't hold me, for I haven't yet ascended to my Father; but go to my brothers, and tell them, 'I am ascending to my Father and your Father, to my God and your God.'"

MATT. 3:15, 5:38-42, 12:3-8; MARK 6:10-11, 15:2; LUKE 18:22, 18:24-25, 23:46; JOHN 12:23-26, 20:17

## Listening

"Behold, a farmer went out to sow. As he sowed, some seeds fell by the roadside, and the birds came and devoured them. Others fell on rocky ground, where they didn't have much soil, and immediately they sprang up, because they had no depth of earth. When the sun had risen, they were scorched. Because they had no root, they withered away. Others fell among thorns. The thorns grew up and choked them. Others fell on good soil, and yielded fruit: some one hundred times as much, some sixty, and some thirty. He who has ears to hear, let him hear." ~ "Listen!" ~ "To you is given the mystery the Kingdom of God, but to those who are outside, all things are done in parables, that 'seeing they may see, and not perceive; and hearing they may hear, and not understand; lest perhaps they should turn again, and their sins should be forgiven them." ~ "Is the lamp brought to be put under a basket or under a bed? Isn't it put on a stand? For there is nothing hidden, except that it should be made known; neither was anything made secret, but that it should come to light. If any man has ears to hear, let him hear." ~ "Take heed what you hear. With whatever measure you measure, it will be measured to you, and more will be given to you who hear. For whoever has, to him will more be given, and he who doesn't have, even that which he has will be taken away from him." ~ "Simon, I have something to tell you." ~ "Be careful therefore how you hear. For whoever has, to him will be given; and whoever doesn't have, from him will be taken away even that which he thinks he has." ~ "Let these words sink into your ears, for the Son of Man will be delivered up into the hands of men." ~ "I don't have a demon, but I honor my Father, and you dishonor me. But I don't seek my own glory. There is one who seeks and judges. Most certainly, I tell you, if a person keeps my word, he will never see death." ~ "Father, I thank you that you listened to me. I know that you always listen to me, but because of the multitude that stands around I said this, that they may believe that you sent me." ~ "He who has an ear, let him hear what the Spirit says to the assemblies. To him who overcomes I will give to eat of the tree of life, which is in the Paradise of my God."

MATT. 13:3-9; MARK 4:3, 4:11-12, 4:21-23, 4:24-25; LUKE 7:40, 8:18, 9:44; JOHN 8:49-51, 11:41-42; REV. 2:7

# *Lonely*

"The foxes have holes, and the birds of the sky have nests, but the Son of Man has nowhere to lay his head." ~ "Brother will deliver up brother to death, and the father his child. Children will rise up against parents, and cause them to be put to death. You will be hated by all men for my name's sake, but he who endures to the end will be saved. But when they persecute you in this city, flee into the next, for most certainly I tell you, you will not have gone through the cities of Israel, until the Son of Man has come." ~ "Most certainly I tell you, that you today, even this night, before the rooster crows twice, you will deny me three times." ~ "Sit here, while I pray" ~ "My soul is exceedingly sorrowful, even to death. Stay here, and watch." ~ "Abba, Father, all things are possible to you. Please remove this cup from me. However, not what I desire, but what you desire." ~ "Simon, are you sleeping? Couldn't you watch one hour? Watch and pray, that you may not enter into temptation. The spirit indeed is willing, but the flesh is weak." ~ "Aren't five sparrows sold for two assaria coins? Not one of them is forgotten by God. But the very hairs of your head are all numbered. Therefore don't be afraid. You are of more value than many sparrows." ~ "Zacchaeus, hurry and come down, for today I must stay at your house." ~ "Today, salvation has come to this house, because he also is a son of Abraham. For the Son of Man came to seek and to save that which was lost." ~ "Peace be to you." ~ "Follow me." ~ "Do you want to be made well?" ~ "Arise, take up your mat, and walk." ~ "You have both seen him, and it is he who speaks with you." ~ "Do you now believe? Behold, the time is coming, yes, and has now come, that you will be scattered, everyone to his own place, and you will leave me alone. Yet I am not alone, the Father is with me. I have told you these things, that in me you may have peace. In the world you have oppression; but cheer up! I have overcome the world." ~ "Peace be to you. As the Father has sent me, even so I send you." ~ "Behold, I stand at the door and knock. If anyone hears my voice and opens the door, then I will come in to him, and will dine with him, and he with me."

MATT. 8:20, 10:21-23; MARK 14:30, 14:32, 14:34, 14:36, 14:37-38; LUKE 12:6-7, 19:5, 19:9-10, 24:36; JOHN 1:43, 5:6, 5:8, 9:37, 16:31-33, 20:21; REV. 3:20

## *Longing to be Loved*

"Aren't two sparrows sold for an assarion coin? Not one of them falls on the ground apart from your Father's will, but the very hairs of your head are all numbered. Therefore don't be afraid. You are of more value than many sparrows." ~ "Come to me, all you who labor and are heavily burdened, and I will give you rest. Take my yoke upon you, and learn from me, for I am gentle and lowly in heart; and you will find rest for your souls. For my yoke is easy, and my burden is light." ~ "I wasn't sent to anyone but the lost sheep of the house of Israel." ~ "Whoever receives this little child in my name receives me. Whoever receives me receives him who sent me. For whoever is least among you all, this one will be great." ~ "Jerusalem, Jerusalem, that kills the prophets, and stones those who are sent to her! How often I wanted to gather your children together, like a hen gathers her own brood under her wings, and you refused! Behold, your house is left to you desolate. I tell you, you will not see me, until you say, 'Blessed is he who comes in the name of the Lord!'" ~ "Isn't it written in your law, 'I said, you are gods?' If he called them gods, to whom the word of God came (and the Scripture can't be broken), do you say of him whom the Father sanctified and sent into the world, 'You blaspheme,' because I said, 'I am the Son of God?' If I don't do the works of my Father, don't believe me. But if I do them, though you don't believe me, believe the works; that you may know and believe that the Father is in me, and I in the Father." ~ "Leave her alone. She has kept this for the day of my burial. For you always have the poor with you, but you don't always have me." ~ "Come and eat breakfast." ~ "Behold, I stand at the door and knock. If anyone hears my voice and opens the door, then I will come in to him, and will dine with him, and he with me."

MATT. 10:29-31, 11:28-29, 15:24; LUKE 9:48, 13:34-35; JOHN 10:34-38, 12:7-8, 21:12; REV. 3:20

## *Loss*

"Blessed are the poor in spirit, for theirs is the Kingdom of Heaven. Blessed are those who mourn, for they shall be comforted." ~ "Cheer up! It is I! Don't be afraid." ~ "How many loaves do you have?" ~ "Don't cry." ~ "Young man, I tell you, arise!" ~ "If anyone desires to come after me, let him deny himself, take up his cross, and follow me. For whoever desires to save his life will lose it, but whoever will lose his life for my sake, the same will save it. For what does it profit a man if he gains the whole world, and loses or forfeits his own self? For whoever will be ashamed of me and of my words, of him will the Son of Man be ashamed, when he comes in his glory, and the glory of the Father, and of the holy angels. But I tell you the truth: There are some of those who stand here, who will in no way taste of death, until they see the Kingdom of God." ~ "Zacchaeus, hurry and come down, for today I must stay at your house." ~ "Today, salvation has come to this house, because he also is a son of Abraham. For the Son of Man came to seek and to save that which was lost." ~ "Peace be to you." ~ "It is I. Don't be afraid." ~ "Do you now believe? Behold, the time is coming, yes, and has now come, that you will be scattered, everyone to his own place, and you will leave me alone. Yet I am not alone, because the Father is with me. I have told you these things, that in me you may have peace. In the world you have oppression; but cheer up! I have overcome the world." ~ "Don't be afraid. I am the first and the last, and the Living one. I was dead, and behold, I am alive forevermore. Amen. I have the keys of Death and of Hades."

MATT. 5:3-4, 14:27, 15:34; LUKE 7:13, 7:14, 9:23-27, 19:5, 19:9-10, 24:36; JOHN 6:20, 16:31-33; REV. 1:17-18

## *Lost*

"I wasn't sent to anyone but the lost sheep of the house of Israel." ~ "See that you don't despise one of these little ones, for I tell you that in heaven their angels always see the face of my Father who is in heaven. For the Son of Man came to save that which was lost." ~ "What do you think? If a man has one hundred sheep, and one of them goes astray, doesn't he leave the ninety-nine, go to the mountains, and seek that which has gone astray? If he finds it, most certainly I tell you, he rejoices over it more than over the ninety-nine which have not gone astray. Even so it is not the will of your Father who is in heaven that one of these little ones should perish." ~ "Let these words sink into your ears, for the Son of Man will be delivered up into the hands of men." ~ "When you make a dinner or a supper, don't call your friends, nor your brothers, nor your kinsmen, nor rich neighbors, or perhaps they might also return the favor, and pay you back. But when you make a feast, ask the poor, the maimed, the lame, or the blind; and you will be blessed, because they don't have the resources to repay you. For you will be repaid in the resurrection of the righteous." ~ "Which of you men, if you had one hundred sheep, and lost one of them, wouldn't leave the ninety-nine in the wilderness, and go after the one that was lost, until he found it? When he has found it, he carries it on his shoulders, rejoicing. When he comes home, he calls together his friends and his neighbors, saying to them, 'Rejoice with me, for I have found my sheep which was lost!'" ~ "He said to him, 'Son, you are always with me, and all that is mine is yours. But it was appropriate to celebrate and be glad, for this, your brother, was dead, and is alive again. He was lost, and is found.'" ~ "Peace be to you." ~ "It is I. Don't be afraid." ~ "I am the way, the truth, and the life. No one comes to the Father, except through me. If you had known me, you would have known my Father also. From now on, you know him, and have seen him." ~ "While I was with them in the world, I kept them in your name. Those whom you have given me I have kept. None of them is lost, except the son of destruction, that the Scripture might be fulfilled. But now I come to you, and I say these things in the world, that they may have my joy made full in themselves. I have given them your word. The world hated them, because they are not of the world, even as I am not of the world." ~ "Behold, I stand at the door and knock. If anyone hears my voice and opens the door, then I will come in to him, and will dine with him, and he with me."

MATT. 15:24, 18:10-11, 18:12-14; LUKE 9:44, 14:12-14, 15:4-6, 15:31-32, 24:36; JOHN 6:20. 14:6-7, 17:12-14; REV. 3:20

## *Love*

"Don't think that I came to send peace on the earth. I didn't come to send peace, but a sword. For I came to set a man at odds against his father, and a daughter against her mother, and a daughter-in-law against her mother-in-law. A man's foes will be those of his own household. He who loves father or mother more than me is not worthy of me; and he who loves son or daughter more than me isn't worthy of me. He who doesn't take his cross and follow after me, isn't worthy of me. He who seeks his life will lose it; and he who loses his life for my sake will find it. He who receives you receives me, and he who receives me receives him who sent me. He who receives a prophet in the name of a prophet will receive a prophet's reward. He who receives a righteous man in the name of a righteous man will receive a righteous man's reward. Whoever gives one of these little ones just a cup of cold water to drink in the name of a disciple, most certainly I tell you he will in no way lose his reward." ~ "The greatest is, 'Hear, Israel, the Lord our God, the Lord is one: you shall love the Lord your God with all your heart, and with all your soul, and with all your mind, and with all your strength.' This is the first commandment. The second is like this, 'You shall love your neighbor as yourself.' There is no other commandment greater than these." ~ "A certain lender had two debtors. The one owed five hundred denarii, and the other fifty. When they couldn't pay, he forgave them both. Which of them therefore will love him most?" ~ "You have judged correctly." ~ "Do you see this woman? I entered into your house, and you gave me no water for my feet, but she has wet my feet with her tears, and wiped them with the hair of her head. You gave me no kiss, but she, since the time I came in, has not ceased to kiss my feet. You didn't anoint my head with oil, but she has anointed my feet with ointment. Therefore I tell you, her sins, which are many, are forgiven, for she loved much. But to whom little is forgiven, the same loves little." ~ "Your sins are forgiven." ~ "If anyone comes to me, and doesn't disregard his own father, mother, wife, children, brothers, and sisters, yes, and his own life also, he can't be my disciple. Whoever doesn't bear his own cross, and come after me, can't be my disciple. For which of you, desiring to build a tower, doesn't first sit down and count the cost, to see if he has enough to complete it? Or perhaps, when he has laid a foundation, and is not able to finish, everyone who sees begins to mock him, saying, 'This man began to build, and wasn't able to finish.' Or what king, as he goes to encounter another king in war, will not sit down first and consider whether he is able with ten thousand to meet him who comes against him with twenty thousand? Or else, while the other is yet a great way off, he sends an envoy, and asks for conditions of peace. So therefore whoever of you who doesn't renounce all that he has, he can't be my disciple. Salt is good, but if the salt becomes flat and tasteless, with what do you season it? It is fit neither for the soil nor for the manure pile. It is thrown out. He who has ears to hear, let him hear." ~ "For God so loved the world, that he gave his one and only Son, that whoever believes in him should not perish, but have eternal life. For God didn't send his Son into the world to judge the world, but that the world should be saved through him." ~ "Now the Son of Man has been glorified, and God has been glorified in him. If God has been glorified in him, God will also glorify him in himself, and he will glorify him immediately. Little children, I will be with you a little while longer. You will seek me, and as I said to the Jews, 'Where I am going, you can't come,' so now I tell you. A new commandment I give to you, that you love one another, just like I have loved you; that you also love one another." ~ "Simon, son of Jonah, do you love me more than these?" ... "Feed my lambs." ~ "Simon, son of Jonah, do you love me?" ... "Tend my sheep." ~ "Simon, son of Jonah, do you have affection for me?" ... "Do you have affection for me?" ... "Feed my sheep."

MATT. 10:34-42; MARK 12:29-31; LUKE 7:41-42, 7:43, 7:44-47, 7:48. 14:26-35; JOHN 3:16-17, 13:31-35, 21:15, 21:16, 21:17

## *Major Decisions*

"Enter in by the narrow gate; for wide is the gate and broad is the way that leads to and many are those who enter in by it. How narrow is the gate, and restricted is the way that leads to life! Few are those who find it." ~ "Can the friends of the bridegroom mourn, as long as the bridegroom is with them? But the days will come when the bridegroom will be taken away from them, and then they will fast. No one puts a piece of unshrunk cloth on an old garment; for the patch would tear away from the garment, and a worse hole is made. Neither do people put new wine into old wineskins, or else the skins would burst, the wine be spilled, and the skins ruined. No, they put new wine into fresh wineskins, and both are preserved." ~ "What do you want?" ~ "Stand up." ~ "Whoever wants to come after me, let him deny himself, and take up his cross, and follow me. For whoever wants to save his life will lose it; and whoever will lose his life for my sake and the sake of the Good News will save it. For what does it profit a man, to gain the whole world, and forfeit his life? For what will a man give in exchange for his life? For whoever will be ashamed of me and of my words in this adulterous and sinful generation, the Son of Man also will be ashamed of him, when he comes in the glory of his Father with the holy angels." ~ "Follow me!" ~ "Let's go over to the other side of the lake." ~ "Where is your faith?" ~ "No one, having put his hand to the plow, and looking back, is fit for the Kingdom of God." ~ "Aren't there twelve hours of daylight? If a man walks in the day, he doesn't stumble, because he sees the light of this world. But if a man walks in the night, he stumbles, because the light isn't in him." ~ "In that day you will ask me no questions. Most certainly

I tell you, whatever you may ask of the Father in my name, he will give it to you. Until now, you have asked nothing in my name. Ask, and you will receive, that your joy may be made full. I have spoken these things to you in figures of speech. But the time is coming when I will no more speak to you in figures of speech, but will tell you plainly about the Father. In that day you will ask in my name; and I don't say to you, that I will pray to the Father for you, for the Father himself loves you, because you have loved me, and have believed that I came forth from God. I came out from the Father, and have come into the world. Again, I leave the world, and go to the Father." ~ "Peace be to you." ~ "To the angel of the assembly in Philadelphia write: 'He who is holy, he who is true, he who has the key of David, he who opens and no one can shut, and who shuts and no one opens, says these things.'"

MATT. 7:13-14, 9:15-17, 20:21; MARK 3:3, 8:34-38; LUKE 5:27, 8:22, 8:25, 9:62; JOHN 11:9-10, 16:23-28, 20:26; REV. 3:7

## Marriage

"You have heard that it was said, 'You shall not commit adultery' but I tell you that everyone who gazes at a woman to lust after her has committed adultery with her already in his heart." ~ "It was also said, 'Whoever shall put away his wife, let him give her a writing of divorce' but I tell you that whoever puts away his wife, except for the cause of sexual immorality, makes her an adulteress; and whoever marries her when she is put away commits adultery." ~ "Haven't you read that he who made them from the beginning made them male and female, and said, 'For this cause a man shall leave his father and mother, and shall join to his wife; and the two shall become one flesh?' So that they are no more two, but one flesh. What therefore God has joined together, don't let man tear apart." ~ "Moses, because of the hardness of your hearts, allowed you to divorce your wives, but from the beginning it has not been so. I tell you that whoever divorces his wife, except for sexual immorality, and marries another, commits adultery; and he who marries her when she is divorced commits adultery." ~ "You are mistaken, not knowing the Scriptures, nor the power of God. For in the resurrection they neither marry, nor are given in marriage, but are like God's angels in heaven." ~ "For your hardness of heart, he wrote you this commandment. But from the beginning of the creation, God made them male and female. For this cause a man will leave his father and mother, and will join to his wife, and the two will become one flesh, so that they are no longer two, but one flesh. What therefore God has joined together, let no man separate." ~ "The children of this age marry, and are given in marriage. But those who are considered worthy to attain to that age and the resurrection from the dead, neither marry, nor are given in marriage. For they can't die any more, for they are like the angels, and are children of God, being children of the resurrection. But that the dead are raised, even Moses showed at the bush, when he called the Lord 'The God of Abraham, the God of Isaac, and the God of Jacob.' Now he is not the God of the dead, but of the living, for all are alive to him." ~ "Peace be to you."

MATT. 5:27-28, 5:31-32, 19:4-6, 19:8-9, 22:29-30; MARK 10:5-9; LUKE 20:34-38; JOHN 20:19

## *Meaning of Life*

"Let's go elsewhere into the next towns, that I may preach there also, because I came out for this reason." ~ "The greatest is, 'Hear, Israel, the Lord our God, the Lord is one: you shall love the Lord your God with all your heart, and with all your soul, and with all your mind, and with all your strength.' This is the first commandment. The second is like this, 'You shall love your neighbor as yourself.' There is no other commandment greater than these." ~ "Why do you call me, 'Lord, Lord,' and don't do the things which I say? Everyone who comes to me, and hears my words, and does them, I will show you who he is like. He is like a man building a house, who dug and went deep, and laid a foundation on the rock. When a flood arose, the stream broke against that house, and could not shake it, because it was founded on the rock. But he who hears, and doesn't do, is like a man who built a house on the earth without a foundation, against which the stream broke, and immediately it fell, and the ruin of that house was great." ~ "What is written in the law? How do you read it?" ~ "You have answered correctly. Do this, and you will live." ~ "What are you looking for?" ~ "Come, and see." ~ "You search the Scriptures, because you think that in them you have eternal life; and these are they which testify about me. Yet you will not come to me, that you may have life. I don't receive glory from men. But I know you, that you don't have God's love in yourselves. I have come in my Father's name, and you don't receive me. If another comes in his own name, you will receive him. How can you believe, who receive glory from one another, and you don't seek the glory that comes from the only God?" ～ "Don't murmur among yourselves. No one can come to me unless the Father who sent me draws him, and I will raise him up in the last day. It is written in the prophets, 'They will all be taught by God.' Therefore everyone who hears from the Father, and has learned, comes to me. Not that anyone has seen the Father, except he who is from God. He has seen the Father. Most certainly, I tell you, he who believes in me has eternal life. I am the bread of life. Your fathers ate the manna in the wilderness, and they died. This is the bread which comes down out of heaven, that anyone may eat of it and not die. I am the living bread which came down out of heaven. If anyone eats of this bread, he will live forever. Yes, the bread which I will give for the life of the world is my flesh."

MARK 1:38, 12:29-31; LUKE 6:46-49, 10:26, 10:28; JOHN 1:38, 1:39, 5:39-44, 6:43-51

## Mercy

"Blessed are the merciful, for they shall obtain mercy." ～ "Those who are healthy have no need for a physician, but those who are sick do. But you go and learn what this means: 'I desire mercy, and not sacrifice,' for I came not to call the righteous, but sinners to repentance." ～ "Woe to you, scribes and Pharisees, hypocrites! For you tithe mint, dill, and cumin, and have left undone the weightier matters of the law: justice, mercy, and faith. But you ought to have done these, and not to have left the other undone." ～ "Go and do likewise." ～ "Father, forgive them, for they don't know what they are doing." ～ "For God so loved the world, that he gave his one and only Son, that whoever believes in him should not perish, but have eternal life. For God didn't send his Son into the world to judge the world, but that the world should be saved through him." ～ "Neither do I condemn you. Go your way. From now on, sin no more."

MATT. 5:7, 9:12-13, 23:23; LUKE 10:37, 23:34; JOHN 3:16-17, 8:11

## Ministry

"Don't go among the Gentiles, and don't enter into any city of the Samaritans. Rather, go to the lost sheep of the house of Israel. As you go, preach, saying, 'The Kingdom of Heaven is at hand!' Heal the sick, cleanse the lepers, and cast out demons. Freely you received, so freely give." ~ "Into whatever city or village you enter, find out who in it is worthy; and stay there until you go on. As you enter into the household, greet it. If the household is worthy, let your peace come on it, but if it isn't worthy, let your peace return to you. Whoever doesn't receive you, nor hear your words, as you go out of that house or that city, shake off the dust from your feet. Most certainly I tell you, it will be more tolerable for the land of Sodom and Gomorrah in the day of judgment than for that city." ~ "Let the children be filled first, for it is not appropriate to take the children's bread and throw it to the dogs." ~ "Why were you looking for me? Didn't you know that I must be in my Father's house?" ~ "Doubtless you will tell me this parable, 'Physician, heal yourself! Whatever we have heard done at Capernaum, do also here in your hometown.'" ~ "Most certainly I tell you, no prophet is acceptable in his hometown. But truly I tell you, there were many widows in Israel in the days of Elijah, when the sky was shut up three years and six months, when a great famine came over all the land. Elijah was sent to none of them, except to Zarephath, in the land of Sidon, to a woman who was a widow. There were many lepers in Israel in the time of Elisha the prophet, yet not one of them was cleansed, except Naaman, the Syrian." ~ "The harvest is indeed plentiful, but the laborers are few. Pray therefore to the Lord of the harvest, that he may send out laborers into his harvest. Go your ways. Behold, I send you out as lambs among wolves. Carry no purse, nor wallet, nor sandals. Greet no one on the way. Into whatever house you enter, first say, 'Peace be to this house.' If a son of peace is there, your peace will rest on him; but if not, it will return to you. Remain in that same house, eating and drinking the things they give, for the laborer is worthy of his wages. Don't go from house to house. Into whatever city you enter, and they receive you, eat the things that are set before you. Heal the sick who are therein, and tell them, 'The Kingdom of God has come near to you.' But into whatever city you enter, and they don't receive you, go out into its streets and say, 'Even the dust from your city that clings to us, we wipe off against you. Nevertheless know this, that the Kingdom of God has come near to you.' I tell you, it will be more tolerable in that day for Sodom than for that city." ~ "From that time the Good News of the Kingdom of God is preached, and everyone is forcing his way into it." ~ "My food is to do the will of him who sent me, and to accomplish his work.

Don't you say, 'There are yet four months until the harvest?' Behold, I tell you, lift up your eyes, and look at the fields, that they are white for harvest already. He who reaps receives wages, and gathers fruit to eternal life; that both he who sows and he who reaps may rejoice together. For in this the saying is true, 'One sows, and another reaps.' I sent you to reap that for which you haven't labored. Others have labored, and you have entered into their labor." ~ "Who are you looking for?" ~ "It is more blessed to give than to receive." ~ "Hurry and get out of Jerusalem quickly, because they will not receive testimony concerning me from you."

MATT. 10:5-8, 11-15; MARK 7:27; LUKE 2:49. 4:23, 4:24-27, 10:2-12, 16:16; JOHN 4:34-38, 18:4; ACTS 20:35, 22:18

# *Money*

"If you want to be perfect, go, sell what you have, and give to the poor, and you will have treasure in heaven; and come, follow me." ~ "Give therefore to Caesar the things that are Caesar's, and to God the things that are God's." ~ "For it is like a man, going into another country, who called his own servants, and entrusted his goods to them. To one he gave five talents, to another two, to another one; to each according to his own ability. Then he went on his journey. Immediately he who received the five talents went and traded with them, and made another five talents. In the same way, he also who got the two gained another two. But he who received the one went away and dug in the earth, and hid his lord's money." ~ "Now after a long time the lord of those servants came, and reconciled accounts with them. He who received the five talents came and brought another five talents, saying, 'Lord, you delivered to me five talents. Behold, I have gained another five talents besides them.'" ~ "His lord said to him, 'Well done, good and faithful servant. You have been faithful over a few things, I will set you over many things. Enter into the joy of your lord.'" ~ "He also who got the two talents came and said, 'Lord, you delivered to me two talents. Behold, I have gained another two talents besides them.'" ~ "His lord said to him, 'Well done, good and faithful servant. You have been faithful over a few things, I will set you over many things. Enter into the joy of your lord.'" ~ "He also who had received the one talent came and said, 'Lord, I knew you that you are a hard man, reaping where you did not sow, and gathering where you did not scatter. I was afraid, and went away and hid your talent in the earth. Behold, you have what is yours.'" ~ "But his lord answered him, 'You wicked and slothful servant. You knew that I reap where I didn't sow, and gather where I didn't scatter. You ought therefore to have deposited my money with the bankers, and at my coming I should have received back my own with interest. Take away therefore the talent from him, and give it to him who has the ten talents. For to everyone who has will be given, and he will have abundance, but from him who doesn't have, even that which he has will be taken away. Throw out the unprofitable servant into the outer darkness, where there will be weeping and gnashing of teeth.'" ~ "One thing you lack. Go, sell whatever you have, and give to the poor, and you will have treasure in heaven; and come, follow me, taking up the cross." ~ "How difficult it is for those who have riches to enter into the Kingdom of God!" ~ "Children, how hard is it for those who trust in riches to enter into the Kingdom of God! It is easier for a camel to go through a needle's eye than for a rich man to enter into the Kingdom of God." ~ "Render to Caesar the things that are Caesar's, and to God the things that are God's." ~ "Man, who made me a judge or an arbitrator over you?" ~ "Beware! Keep yourselves from covetousness, for a man's life doesn't consist of the abundance of the things which he possesses." ~ "The ground of a certain rich man brought forth abundantly. He reasoned within himself, saying, 'What will I do, because I don't have room to store my crops?' He said, 'This is what I will do. I will pull down my barns, and build bigger ones, and there I will store all my grain and my goods. I will tell my soul, 'Soul, you have many goods laid up for many years. Take your ease, eat, drink, be merry.'" ~ "But God said to him, 'You foolish one, tonight your soul is required of you. The things which you have prepared— whose will they be?' So is he who lays up treasure for himself, and is not rich toward God." ~ "To the angel of the assembly in Laodicea write: "The Amen, the Faithful and True Witness, the Head of God's creation, says these things" ~ "I know your works, that you are neither cold nor hot. I wish you were cold or hot. So, because you are lukewarm, and neither hot nor cold, I will vomit you out of my mouth. Because you say, 'I am rich, and have gotten riches, and have need of nothing;' and don't know that you are the wretched one, miserable, poor, blind, and naked; I counsel you to buy from me gold refined by fire, that you may become rich; and white garments, that you may clothe yourself, and that the shame of your nakedness may not be revealed; and eye salve to anoint your eyes, that you may see. As many as I love, I reprove and chasten. Be zealous therefore, and repent."

MATT, 19-21, 22:21, 25:14-18, 25:19-20, 25:21, 25:22, 25:23, 25:24-25, 25:26-30; MARK 10:21, 10:23, 10:24-25. 12:17; LUKE 12:14, 12:15, 12:16-19, 12:20-21; REV, 3:14, 3:15-19

# Obedience

"Put your sword back into its place, for all those who take the sword will die by the sword. Or do you think that I couldn't ask my Father, and he would even now send me more than twelve legions of angels? How then would the Scriptures be fulfilled that it must be so?" ~ "Be careful that no one leads you astray. For many will come in my name, saying, 'I am he!' and will lead many astray." ~ "Abba, Father, all things are possible to you. Please remove this cup from me. However, not what I desire, but what you desire." ~ "My mother and my brothers are these who hear the word of God, and do it." ~ "Leave the dead to bury their own dead, but you go and announce the Kingdom of God." ~ "My Father is still working, so I am working, too." ~ "Do you have affection for me?" . . . "Feed my sheep." ~ "Most certainly I tell you, when you were young, you dressed yourself, and walked where you wanted to. But when you are old, you will stretch out your hands, and another will dress you, and carry you where you don't want to go." ~ "Follow me." ~ "Saul, Saul, why do you persecute me?" ~ "I am Jesus, whom you are persecuting. But rise up, and enter into the city, and you will be told what you must do." ~ "Ananias!" ~ "Arise, and go to the street which is called Straight, and inquire in the house of Judah for one named Saul, a man of Tarsus. For behold, he is praying, and in a vision he has seen a man named Ananias coming in, and laying his hands on him, that he might receive his sight."

MATT. 26:52-54; MARK 13:5-6, 14:36; LUKE 8:21. 9:60; JOHN 5:17. 21:17, 21:18, 21:19; ACTS 9:4, 9:5-6, 9:10, 9:11-12

# Patience

"Many false prophets will arise, and will lead many astray. Because iniquity will be multiplied, the love of many will grow cold. But he who endures to the end, the same will be saved. This Good News of the Kingdom will be preached in the whole world for a testimony to all the nations, and then the end will come." ~

"That in the good ground, these are such as in an honest and good heart, having heard the word, hold it tightly, and bring forth fruit with patience." ~ "On the contrary, blessed are those who hear the word of God, and keep it." ~ "A certain man had a fig tree planted in his vineyard, and he came seeking fruit on it, and found none. He said to the vine dresser, 'Behold, these three years I have come looking for fruit on this fig tree, and found none. Cut it down. Why does it waste the soil?' He answered, 'Lord, leave it alone this year also, until I dig around it, and fertilize it. If it bears fruit, fine; but if not, after that, you can cut it down.'" ~ "Do you inquire among yourselves concerning this, that I said, 'A little while, and you won't see me, and again a little while, and you will see me?' Most certainly I tell you, that you will weep and lament, but the world will rejoice. You will be sorrowful, but your sorrow will be turned into joy. A woman, when she gives birth, has sorrow, because her time has come. But when she has delivered the child, she doesn't remember the anguish any more, for the joy that a human being is born into the world. Therefore you now have sorrow, but I will see you again, and your heart will rejoice, and no one will take your joy away from you." ~ "Don't depart from Jerusalem, but wait for the promise of the Father, which you heard from me. For John indeed baptized in water, but you will be baptized in the Holy Spirit not many days from now." ~ "To the angel of the assembly in Ephesus write: 'He who holds the seven stars in his right hand, he who walks among the seven golden lampstands says these things.'" ~ "I know your works, and your toil and perseverance, and that you can't tolerate evil men, and have tested those who call themselves apostles, and they are not, and found them false. You have perseverance and have endured for my name's sake, and have not grown weary. But I have this against you, that you left your first love. Remember therefore from where you have fallen, and repent and do the first works; or else I am coming to you swiftly, and will move your lampstand out of its place, unless you repent. But this you have, that you hate the works of the Nicolaitans, which I also hate. He who has an ear, let him hear what the Spirit says to the assemblies. To him who overcomes I will give to eat of the tree of life, which is in the Paradise of my God." ~ "Yes, I come quickly."

MATT. 24:11-14; LUKE 8:15, 11:28, 13:6-9; JOHN 16:19-22; ACTS 1:4-5; REV. 2:1, 2:2-7, 22:20

# Peace

"Blessed are the gentle, for they shall inherit the earth. Blessed are those who hunger and thirst after righteousness, for they shall be filled." ~ "Come to me, all you who labor and are heavily burdened, and I will give you rest. Take my yoke upon you, and learn from me, for I am gentle and lowly in heart; and you will find rest for your souls. For my yoke is easy, and my burden is light." ~ "You come apart into a deserted place, and rest awhile." ~ "Don't seek what you will eat or what you will drink; neither be anxious. For the nations of the world seek after all of these things, but your Father knows that you need these things. But seek God's Kingdom, and all these things will be added to you. Don't be afraid, little flock, for it is your Father's good pleasure to give you the Kingdom." ~ "What is the Kingdom of God like? To what shall I compare it? It is like a grain of mustard seed, which a man took, and put in his own garden. It grew, and became a large tree, and the birds of the sky lodged in its branches." ~ "I am he, the one who speaks to you." ~ "Peace I leave with you. My peace I give to you; not as the world gives, give I to you. Don't let your heart be troubled, neither let it be fearful. You heard how I told you, 'I go away, and I come to you.' If you loved me, you would have rejoiced, because I said 'I am going to my Father;' for the Father is greater than I. Now I have told you before it happens so that, when it happens, you may believe. I will no more speak much with you, for the prince of the world comes, and he has nothing in me. But that the world may know that I love the Father, and as the Father commanded me, even so I do. Arise, let us go from here."

MATT. 5:5-6, 11:28-29; MARK 6:31; LUKE 12:29-32, 13:18-19; JOHN 4:26, 14:27-31

# Persecution

"Blessed are those who have been persecuted for righteousness' sake, for theirs is the Kingdom of Heaven." ~ "Blessed are you when people reproach you, persecute you, and say all kinds of evil against you falsely, for my sake. Rejoice, and be exceedingly glad, for great is your reward in heaven. For that is how they persecuted the prophets who were before you." ~ "Be careful that no one leads you astray. For many will come in my name, saying, 'I am the Christ,' and will lead many astray. You will hear of wars and rumors of wars. See that you aren't troubled, for all this must happen, but the end is not yet. For nation will rise against nation, and kingdom against kingdom; and there will be famines, plagues, and earthquakes in various places. But all these things are the beginning of birth pains. Then they will deliver you up to oppression, and will kill you. You will be hated by all of the nations for my name's sake. Then many will stumble, and will deliver up one another, and will hate one another. Many false prophets will arise, and will lead many astray. Because iniquity will be multiplied, the love of many will grow cold. But he who endures to the end, the same will be saved. This Good News of the Kingdom will be preached in the whole world for a testimony to all the nations, and then the end will come." ~ "The Son of Man must suffer many things, and be rejected by the elders, chief priests, and scribes, and be killed, and the third day be raised up." ~ "It is I. Don't be afraid." ~ "I have shown you many good works from my Father. For which of those works do you stone me?" ~ "Of those whom you have given me, I have lost none." ~ "If I have spoken evil, testify of the evil; but if well, why do you beat me?" ~ "Saul, Saul, why are you persecuting me?" ~ "I am Jesus of Nazareth, whom you persecute." ~ "To the angel of the assembly in Smyrna write: "The first and the last, who was dead, and has come to life says these things" ~ "I know your works, oppression, and your poverty (but you are rich), and the blasphemy of those who say they are Jews, and they are not, but are a synagogue of Satan. Don't be afraid of the things which you are about to suffer. Behold, the devil is about to throw some of you into prison, that you may be tested; and you will have oppression for ten days. Be faithful to death, and I will give you the crown of life. He who has an ear, let him hear what the Spirit says to the assemblies. He who overcomes won't be harmed by the second death."

MATT. 5:10, 5:11-12, 24:4-14; LUKE 9:22; JOHN 6:20, 10:31, 18:9, 18:23; ACTS 22:7, 22:8; REV. 2:8, 2:9-11

# Power

"Blessed are the poor in spirit, for theirs is the Kingdom of Heaven." ~ "Bring us not into temptation, but deliver us from the evil one. For yours is the Kingdom, the power, and the glory forever. Amen.'" ~ "You are mistaken, not knowing the Scriptures, nor the power of God." ~ "But that you may know that the Son of Man has authority on earth to forgive sins" ..."I tell you, arise, take up your mat, and go to your house." ~ "If any man wants to be first, he shall be last of all, and servant of all." ~ "Everyone who drinks of this water will thirst again, but whoever drinks of the water that I will give him will never thirst again; but the water that I will give him will become in him a well of water springing up to eternal life." ~ "Therefore the Father loves me, because I lay down my life, that I may take it again. No one takes it away from me, but I lay it down by myself. I have power to lay it down, and I have power to take it again. I received this commandment from my Father." ~ "My grace is sufficient for you, for my power is made perfect in weakness."

MATT 5:3; 6:13; 22:29; MARK 2:10-11; 9:35; JOHN 4:13-14; 10:17-18; 2 COR 12:9

# Prayer

"When you pray, you shall not be as the hypocrites, for they love to stand and pray in the synagogues and in the corners of the streets, that they may be seen by men. Most certainly, I tell you, they have received their reward. But you, when you pray, enter into your inner room, and having shut your door, pray to your Father who is in secret, and your Father who sees in secret will reward you openly. In praying, don't use vain repetitions, as the Gentiles do; for they think that they will be heard for their much speaking. Therefore don't be like them, for your Father knows what things you need, before you ask him. Pray like this: 'Our Father in heaven, may your name be kept holy. Let your Kingdom come. Let your will be done, as in heaven, so on earth. Give us today our daily bread. Forgive us our debts, as we also forgive our debtors. Bring us not into temptation, but deliver us from the evil one. For yours is the Kingdom, the power, and the glory forever. Amen.'" ~ "Most certainly I tell you, if you have faith, and don't doubt, you will not only do what was done to the fig tree, but even if you told this mountain, 'Be taken up and cast into the sea,' it would be done. All things, whatever you ask in prayer, believing, you will receive." ~ "Isn't it written, 'My house will be called a house of prayer for all the nations?' But you have made it a den of robbers!" ~ "Have faith in God. For most certainly I tell you, whoever may tell this mountain, 'Be taken up and cast into the sea,' and doesn't doubt in his heart, but believes that what he says is happening; he shall have whatever he says. Therefore I tell you, all things whatever you pray and ask for, believe that you have received them, and you shall have them. Whenever you stand praying, forgive, if you have anything against anyone; so that your Father, who is in heaven, may also forgive you your transgressions. But if you do not forgive, neither will your Father in heaven forgive your transgressions." ~ "Pray that you don't enter into temptation." ~ "Why do you sleep? Rise and pray that you may not enter into temptation." ~ "Arise, and go to the street which is called Straight, and inquire in the house of Judah for one named Saul, a man of Tarsus. For behold, he is praying, and in a vision he has seen a man named Ananias coming in, and laying his hands on him, that he might receive his sight."

MATT, 6:5-13, 21:21-22; MARK 11:17, 11:22-26; LUKE 22:40, 22:46; ACTS 9:11-12

## Priorities

"Again, the Kingdom of Heaven is like a man who is a merchant seeking fine pearls, who having found one pearl of great price, he went and sold all that he had, and bought it." ~ "Render to Caesar the things that are Caesar's, and to God the things that are God's." ~ "The greatest is, 'Hear, Israel, the Lord our God, the Lord is one: you shall love the Lord your God with all your heart, and with all your soul, and with all your mind, and with all your strength.' This is the first commandment. The second is like this, 'You shall love your neighbor as yourself.' There is no other commandment greater than these." ~ "You are not far from the Kingdom of God." ~ "Leave her alone. Why do you trouble her? She has done a good work for me. For you always have the poor with you, and whenever you want to, you can do them good; but you will not always have me. She has done what she could. She has anointed my body beforehand for the burying. Most certainly I tell you, wherever this Good News may be preached throughout the whole world, that which this woman has done will also be spoken of for a memorial of her." ~ "Those on the rock are they who, when they hear, receive the word with joy; but these have no root, who believe for a while, then fall away in time of temptation. That which fell among the thorns, these are those who have heard, and as they go on their way they are choked with cares, riches, and pleasures of life, bring no fruit to maturity. That in the good ground, these are such as in an honest and good heart, having heard the word, hold it tightly, and bring forth fruit with patience." ~ "The harvest is indeed plentiful, but the laborers are few. Pray therefore to the

Lord of the harvest, that he may send out laborers into his harvest. Go your ways. Behold, I send you out as lambs among wolves. Carry no purse, nor wallet, nor sandals. Greet no one on the way. Into whatever house you enter, first say, 'Peace be to this house.' If a son of peace is there, your peace will rest on him; but if not, it will return to you. Remain in that same house, eating and drinking the things they give, for the laborer is worthy of his wages. Don't go from house to house. Into whatever city you enter, and they receive you, eat the things that are set before you. Heal the sick who are therein, and tell them, 'The Kingdom of God has come near to you.' But into whatever city you enter, and they don't receive you, go out into its streets and say, 'Even the dust from your city that clings to us, we wipe off against you. Nevertheless know this, that the Kingdom of God has come near to you.' I tell you, it will be more tolerable in that day for Sodom than for that city." ~ "Martha, Martha, you are anxious and troubled about many things, but one thing is needed. Mary has chosen the good part, which will not be taken away from her." ~ "You don't also want to go away, do you?"

MATT, 13:45-46; MARK 12:17, 12:29-31, 12:34, 14:6-9; LUKE 8:13-15, 10:2-12, 10:41-42; JOHN 6:67

## Protection

"Behold, I am with you always, even to the end of the age." ~ "By your endurance you will win your lives." ~ "I told you, and you don't believe. The works that I do in my Father's name, these testify about me. But you don't believe, because you are not of my sheep, as I told you. My sheep hear my voice, and I know them, and they follow me. I give eternal life to them. They will never perish, and no one will snatch them out of my hand. My Father, who has given them to me, is greater than all. No one is able to snatch them out of my Father's hand. I and the Father are one." ~ "I am no more in the world, but these are in the world, and I am coming to you. Holy Father, keep them through your name which you have given me, that they may be one, even as we are. While I was with them in the world, I kept them in your name. Those whom you have given me I have kept. None of them is lost, except the son of destruction, that the Scripture might be fulfilled." ~ "Depart, for I will send you out far from here to the Gentiles." MATT. 28:20, LUKE 21:19; JOHN 10:25-30, 17:11-12; ACTS 22:21

# *Provision*

"Don't take any gold, nor silver, nor brass in your money belts. Take no bag for your journey, neither two coats, nor shoes, nor staff: for the laborer is worthy of his food." ~ "Therefore the children are exempt. But, lest we cause them to stumble, go to the sea, cast a hook, and take up the first fish that comes up. When you have opened its mouth, you will find a stater coin. Take that, and give it to them for me and you." ~ "Go and tell John the things which you have seen and heard: that the blind receive their sight, the lame walk, the lepers are cleansed, the deaf hear, the dead are raised up, and the poor have good news preached to them. Blessed is he who finds no occasion for stumbling in me." ~ "Therefore I tell you, don't be anxious for your life, what you will eat, nor yet for your body, what you will wear. Life is more than food, and the body is more than clothing. Consider the ravens: they don't sow, they don't reap, they have no warehouse or barn, and God feeds them. How much more valuable are you than birds! Which of you by being anxious can add a cubit to his height? If then you aren't able to do even the least things, why are you anxious about the rest? Consider the lilies, how they grow. They don't toil, neither do they spin; yet I tell you, even Solomon in all his glory was not arrayed like one of these. But if this is how God clothes the grass in the field, which today exists, and tomorrow is cast into the oven, how much more will he clothe you, O you of little faith? Don't seek what you will eat or what you will drink; neither be anxious. For the nations of the world seek after all of these things, but your Father knows that you need these things. But seek God's Kingdom, and all these things will be added to you. Don't be afraid, little flock, for it is your Father's good pleasure to give you the Kingdom. Sell that which you have, and give gifts to the needy. Make for yourselves purses which don't grow old, a treasure in the heavens that doesn't fail, where no thief approaches, neither moth destroys. For where your treasure is, there will your heart be also." ~ "Where are we to buy bread, that these may eat?" ~ "Have the people sit down." ~ "Gather up the broken pieces which are left over, that nothing be lost." ~ "Most certainly, I tell you, it wasn't Moses who gave you the bread out of heaven, but my Father gives you the true bread out of heaven. For the bread of God is that which comes down out of heaven, and gives life to the world." ~ "Most certainly I tell you, unless you eat the flesh of the Son of Man and drink his blood, you don't have life in yourselves. He who eats my flesh and drinks my blood has eternal life, and I will raise him up at the last day. For my flesh is food indeed, and my blood is drink indeed. He who eats my flesh and drinks my blood lives in me, and I in him. As the living Father sent me, and I live because of the Father; so he who feeds on me, he will also live because of me. This is the bread which came down out of heaven—not as our fathers ate the manna, and died. He who eats this bread will live forever." ~ "Children, have you anything to eat?" ~ "Cast the net on the right side of the boat, and you will find some." ~ "Bring some of the fish which you have just caught."

MATT. 10:9-10, 17:26-27; LUKE 7:22-23, 12:22-34; JOHN 6:5, 6:10, 6:12, 6:32-33, 6:53-58, 21:5, 21:6, 21:10

# *Purpose*

"Repent! For the Kingdom of Heaven is at hand." ~ "'You shall love the Lord your God with all your heart, with all your soul, and with all your mind.' This is the first and great commandment. A second likewise is this, 'You shall love your neighbor as yourself.'" ~ "Come after me, and I will make you into fishers for men." ~ "A certain man made a great supper, and he invited many people. He sent out his servant at supper time to tell those who were invited, 'Come, for everything is ready now.' They all as one began to make excuses. The first said to him, 'I have bought a field, and I must go and see it. Please have me excused.'" ~ "Another said, 'I have bought five yoke of oxen, and I must go try them out. Please have me excused.'" ~ "Another said, 'I have married a wife, and therefore I can't come.'" ~ "That servant came, and told his lord these things. Then the master of the house, being angry, said to his servant, Go out quickly into the streets and lanes of the city, and bring in the poor, maimed, blind, and lame.'" ~ "The servant said, 'Lord, it is done as you commanded, and there is still room.'" ~ "The lord said to the servant, 'Go out into the highways and hedges, and compel them to come in, that my house may be filled. For I tell you that none of those men who were invited will taste of my supper.'" ~ "Most certainly I tell you, there is no one who has left house, or wife, or brothers, or parents, or children, for the Kingdom of God's sake, who will not receive many times more in this time, and in the world to come, eternal life." ~ "I have earnestly desired to eat this Passover with you before I suffer, for I tell you, I will no longer by any means eat of it until it is fulfilled in the Kingdom of God." ~ "Follow me." ~ "I am the bread of life. He who comes to me will not be hungry, and he who believes in me will never be thirsty. But I told you that you have seen me, and yet you don't believe. All those whom the Father gives me will come to me. He who comes to me I will in no way throw out. For I have come down from heaven, not to do my own will, but the will of him who sent me. This is the will of my Father who sent me, that of all he has given to me I should lose nothing, but should raise him up at the last day. This is the will of the one who sent me, that everyone who sees the Son, and believes in him, should have eternal life; and I will raise him up at the last day." ~ "If a man loves me, he will keep my word. My Father will love him, and we will come to him, and make our home with him." ~ "Go your way, for he is my chosen vessel to bear my name before the nations and kings, and the children of Israel. For I will show him how many things he must suffer for my name's sake."

MATT. 4:17, 22:37-39; MARK 1:17; LUKE 14:16-18, 14:19, 14:20, 14:21, 14:22, 14:23-24, 18:29-30, 22:15-16; JOHN 1:43, 6:35-40, 14:23; ACTS 9:15-16

## *Readiness*

"When, therefore, you see the abomination of desolation, which was spoken of through Daniel the prophet, standing in the holy place (let the reader understand), then let those who are in Judea flee to the mountains. Let him who is on the housetop not go down to take out things that are in his house. Let him who is in the field not return back to get his clothes. But woe to those who are with child and to nursing mothers in those days! Pray that your flight will not be in the winter, nor on a Sabbath, for then there will be great oppression, such as has not been from the beginning of the world until now, no, nor ever will be. Unless those days had been shortened, no flesh would have been saved. But for the sake of the chosen ones, those days will be shortened." ~ "As the days of Noah were, so will be the coming of the Son of Man. For as in those days which were before the flood they were eating and drinking, marrying and giving in marriage, until the day that Noah entered into the ship, and they didn't know until the flood came, and took them all away, so will be the coming of the Son of Man. Then two men will be in the field: one will be taken and one will be left; two women grinding at the mill, one will be taken and one will be left. Watch therefore, for you don't know in what hour your Lord comes. But know this, that if the master of the house had known in what watch of the night the thief was coming, he would have watched, and would not have allowed his house to be broken into. Therefore also be ready, for in an hour that you don't expect, the Son of Man will come." ~ "Brother will deliver up brother to death, and the father his child. Children will rise up against parents, and cause them to be put to death. You will be hated by all men for my name's sake, but he who endures to the end, the same will be saved. But when you see the abomination of desolation, spoken of by Daniel the prophet, standing where it ought not (let the reader understand), then let those who are in Judea flee to the mountains, and let him who is on the housetop not go down, nor enter in, to take anything out of his house. Let him who is in the field not return back to take his cloak. But woe to those who are with child and to those who nurse babies in those days! Pray that your flight won't be in the winter. For in those days there will be oppression, such as there has not been the like from the beginning of the creation which God created until now, and never will be. Unless the Lord had shortened the days, no flesh would have been saved; but for the sake of the chosen ones, whom he picked out, he shortened the days. Then if anyone tells you, 'Look, here is the Christ!' or, 'Look, there!' don't believe it. For there will arise false christs and false prophets, and will show signs and wonders, that they may lead astray, if possible, even the chosen ones. But you watch." ~ "Now from the fig tree, learn this parable. When the branch has now become tender, and puts forth its leaves, you know that the summer is near; even so you also, when you see these things coming to pass, know that it is near, at the doors. Most certainly I say to you, this generation will not pass away until all these things happen. Heaven and earth will pass away, but my words will not pass away. But of that day or that hour no one knows, not even the angels in heaven, nor the Son, but only the Father. Watch, keep alert, and pray; for you don't know when the time is." ~ "The days will come, when you will desire to see one of the days of the Son of Man, and you will not see it. They will tell you, 'Look, here!' or 'Look, there!' Don't go away, nor follow after them, for as the lightning, when it flashes out of the one part under the sky, shines to the other part under the sky; so will the Son of Man be in his day. But first, he must suffer many things and be rejected by this generation. As it happened in the days of Noah, even so will it be also in the days of the Son of Man. They ate, they drank, they married, they were given in marriage, until the day that Noah entered into the ship, and the flood came, and destroyed them all. Likewise, even as it happened in the days of Lot: they ate, they drank, they bought, they sold, they planted, they built; but in the day that Lot went out from Sodom, it rained fire and sulfur from the sky, and destroyed them all. It will be the same way in the day that the Son of Man is revealed. In that day, he who will be on the housetop, and his goods in the house, let him not go down to take them away. Let him who is in the field likewise not turn back. Remember Lot's wife! Whoever seeks to save his life loses it, but whoever loses his life preserves it. I tell you, in that night there will be two people in one bed. The one will be taken, and the other will be left. There will be two grinding grain together. One will be taken, and the other will be left." ~ "My time has not yet come, but your time is always ready. The world can't hate you, but it hates me, because I testify about it, that its works are evil. You go up to the feast. I am not yet going up to this feast, because my time is not yet fulfilled." ~ "These things have I spoken to you, so that you wouldn't be caused to stumble. They will put you out of the synagogues. Yes, the time comes that whoever kills you will think that he offers service to God. They will do these things because they have not known the Father, nor me. But I have told you these things, so that when the time comes, you may remember that I told you about them. I didn't tell you these things from the beginning, because I was with you." ~ "Cheer up, Paul, for as you have testified about me at Jerusalem, so you must testify also at Rome." ~ "Behold, I come like a thief. Blessed is he who watches, and keeps his clothes, so that he doesn't walk naked, they see his shame."

MATT. 24:15-22, 24:37-44; MARK 13:12-23, 13:28-33; LUKE 17:22-36; JOHN 7:6-8, 16:1-4; ACTS 23:11; REV. 16:15

## Redemption

"Those who are healthy have no need for a physician, but those who are sick. I came not to call the righteous, but sinners to repentance." ~ "This is my blood of the new covenant, which is poured out for many. Most certainly I tell you, I will no more drink of the fruit of the vine, until that day when I drink it anew in the Kingdom of God." ~ "The Son of Man must suffer many things, and be rejected by the elders, chief priests, and scribes, and be killed, and the third day be raised up." ~ "A certain man had two sons. The younger of them said to his father, 'Father, give me my share of your property.' He divided his livelihood between them. Not many days after, the younger son gathered all of this together and traveled into a far country. There he wasted his property with riotous living. When he had spent all of it, there arose a severe famine in that country, and he began to be in need. He went and joined himself to one of the citizens of that country, and he sent him into his fields to feed pigs. He wanted to fill his belly with the husks that the pigs ate, but no one gave him any. But when he came to himself he said, 'How many hired servants of my father's have bread enough to spare, and I'm dying with hunger! I will get up and go to my father, and will tell him, "Father, I have sinned against heaven, and in your sight. I am no more worthy to be called your son. Make me as one of your hired servants." ~ "He arose, and came to his father. But while he was still far off, his father saw him, and was moved with compassion, and ran, and fell on his neck, and kissed him. The son said to him, 'Father, I have sinned against heaven, and in your sight. I am no longer worthy to be called your son." ~ "But the father said to his servants, 'Bring out the best robe, and put it on him. Put a ring on his hand, and shoes on his feet. Bring the fattened calf, kill it, and let us eat, and celebrate; for this, my son, was dead, and is alive again. He was lost, and is found.' They began to celebrate." ~ "Most certainly I tell you, he who hears my word, and believes him who sent me, has eternal life, and doesn't come into judgment, but has passed out of death into life. Most certainly, I tell you, the hour comes, and now is, when the dead will hear the Son of God's voice; and those who hear will live. For as the Father has life in himself, even so he gave to the Son also to have life in himself. He also gave him authority to execute judgment, because he is a son of man. Don't marvel at this, for the hour comes, in which all that are in the tombs will hear his voice, and will come out; those who have done good, to the resurrection of life; and those who have done evil, to the resurrection of judgment. I can of myself do nothing. As I hear, I judge, and my judgment is righteous; because I don't seek my own will, but the will of my Father who sent me." ~ "What God has cleansed, don't you call unclean."

MARK 2:17, 14:24-25; LUKE 9:22, 15:11-19, 15:20-21, 15:22-24; JOHN 5:24-30; ACTS 11:9

# Rejection

"Woe to you, Chorazin! Woe to you, Bethsaida! For if the mighty works had been done in Tyre and Sidon which were done in you, they would have repented long ago in sackcloth and ashes. But I tell you, it will be more tolerable for Tyre and Sidon on the day of judgment than for you. You, Capernaum, who are exalted to heaven, you will go down to Hades. For if the mighty works had been done in Sodom which were done in you, it would have remained until this day. But I tell you that it will be more tolerable for the land of Sodom, on the day of judgment, than for you." ~ "Did you never read in the Scriptures, 'The stone which the builders rejected, the same was made the head of the corner. This was from the Lord. It is marvelous in our eyes?' Therefore I tell you, the Kingdom of God will be taken away from you, and will be given to a nation bringing forth its fruit. He who falls on this stone will be broken to pieces, but on whomever it will fall, it will scatter him as dust." ~ "As the days of Noah were, so will be the coming of the Son of Man. For as in those days which were before the flood they were eating and drinking, marrying and giving in marriage, until the day that Noah entered into the ship, and they didn't know until the flood came, and took them all away, so will be the coming of the Son of Man." ~ "A man planted a vineyard, put a hedge around it, dug a pit for the winepress, built a tower, rented it out to a farmer, and went into another country. When it was time, he sent a servant to the farmer to get from the farmer his share of the fruit of the vineyard. They took him, beat him, and sent him away empty. Again, he sent another servant to them; and they threw stones at him, wounded him in the head, and sent him away shamefully treated. Again he sent another; and they killed him; and many others, beating some, and killing some. Therefore still having one, his beloved son, he sent him last to them, saying, 'They will respect my son.' But those farmers said among themselves, 'This is the heir. Come, let's kill him, and the inheritance will be ours. They took him, killed him, and cast him out of the vineyard. What therefore will the lord of the vineyard do? He will come and destroy the farmers, and will give the vineyard to others. Haven't you even read this Scripture: 'The stone which the builders rejected, the same was made the head of the corner. This was from the Lord, it is marvelous in our eyes'?" ~ "Whoever receives this little child in my name receives me. Whoever receives me receives him who sent me.

For whoever is least among you all, this one will be great." ~ "Woe to you, Chorazin! Woe to you, Bethsaida! For if the mighty works had been done in Tyre and Sidon which were done in you, they would have repented long ago, sitting in sackcloth and ashes. But it will be more tolerable for Tyre and Sidon in the judgment than for you. You, Capernaum, who are exalted to heaven, will be brought down to Hades. Whoever listens to you listens to me, and whoever rejects you rejects me. Whoever rejects me rejects him who sent me." ~ "My teaching is not mine, but his who sent me. If anyone desires to do his will, he will know about the teaching, whether it is from God, or if I am speaking from myself. He who speaks from himself seeks his own glory, but he who seeks the glory of him who sent him is true, and no unrighteousness is in him. Didn't Moses give you the law, and yet none of you keeps the law? Why do you seek to kill me?"

MATT. 11:21-24, 21:42-44, 24:37-39; MARK 12:1-11; LUKE 9:48, 10:13-16; JOHN 7:16-19

## Relationships

"If therefore you are offering your gift at the altar, and there remember that your brother has anything against you, leave your gift there before the altar, and go your way. First be reconciled to your brother, and then come and offer your gift. Agree with your adversary quickly, while you are with him in the way; lest perhaps the prosecutor deliver you to the judge, and the judge deliver you to the officer, and you be cast into prison. Most certainly I tell you, you shall by no means get out of there, until you have paid the last penny." ~ "Don't give that which is holy to the dogs, neither throw your pearls before the pigs, lest perhaps they trample them under their feet, and turn and tear you to pieces." ~ "If your brother sins against you, go, show him his fault between you and him alone. If he listens to you, you have gained back your brother. But if he doesn't listen, take one or two more with you, that at the mouth of two or three witnesses every word may be established. If he refuses to listen to them, tell it to the assembly. If he refuses to hear the assembly also, let him be to you as a Gentile or a tax collector. Most certainly I tell you, whatever things you bind on earth will have been bound in heaven, and whatever things you release on earth will have been released in heaven. Again, assuredly I tell you, that if two of you will agree on earth concerning anything that they will ask, it will be done for them by my Father who is in heaven.

For where two or three are gathered together in my name, there I am in their midst." ~ "Man, your sins are forgiven you." ~ "Then what is this that is written, 'The stone which the builders rejected, the same was made the chief cornerstone?' Everyone who falls on that stone will be broken to pieces, but it will crush whomever it falls on to dust." ~ "Even if I testify about myself, my testimony is true, for I know where I came from, and where I am going; but you don't know where I came from, or where I am going. You judge according to the flesh. I judge no one. Even if I do judge, my judgment is true, for I am not alone, but I am with the Father who sent me. It's also written in your law that the testimony of two people is valid. I am one who testifies about myself, and the Father who sent me testifies about me." ~ "Peace be to you." ~ "Come and eat breakfast."

MATT. 5:23-26, 7:6, 18:15-20; LUKE 5:20, 20:17-18; JOHN 8:14-18, 20:19; JOHN 21:12

# Repentance

"Those who are healthy have no need for a physician, but those who are sick do. But you go and learn what this means: 'I desire mercy, and not sacrifice,' for I came not to call the righteous, but sinners to repentance." ~ "Which of you men, if you had one hundred sheep, and lost one of them, wouldn't leave the ninety-nine in the wilderness, and go after the one that was lost, until he found it? When he has found it, he carries it on his shoulders, rejoicing. When he comes home, he calls together his friends and his neighbors, saying to them, 'Rejoice with me, for I have found my sheep which was lost!' I tell you that even so there will be more joy in heaven over one sinner who repents, than over ninety-nine righteous people who need no repentance. Or what woman, if she had ten drachma coins, if she lost one drachma coin, wouldn't light a lamp, sweep the house, and seek diligently until she found it? When she has found it, she calls together her friends and neighbors, saying, 'Rejoice with me, for I have found the drachma which I had lost.' Even so, I tell you, there is joy in the presence of the angels of God over one sinner repenting." ~ "Be careful. If your brother sins against you, rebuke him. If he repents, forgive him. If he sins against you seven times in the day, and seven times returns, saying, 'I repent,' you shall forgive him." ~ "Assuredly I tell you, today you will be with me in Paradise." ~ "And to the angel of the assembly in Sardis write: "He who has the seven Spirits of God, and the seven stars says these things: "I know your works, that you have a reputation of being alive, but you are dead. Wake up, and keep the things that remain, which you were about to throw away, for I have found no works of yours perfected before my God. Remember therefore how you have received and heard. Keep it, and repent. If therefore you won't watch, I will come as a thief, and you won't know what hour I will come upon you." ~ "I know your works, that you are neither cold nor hot. I wish you were cold or hot. So, because you are lukewarm, and neither hot nor cold, I will vomit you out of my mouth. Because you say, 'I am rich, and have gotten riches, and have need of nothing;' and don't know that you are the wretched one, miserable, poor, blind, and naked; I counsel you to buy from me gold refined by fire, that you may become rich; and white garments, that you may clothe yourself, and that the shame of your nakedness may not be revealed; and eye salve to anoint your eyes, that you may see. As many as I love, I reprove and chasten. Be zealous therefore, and repent."

MATT. 9:12-13, LUKE 15:4-10, 17:3-4, 23:43; REV. 3:1-3, 3:15-19

## Respect

"Again, it is written, 'You shall not test the Lord, your God.'" ~ "Get behind me, Satan! For it is written, 'You shall worship the Lord your God, and you shall serve him only.'" ~ "A disciple is not above his teacher, nor a servant above his lord. It is enough for the disciple that he be like his teacher, and the servant like his lord. If they have called the master of the house Beelzebul, how much more those of his household! Therefore don't be afraid of them, for there is nothing covered that will not be revealed; and hidden that will not be known. What I tell you in the darkness, speak in the light; and what you hear whispered in the ear, proclaim on the housetops. Don't be afraid of those who kill the body, but are not able to kill the soul. Rather, fear him who is able to destroy both soul and body in Gehenna." ~ "A man planted a vineyard, and rented it out to some farmers, and went into another country for a long time. At the proper season, he sent a servant to the farmers to collect his share of the fruit of the vineyard. But the farmers beat him, and sent him away empty. He sent yet another servant, and they also beat him, and treated him shamefully, and sent him away empty. He sent yet a third, and they also wounded him, and threw him out. The lord of the vineyard said, 'What shall

I do? I will send my beloved son. It may be that seeing him, they will respect him.'" ~ "But when the farmers saw him, they reasoned among themselves, saying, 'This is the heir. Come, let's kill him, that the inheritance may be ours.' They threw him out of the vineyard, and killed him. What therefore will the lord of the vineyard do to them? He will come and destroy these farmers, and will give the vineyard to others." ~ "Then what is this that is written, 'The stone which the builders rejected, the same was made the chief cornerstone?' Everyone who falls on that stone will be broken to pieces, but it will crush whomever it falls on to dust."

MATT. 4:7, 4:10, 10:24-28; LUKE 20:9-13, 20:14-16, 20:17-18

## *Righteousness*

"Blessed are those who have been persecuted for righteousness' sake, for theirs is the Kingdom of Heaven." ~ "Don't think that I came to destroy the Torah or the Prophets. I didn't come to destroy, but to fulfill. For most certainly, I tell you, until heaven and earth pass away, not even one smallest letter or one tiny pen stroke shall in any way pass away from the Torah, until all things are accomplished. Whoever, therefore, shall break one of these least commandments, and teach others to do so, shall be called least in the Kingdom of Heaven; but whoever shall do and teach them shall be called great in the Kingdom of Heaven. For I tell you that unless your righteousness exceeds that of the scribes and Pharisees, there is no way you will enter into the Kingdom of Heaven." ~ "Therefore don't be anxious, saying, 'What will we eat?', 'What will we drink?' or, 'With what will we be clothed?' For the Gentiles seek after all these things; for your heavenly Father knows that you need all these things. But seek first God's Kingdom, and his righteousness; and all these things will be given to you as well. Therefore don't be anxious for tomorrow, for tomorrow will be anxious for itself. Each day's own evil is sufficient." ~ "Those who are healthy have no need for a physician, but those who are sick do. I have not come to call the righteous, but sinners to repentance." ~ "John indeed baptized in water, but you will be baptized in the Holy Spirit."

MATT. 5:10, 5:17-20, 6:31-34; LUKE 5:31-32; ACTS 11:16

# Satan

"Get behind me, Satan! You are a stumbling block to me, for you are not setting your mind on the things of God, but on the things of men." ~ "This kind can come out by nothing, except by prayer and fasting." ~ "Get behind me Satan! For it is written, 'You shall worship the Lord your God, and you shall serve him only.'" ~ "It has been said, 'You shall not tempt the Lord your God.'" ~ "Be silent, and come out of him!" ~ "Now the parable is this: The seed is the word of God. Those along the road are those who hear, then the devil comes, and takes away the word from their heart, that they may not believe and be saved." ~ "I saw Satan having fallen like lightning from heaven. Behold, I give you authority to tread on serpents and scorpions, and over all the power of the enemy. Nothing will in any way hurt you. Nevertheless, don't rejoice in this, that the spirits are subject to you, but rejoice that your names are written in heaven." ~ "Every kingdom divided against itself is brought to desolation. A house divided against itself falls. If Satan also is divided against himself, how will his kingdom stand? For you say that I cast out demons by Beelzebul. But if I cast out demons by Beelzebul, by whom do your children cast them out? Therefore will they be your judges. But if I by the finger of God cast out demons, then the Kingdom of God has come to you." ~ "Simon, Simon, behold, Satan asked to have you, that he might sift you as wheat, but I prayed for you, that your faith wouldn't fail. You, when once you have turned again, establish your brothers." ~ "If God were your father, you would love me, for I came out and have come from God. For I haven't come of myself, but he sent me. Why don't you understand my speech? Because you can't hear my word. You are of your father, the devil, and you want to do the desires of your father. He was a murderer from the beginning, and doesn't stand in the truth, because there is no truth in him. When he speaks a lie, he speaks on his own; for he is a liar, and its father. But because I tell the truth, you don't believe me. Which of you convicts me of sin? If I tell the truth, why do you not believe me? He who is of God hears the words of God. For this cause you don't hear, because you are not of God."

MATT. 16:23; MARK 9:29; LUKE 4:8-12, 4:35, 8:11-12, 10:18-20, 11:17-20, 22:30-31; JOHN 8:42-47

# Self-Control

"If your right eye causes you to stumble, pluck it out and throw it away from you. For it is more profitable for you that one of your members should perish, than for your whole body to be cast into Gehenna. If your right hand causes you to stumble, cut it off, and throw it away from you. For it is more profitable for you that one of your members should perish, than for your whole body to be cast into Gehenna." ~ "Woe to the world because of occasions of stumbling! For it must be that the occasions come, but woe to that person through whom the occasion comes!" ~ "Follow me." ~ "I am the true vine, and my Father is the farmer. Every branch in me that doesn't bear fruit, he takes away. Every branch that bears fruit, he prunes, that it may bear more fruit. You are already pruned clean because of the word which I have spoken to you. Remain in me, and I in you. As the branch can't bear fruit by itself, unless it remains in the vine, so neither can you, unless you remain in me. I am the vine. You are the branches. He who remains in me, and I in him, the same bears much fruit, for apart from me you can do nothing. If a man doesn't remain in me, he is thrown out as a branch, and is withered; and they gather them, throw them into the fire, and they are burned. If you remain in me, and my words remain in you, you will ask whatever you desire, and it will be done for you."

MATT. 5:29-30, 18:7; JOHN 1:43, 15:1-7

# Serving

"Take nothing for your journey— neither staffs, nor wallet, nor bread, nor money; neither have two coats apiece. Into whatever house you enter, stay there, and depart from there. As many as don't receive you, when you depart from that city, shake off even the dust from your feet for a testimony against them." ~ "You give them something to eat." ~ "Make them sit down in groups of about fifty each." ~ "If you had faith like a grain of mustard seed, you would tell this sycamore tree, 'Be uprooted, and be planted in the sea,' and it would obey you. But who is there among you, having a servant plowing or keeping sheep, that will say, when he comes in from the field, 'Come immediately and sit down at the table,' and will not rather tell him, 'Prepare my supper, clothe yourself properly, and serve me, while I eat and drink. Afterward you shall eat and drink'? Does he thank that servant because he did the things that were commanded? I think not. Even so you also, when you have done all the things that are commanded you, say, 'We are unworthy servants. We have done our duty.'" ~ "Fill the water pots with water." ~ "If I don't wash you, you have no part with me." ~ "Do you know what I have done to you?" ~ "You call me, 'Teacher' and 'Lord.' You say so correctly, for so I am. If I then, the Lord and the Teacher, have washed your feet, you also ought to wash one another's feet. For I have given you an example, that you also should do as I have done to you. Most certainly I tell you, a servant is not greater than his lord, neither one who is sent greater than he who sent him." ~ "If you know these things, blessed are you if you do them." ~ "To the angel of the assembly in Thyatira write: 'The Son of God, who has his eyes like a flame of fire, and his feet are like burnished brass, says these things.'" ~ "I know your works, your love, faith, service, patient endurance, and that your last works are more than the first. But I have this against you, that you tolerate your woman, Jezebel, who calls herself a prophetess. She teaches and seduces my servants to commit sexual immorality, and to eat things sacrificed to idols. I gave her time to repent, but she refuses to repent of her sexual immorality. Behold, I will throw her into a bed, and those who commit adultery with her into great oppression, unless they repent of her works."

LUKE 9:3-5, 9:13, 9:14, 17:6-10; JOHN 2:7, 13:8, 13:12, 13:13-16, 13:17; REV. 2:18, 2:19-22

## *Sexuality*

"Not all men can receive this saying, but those to whom it is given. For there are eunuchs who were born that way from their mother's womb, and there are eunuchs who were made eunuchs by men; and there are eunuchs who made themselves eunuchs for the Kingdom of Heaven's sake. He who is able to receive it, let him receive it." ~ "Isn't this because you are mistaken, not knowing the Scriptures, nor the power of God? For when they will rise from the dead, they neither marry, nor are given in marriage, but are like angels in heaven." ~ "Peace be to you." ~ "Follow me." ~ "My grace is sufficient for you, for my power is made perfect in weakness." ~ "I counsel you to buy from me gold refined by fire, that you may become rich; and white garments, that you may clothe yourself, and that the shame of your nakedness may not be revealed; and eye salve to anoint your eyes, that you may see. As many as I love, I reprove and chasten. Be zealous therefore, and repent. Behold, I stand at the door and knock. If anyone hears my voice and opens the door, then I will come in to him, and will dine with him, and he with me. He who overcomes, I will give to him to sit down with me on my throne, as I also overcame, and sat down with my Father on his throne."

MATT. 19:11-12; MARK 12:24-25; LUKE 24:36; JOHN 1:43; 2 COR. 12:9; REV. 2:19-21

## Sin

"Hear another parable. There was a man who was a master of a household, who planted a vineyard, set a hedge about it, dug a winepress in it, built a tower, leased it out to farmers, and went into another country. When the season for the fruit drew near, he sent his servants to the farmers, to receive his fruit. The farmers took his servants, beat one, killed another, and stoned another. Again, he sent other servants more than the first: and they treated them the same way. But afterward he sent to them his son, saying, 'They will respect my son.' But the farmers, when they saw the son, said among themselves, 'This is the heir. Come, let's kill him, and seize his inheritance.' So they took him, and threw him out of the vineyard, and killed him. When therefore the lord of the vineyard comes, what will he do to those farmers?" ~ "Why are you reasoning so in your hearts? Which is easier to say, 'Your sins are forgiven you;' or to say, 'Arise and walk?' But that you may know that the Son of Man has authority on earth to forgive sins" … "I tell you, arise, and take up your cot, and go to your house." ~ "Your faith has saved you. Go in peace." ~ "Do you think that these Galileans were worse sinners than all the other Galileans, because they suffered such things? I tell you, no, but unless you repent, you will all perish in the same way. Or those eighteen, on whom the tower in Siloam fell, and killed them; do you think that they were worse offenders than all the men who dwell in Jerusalem? I tell you, no, but, unless you repent, you will all perish in the same way." ~ "Which of you men, if you had one hundred sheep, and lost one of them, wouldn't leave the ninety-nine in the wilderness, and go after the one that was lost, until he found it? When he has found it, he carries it on his shoulders, rejoicing. When he comes home, he calls together his friends and his neighbors, saying to them, 'Rejoice with me, for I have found my sheep which was lost!' I tell you that even so there will be more joy in heaven over one sinner who repents, than over ninety-nine righteous people who need no repentance. Or what woman, if she had ten drachma coins, if she lost one drachma coin, wouldn't light a lamp, sweep the house, and seek diligently until she found it? When she has found it, she calls together her friends and neighbors, saying, 'Rejoice with me, for I have found the drachma which I had lost.' Even so, I tell you, there is joy in the presence of the angels of God over one sinner repenting." ~ "He said to him, 'Son, you are always with me, and all that is mine is yours. But it was appropriate to celebrate and be glad, for this, your brother, was dead, and is alive again. He was lost, and is found.'" ~ "Father, forgive them, for they don't know what they are doing." ~ "Assuredly I tell you, today you will be with me in Paradise."

MATT. 21:33-40; LUKE 5:22-24, 7:50, 13:2-5, 15:4-10, 15:31-32, 23:34, 23:43

## *Single*

"Who is my mother? Who are my brothers?" ..."Behold, my mother and my brothers! For whoever does the will of my Father who is in heaven, he is my brother, and sister, and mother." ~ "Most certainly I tell you that you who have followed me, in the regeneration when the Son of Man will sit on the throne of his glory, you also will sit on twelve thrones, judging the twelve tribes of Israel. Everyone who has left houses, or brothers, or sisters, or father, or mother, or wife, or children, or lands, for my name's sake, will receive one hundred times, and will inherit eternal life. But many will be last who are first; and first who are last." ~ "Isn't this because you are mistaken, not knowing the Scriptures, nor the power of God? For when they will rise from the dead, they neither marry, nor are given in marriage, but are like angels in heaven. But about the dead, that they are raised; haven't you read in the book of Moses, about the Bush, how God spoke to him, saying, 'I am the God of Abraham, the God of Isaac, and the God of Jacob'? He is not the God of the dead, but of the living. You are therefore badly mistaken." ~ "Follow me." ~ "Peace be to you." ~ "My grace is sufficient for you, for my power is made perfect in weakness." ~ "Behold, I stand at the door and knock. If anyone hears my voice and opens the door, then I will come in to him, and will dine with him, and he with me."

MATT 12:48-50; 19:28-30; MARK 12:24-27; JOHN 1:43, 20:21; 2 COR. 12:9; REV. 3:20

# Spiritual Perception

"Therefore I speak to them in parables, because seeing they don't see, and hearing, they don't hear, neither do they understand." ~ "But blessed are your eyes, for they see; and your ears, for they hear." ~ "Why do you reason that it's because you have no bread? Don't you perceive yet, neither understand? Is your heart still hardened? Having eyes, don't you see? Having ears, don't you hear? Don't you remember? When I broke the five loaves among the five thousand, how many baskets full of broken pieces did you take up?" ~ "When the seven loaves fed the four thousand, how many baskets full of broken pieces did you take up?" ~ "Don't you understand, yet?" ~ "Who do men say that I am?" ~ "But who do you say that I am?" ~ "No one, when he has lit a lamp, puts it in a cellar or under a basket, but on a stand, that those who come in may see the light. The lamp of the body is the eye. Therefore when your eye is good, your whole body is also full of light; but when it is evil, your body also is full of darkness. Therefore see whether the light that is in you isn't darkness. If therefore your whole body is full of light, having no part dark, it will be wholly full of light, as when the lamp with its bright shining gives you light." ~ "Receive your sight. Your faith has healed you." ~ "Woman, believe me, the hour comes, when neither in this mountain, nor in Jerusalem, will you worship the Father. You worship that which you don't know. We worship that which we know; for salvation is from the Jews. But the hour comes, and now is, when the true worshipers will worship the Father in spirit and truth, for the Father seeks such to be his worshipers. God is spirit, and those who worship him must worship in spirit and truth." ~ "Does this cause you to stumble? Then what if you would see the Son of Man ascending to where he was before? It is the spirit who gives life. The flesh profits nothing. The words that I speak to you are spirit, and are life. But there are some of you who don't believe." ~ "What God has cleansed, you must not call unclean."

MATT. 13:13, 13:16; MARK 8:17-19, 8:20,8:21, 8:27, 8:29; LUKE 11:33-36, 18:42; JOHN 4:21-24, 6:61-64; ACTS 10:15

# Spiritual Warfare

"Because of your unbelief. For most certainly I tell you, if you have faith as a grain of mustard seed, you will tell this mountain, 'Move from here to there,' and it will move; and nothing will be impossible for you. But this kind doesn't go out except by prayer and fasting." ~ "Be quiet, and come out of him!" ~ "Come out of the man, you unclean spirit!" ~ "What is your name?" ~ "Get behind me, Satan! For you have in mind not the things of God, but the things of men." ~ "How long has it been since this has come to him?" ~ "If you can believe, all things are possible to him who believes." ~ "You mute and deaf spirit, I command you, come out of him, and never enter him again!" ~ "This kind can come out by nothing, except by prayer and fasting." ~ "He that is not with me is against me. He who doesn't gather with me scatters. The unclean spirit, when he has gone out of the man, passes through dry places, seeking rest, and finding none, he says, 'I will turn back to my house from which I came out.' When he returns, he finds it swept and put in order. Then he goes, and takes seven other spirits more evil than himself, and they enter in and dwell there. The last state of that man becomes worse than the first." ~ "That is enough."

MATT. 17:20-21; MARK 1:25, 5:8, 5:9, 8:33, 9:21, 9:23, 9:25, 9:29; LUKE 11:23-26, 22:38

## *Strength*

"Aren't two sparrows sold for an assarion coin? Not one of them falls on the ground apart from your Father's will, but the very hairs of your head are all numbered. Therefore don't be afraid. You are of more value than many sparrows." ~ "You shall love the Lord your God with all your heart, and with all your soul, and with all your mind, and with all your strength.' This is the first commandment." ~ "Simon, Simon, behold, Satan asked to have you, that he might sift you as wheat, but I prayed for you, that your faith wouldn't fail. You, when once you have turned again, establish your brothers." ~ "Everyone who drinks of this water will thirst again, but whoever drinks of the water that I will give him will never thirst again; but the water that I will give him will become in him a well of water springing up to eternal life." ~ "Do you now believe? Behold, the time is coming, yes, and has now come, that you will be scattered, everyone to his own place, and you will leave me alone. Yet I am not alone, because the Father is with me. I have told you these things, that in me you may have peace. In the world you have oppression; but cheer up! I have overcome the world." ~ "My grace is sufficient for you, for my power is made perfect in weakness."

MATT. 10:29-31; MARK 12:30; LUKE 22:31; JOHN 4:13-14; 16:31-33; 2 COR. 12:9

## *Success*

"His lord said to him, 'Well done, good and faithful servant. You have been faithful over a few things, I will set you over many things. Enter into the joy of your lord." ~ "Listen! Behold, the farmer went out to sow, and it happened, as he sowed, some seed fell by the road, and the birds came and devoured it. Others fell on the rocky ground, where it had little soil, and immediately it sprang up, because it had no depth of soil. When the sun had risen, it was scorched; and because it had no root, it withered away. Others fell among the thorns, and the thorns grew up, and choked it, and it yielded no fruit. Others fell into the good ground, and yielded fruit, growing up and increasing. Some brought forth thirty times, some sixty times, and some one hundred times as much." ~ "Whoever has ears to hear, let him hear." ~ "Don't you understand this parable? How will you understand all of the parables? The farmer sows the word. The ones by the road are the ones where the word is sown; and when they have heard, immediately Satan comes, and takes away the word which has been sown in them. These in the same way are those who are sown on the rocky places, who, when they have heard the word, immediately receive it with joy. They have no root in themselves, but are short-lived. When oppression or persecution arises because of the word, immediately they stumble. Others are those who are sown among the thorns. These are those who have heard the word, and the cares of this age, and the deceitfulness of riches, and the lusts of other things entering in choke the word, and it becomes unfruitful. Those which were sown on the good ground are those who hear the word, and accept it, and bear fruit, some thirty times, some sixty times, and some one hundred times." ~ "I am. You will see the Son of Man sitting at the right hand of Power, and coming with the clouds of the sky." ~ "If anyone desires to come after me, let him deny himself, take up his cross, and follow me. For whoever desires to save his life will lose it, but whoever will lose his life for my sake, the same will save it. For what does it profit a man if he gains the whole world, and loses or forfeits his own self? For whoever will be ashamed of me and of my words, of him will the Son of Man be ashamed, when he comes in his glory, and the glory of the Father, and of the holy angels. But I tell you the truth: There are some of those who stand here, who will in no way taste of death, until they see the Kingdom of God." ~ "The things which are impossible with men are possible with God." ~

"Most certainly I tell you, you seek me, not because you saw signs, but because you ate of the loaves, and were filled. Don't work for the food which perishes, but for the food which remains to eternal life, which the Son of Man will give to you. For God the Father has sealed him." ~ "This is the work of God, that you believe in him whom he has sent."

MATT. 25:23; MARK 4:3-8, 4:9, 13-20, 14:62; LUKE 9:23-27, 18:27; JOHN 6:26-27, 6:29

# *Suffering*

"If anyone desires to come after me, let him deny himself, and take up his cross, and follow me. For whoever desires to save his life will lose it, and whoever will lose his life for my sake will find it. For what will it profit a man, if he gains the whole world, and forfeits his life? Or what will a man give in exchange for his life? For the Son of Man will come in the glory of his Father with his angels, and then he will render to everyone according to his deeds. Most certainly I tell you, there are some standing here who will in no way taste of death, until they see the Son of Man coming in his Kingdom." ~ "Eloi, Eloi, lama sabachthani?" … "My God, my God, why have you forsaken me?" ~ "Strive to enter in by the narrow door, for many, I tell you, will seek to enter in, and will not be able. When once the master of the house has risen up, and has shut the door, and you begin to stand outside, and to knock at the door, saying, 'Lord, Lord, open to us!' then he will answer and tell you, 'I don't know you or where you come from.' Then you will begin to say, 'We ate and drank in your presence, and you taught in our streets.' He will say, 'I tell you, I don't know where you come from. Depart from me, all you workers of iniquity.' There will be weeping and gnashing of teeth, when you see Abraham, Isaac, Jacob, and all the prophets, in the Kingdom of God, and yourselves being thrown outside. They will come from the east, west, north, and south, and will sit down in the Kingdom of God. Behold, there are some who are last who will be first, and there are some who are first who will be last." ~ "Foolish men, and slow of heart to believe in all that the prophets have spoken! Didn't the Christ have to suffer these things and to enter into his glory?" ~ "Do you want to be made well?" ~ "Arise, take up your mat, and walk." ~ "It is I. Don't be afraid." ~ "You will be made free." ~ "I am thirsty."

MATT. 16:24-28; MARK 15:34; LUKE 13:24-30, 13:24:25-26; JOHN 5:6, 5:8, 6:20, 8:33, 19:28

# Suicide

"Man, your sins are forgiven you." ~ "You don't know what I am doing now, but you will understand later." ~ "Peace I leave with you. My peace I give to you; not as the world gives, give I to you. Don't let your heart be troubled, neither let it be fearful." ~ "I have yet many things to tell you, but you can't bear them now. However when he, the Spirit of truth, has come, he will guide you into all truth, for he will not speak from himself; but whatever he hears, he will speak. He will declare to you things that are coming. He will glorify me, for he will take from what is mine, and will declare it to you. All things whatever the Father has are mine; therefore I said that he takes of mine, and will declare it to you. A little while, and you will not see me. Again a little while, and you will see me." ~ "Peace be to you."

LUKE 5:20; JOHN 13:7, 14:27, 16:12-16, 20:26

# Taxes

"Why do you test me, you hypocrites? Show me the tax money" ~ "Whose is this image and inscription?" ~ "Why do you test me? Show me a denarius. Whose image and inscription are on it?" ~ "Then give to Caesar the things that are Caesar's, and to God the things that are God's."

MATT. 22:18, 22:20; LUKE 20:23-24, 20:25

# Tolerance

"If therefore you are offering your gift at the altar, and there remember that your brother has anything against you, leave your gift there before the altar, and go your way. First be reconciled to your brother, and then come and offer your gift." ~ "Elijah indeed comes first, and will restore all things, but I tell you that Elijah has come already, and they didn't recognize him, but did to him whatever they wanted to. Even so the Son of Man will also suffer by them." ~ "Faithless and perverse generation! How long will I be with you? How long will I bear with you? Bring him here to me." ~ "Didn't Moses give you the law, and yet none of you keeps the law? Why do you seek to kill me?" ~ "He who is without sin among you, let him throw the first stone at her."

MATT. 5:23-24, 17:11-12, 17:17; JOHN 7:19, 8:7

# Trust

"Which of you, by being anxious, can add one moment to his lifespan? Why are you anxious about clothing? Consider the lilies of the field, how they grow. They don't toil, neither do they spin, yet I tell you that even Solomon in all his glory was not dressed like one of these. But if God so clothes the grass of the field, which today exists, and tomorrow is thrown into the oven, won't he much more clothe you, you of little faith?" ~ "With men this is impossible, but with God all things are possible." ~ "For it is like a man, going into another country, who called his own servants, and entrusted his goods to them. To one he gave five talents, to another two, to another one; to each according to his own ability. Then he went on his journey. Immediately he who received the five talents went and traded with them, and made another five talents. In the same way, he also who got the two gained another two. But he who received the one went away and dug in the earth, and hid his lord's money. Now after a long time the lord of those servants came, and reconciled accounts with them. He who received the five talents came and brought another five talents, saying, 'Lord, you delivered to me five talents. Behold, I have gained another five talents besides them.' His lord said to him, 'Well done, good and faithful servant. You have been faithful over a few things, I will set you over many things. Enter into the joy of your lord.' "He also who got the two talents came and said, 'Lord, you delivered to me two talents. Behold, I have gained another two talents besides them.' "His lord said to him, 'Well done, good and faithful servant. you have been faithful over a few things, I will set you over many things. Enter into the joy of your lord.' He also who had received the one talent came and said, 'Lord, I knew you that you are a hard man, reaping where you did not sow, and gathering where you did not scatter. I was afraid, and went away and hid your talent in the earth. Behold, you have what is yours.' But his lord answered him, 'You wicked and slothful servant. You knew that I reap where I didn't sow, and gather where I didn't scatter. You ought therefore to have deposited my money with the bankers, and at my coming I should have received back my own with interest. Take away therefore the talent from him, and give it to him who has the ten talents. For to everyone who has will be given, and he will have abundance, but from him who doesn't have, even that which he has will be taken away. Throw out the unprofitable servant into the outer darkness, where there will be weeping and gnashing of teeth.'" ~ "He who is faithful in a very little is faithful also in much. He who is dishonest in a very little is also dishonest in much. If therefore you have not been faithful in the unrighteous mammon, who will commit to your trust the true riches?" ~ "Whoever seeks to save his life loses it, but whoever loses his life preserves it. I tell you, in that night there will be two people in one bed. The one will be taken, and the other will be left. There will be two grinding grain together. One will be taken, and the other will be left." ~ "Arise, take up your mat, and walk." ~ "It is I. Don't be afraid." ~ "If I desire that he stay until I come, what is that to you? You follow me." ~ "It isn't for you to know times or seasons which the Father has set within his own authority. But you will receive power when the Holy Spirit has come upon you. you will be witnesses to me in Jerusalem, in all Judea and Samaria, and to the uttermost parts of the earth."

MATT. 6:27-30; 19:26; 25:14-30; LUKE 16:10-11; 17:33-35; JOHN 5:8, 6:20, 21:22; ACTS 1:7-8

# Truth

"Don't think that I came to destroy the law or the prophets. I didn't come to destroy, but to fulfill. For most certainly, I tell you, until heaven and earth pass away, not even one smallest letter or one tiny pen stroke shall in any way pass away from the law, until all things are accomplished." ~ "Again you have heard that it was said to them of old time, 'You shall not make false vows, but shall perform to the Lord your vows,' but I tell you, don't swear at all: neither by heaven, for it is the throne of God; nor by the earth, for it is the footstool of his feet; nor by Jerusalem, for it is the city of the great King. Neither shall you swear by your head, for you can't make one hair white or black. But let your 'Yes' be 'Yes' and your 'No' be 'No.' Whatever is more than these is of the evil one." ~ "The lamp of the body is the eye. If therefore your eye is sound, your whole body will be full of light. But if your eye is evil, your whole body will be full of darkness. If therefore the light that is in you is darkness, how great is the darkness!" ~ "Heaven and earth will pass away, but my words will not pass away." ~ "But it is easier for heaven and earth to pass away, than for one tiny stroke of a pen in the law to fall." ~ "See the fig tree, and all the trees. When they are already budding, you see it and know by your own selves that the summer is already near. Even so you also, when you see these things happening, know that the Kingdom of God is near.

Most certainly I tell you, this generation will not pass away until all things are accomplished. Heaven and earth will pass away, but my words will by no means pass away." ~ "This is the judgment, that the light has come into the world, and men loved the darkness rather than the light; for their works were evil. For everyone who does evil hates the light, and doesn't come to the light, lest his works would be exposed. But he who does the truth comes to the light, that his works may be revealed, that they have been done in God." ~ "Don't murmur among yourselves. No one can come to me unless the Father who sent me draws him, and I will raise him up in the last day. It is written in the prophets, 'They will all be taught by God.' Therefore everyone who hears from the Father, and has learned, comes to me. Not that anyone has seen the Father, except he who is from God. He has seen the Father. Most certainly, I tell you, he who believes in me has eternal life. I am the bread of life. Your fathers ate the manna in the wilderness, and they died. This is the bread which comes down out of heaven, that anyone may eat of it and not die. I am the living bread which came down out of heaven. If anyone eats of this bread, he will live forever. Yes, the bread which I will give for the life of the world is my flesh." ~ "If God were your father, you would love me, for I came out and have come from God. For I haven't come of myself, but he sent me. Why don't you understand my speech? Because you can't hear my word. You are of your father, the devil, and you want to do the desires of your father. He was a murderer from the beginning, and doesn't stand in the truth, because there is no truth in him. When he speaks a lie, he speaks on his own; for he is a liar, and its father. But because I tell the truth, you don't believe me. Which of you convicts me of sin? If I tell the truth, why do you not believe me? He who is of God hears the words of God. For this cause you don't hear, because you are not of God." ~ "I have given them your word. The world hated them, because they are not of the world, even as I am not of the world. I pray not that you would take them from the world, but that you would keep them from the evil one. They are not of the world even as I am not of the world. Sanctify them in your truth. Your word is truth. As you sent me into the world, even so I have sent them into the world. For their sakes I sanctify myself, that they themselves also may be sanctified in truth." ~ "I am the Alpha and the Omega" . . . "who is and who was and who is to come, the Almighty."

MATT. 5:17-18, 5:33-37, 6:22-23; MARK 13:31; LUKE 16:17, 21:29-33; JOHN 3:19-21, 6:43-51, 8:42-47, 17:14-19; REV. 1:8

# Understanding

"Hear, then, the parable of the farmer. When anyone hears the word of the Kingdom, and doesn't understand it, the evil one comes, and snatches away that which has been sown in his heart. This is what was sown by the roadside. What was sown on the rocky places, this is he who hears the word, and immediately with joy receives it; yet he has no root in himself, but endures for a while. When oppression or persecution arises because of the word, immediately he stumbles. What was sown among the thorns, this is he who hears the word, but the cares of this age and the deceitfulness of riches choke the word, and he becomes unfruitful. What was sown on the good ground, this is he who hears the word, and understands it, who most certainly bears fruit, and brings forth, some one hundred times as much, some sixty, and some thirty." ~ "Therefore every scribe who has been made a disciple in the Kingdom of Heaven is like a man who is a householder, who brings out of his treasure new and old things." ~ "Can the groomsmen fast while the bridegroom is with them? As long as they have the bridegroom with them, they can't fast. But the days will come when the bridegroom will be taken away from them, and then will they fast in that day. No one sews a piece of unshrunk cloth on an old garment, or else the patch shrinks and the new tears away from the old, and a worse hole is made. No one puts new wine into old wineskins, or else the new wine will burst the skins, and the wine pours out, and the skins will be destroyed; but they put new wine into fresh wineskins." ~ "To you is given the mystery of the Kingdom of God, but to those who are outside, all things are done in parables, that 'seeing they may see, and not perceive; and hearing they may hear, and not understand; lest perhaps they should turn again, and their sins should be forgiven them.'" ~ "To you it is given to know the mysteries of the Kingdom of God, but to the rest in parables; that 'seeing they may not see, and hearing they may not understand.'" ~ "Behold, we are going up to Jerusalem, and all the things that are written through the prophets concerning the Son of Man will be completed. For he will be delivered up to the Gentiles, will be mocked, treated shamefully, and spit on. They will scourge and kill him. On the third day, he will rise again." ~ "But the hour comes, and now is, when the true worshipers will worship the Father in spirit and truth, for the Father seeks such to be his worshipers. God is spirit, and those who worship him must worship in spirit and truth." ~ "For this cause have I said to you that no one can come to me, unless it is given to him by my Father." ~ "I am the light of the world. He who follows me will not walk in the darkness, but will have the light of life." ~ "You don't know what I am doing now, but you will understand later." ~ "He who has an ear, let him hear what the Spirit says to the assemblies. To him who overcomes I will give to eat of the tree of life, which is in the Paradise of my God."

MATT. 13:18-23, 13:52; MARK 2:19-22, 4:11-12; LUKE 8:10, 18:31-33; JOHN 4:23-24, 6:65, 8:12, 13:7; REV. 2:7

## Unforgivable Sin

"He who is not with me is against me, and he who doesn't gather with me, scatters. Therefore I tell you, every sin and blasphemy will be forgiven men, but the blasphemy against the Spirit will not be forgiven men. Whoever speaks a word against the Son of Man, it will be forgiven him; but whoever speaks against the Holy Spirit, it will not be forgiven him, neither in this age, nor in that which is to come." ~ "How can Satan cast out Satan? If a kingdom is divided against itself, that kingdom cannot stand. If a house is divided against itself, that house cannot stand. If Satan has risen up against himself, and is divided, he can't stand, but has an end. But no one can enter into the house of the strong man to plunder, unless he first binds the strong man; and then he will plunder his house. Most certainly I tell you, all sins of the descendants of man will be forgiven, including their blasphemies with which they may blaspheme; but whoever may blaspheme against the Holy Spirit never has forgiveness, but is guilty of an eternal sin" ~ "I tell you, everyone who confesses me before men, him will the Son of Man also confess before the angels of God; but he who denies me in the presence of men will be denied in the presence of the angels of God. Everyone who speaks a word against the Son of Man will be forgiven, but those who blaspheme against the Holy Spirit will not be forgiven."

MATT. 12:30-32; MARK 3:23-29; LUKE 12:8-10

## Universe

"The wind blows where it wants to, and you hear its sound, but don't know where it comes from and where it is going. So is everyone who is born of the Spirit." ~ "Most certainly, I tell you, before Abraham came into existence, I AM." ~ "I am

the Alpha and the Omega," ... "who is and who was and who is to come, the
Almighty." ~ "Don't be afraid. I am the first and the last, and the Living one. I
was dead, and behold, I am alive forevermore. Amen. I have the keys of Death and
of Hades." ~ "To the angel of the assembly in Philadelphia write: "He who is holy,
he who is true, he who has the key of David, he who opens and no one can shut,
and who shuts and no one opens, says these things" ~ "To the angel of the
assembly in Laodicea write: "The Amen, the Faithful and True Witness, the Head
of God's creation, says these things." ~ "Behold, I am making all things new" . .
. "Write, for these words of God are faithful and true" . . . "It is done! I am the
Alpha and the Omega, the Beginning and the End. I will give freely to him who is
thirsty from the spring of the water of life." ~ "I am the Alpha and the Omega,
the First and the Last, the Beginning and the End." ~ "Yes, I come quickly."

JOHN 3:8, 8:58; REV. 1:8, 1:17-18, 3:7, 3:14, 21:5-6, 22:13, 22:20

# *Vindication*

"He who sows the good seed is the Son of Man, the fild is the world; and the good
seed, these are the children of the Kingdom; and the darnel weeds are the children
of the evil one. The enemy who sowed them is the devil. The harvest is the end of
the age, and the reapers are angels. As therefore the darnel weeds are gathered up
and burned with fire; so will it be at the end of this age. The Son of Man will send
out his angels, and they will gather out of his Kingdom all things that cause
stumbling, and those who do iniquity, and will cast them into the furnace of fire.
There will be weeping and the gnashing of teeth. Then the righteous will shine
forth like the sun in the Kingdom of their Father. He who has ears to hear, let him
hear." ~ "This is an evil generation. It seeks after a sign. No sign will be given to
it but the sign of Jonah, the prophet. For even as Jonah became a sign to the
Ninevites, so will also the Son of Man be to this generation. The Queen of the
South will rise up in the judgment with the men of this generation, and will
condemn them: for she came from the ends of the earth to hear the wisdom of
Solomon; and behold, one greater than Solomon is here. The men of Nineveh will
stand up in the judgment with this generation, and will condemn it: for they
repented at the preaching of Jonah, and behold, one greater than Jonah is here."
~ "Behold, there are some who are last who will be first, and there are some who

are first who will be last." ~ "But now I am going to him who sent me, and none of you asks me, 'Where are you going?' But because I have told you these things, sorrow has filled your heart. Nevertheless I tell you the truth: It is to your advantage that I go away, for if I don't go away, the Counselor won't come to you. But if I go, I will send him to you. When he has come, he will convict the world about sin, about righteousness, and about judgment; about sin, because they don't believe in me; about righteousness, because I am going to my Father, and you won't see me any more; about judgment, because the prince of this world has been judged." ~ "Behold, I am making all things new." ... "Write, for these words of God are faithful and true."

MATT. 13:37-43; LUKE 11:29-32, 13:30; JOHN 16:5-11; REV. 21:5

# *War*

"When you hear of wars and rumors of wars, don't be troubled. For those must happen, but the end is not yet. For nation will rise against nation, and kingdom against kingdom. There will be earthquakes in various places. There will be famines and troubles. These things are the beginning of birth pains. But watch yourselves, for they will deliver you up to councils. You will be beaten in synagogues. You will stand before rulers and kings for my sake, for a testimony to them. The Good News must first be preached to all the nations. When they lead you away and deliver you up, don't be anxious beforehand, or premeditate what you will say, but say whatever will be given you in that hour. For it is not you who speak, but the Holy Spirit." ~ "It is like a man, traveling to another country, having left his house, and given authority to his servants, and to each one his work, and also commanded the doorkeeper to keep watch. Watch therefore, for you don't know when the lord of the house is coming, whether at evening, or at midnight, or when the rooster crows, or in the morning; lest coming suddenly he might find you sleeping. What I tell you, I tell all: Watch." ~ "Watch out that you don't get led astray, for many will come in my name, saying, 'I am he,' and, 'The time is at hand.' Therefore don't follow them. When you hear of wars and disturbances, don't be terrified, for these things must happen first, but the end won't come immediately." ~ "Nation will rise against nation, and kingdom against kingdom. There will be great earthquakes, famines, and plagues in various places. There will be terrors and great signs from heaven. But before all these things, they will lay their hands on you and will persecute you, delivering you up to synagogues and prisons, bringing you before kings and governors for my name's sake. It will turn out as a testimony for you. Settle it therefore in your hearts not to meditate beforehand how to answer, for I will give you a mouth and wisdom which all your adversaries will not be able to withstand or to contradict. You will be handed over even by parents, brothers, relatives, and friends. They will cause some of you to be put to death. You will be hated by all men for my name's sake. And not a hair of your head will perish. By your endurance you will win your lives. But when you see Jerusalem surrounded by armies, then know that its desolation is at hand. Then let those who are in Judea flee to the mountains. Let those who are in the midst of her depart. Let those who are in the country not enter therein. For these are days of vengeance, that all things which are written may be fulfilled. Woe to those who are pregnant and to those who nurse infants in those days! For there will be great distress in the land, and wrath to this people. They will fall by the edge of the sword, and will be led captive into all the nations. Jerusalem will be trampled down by the Gentiles, until the times of the Gentiles are fulfilled. There will be signs in the sun, moon, and stars; and on the earth anxiety of nations, in perplexity for the roaring of the sea and the waves; men fainting for fear, and for expectation of the things which are coming on the world: for the powers of the heavens will be shaken. Then they will see the Son of Man coming in a cloud with power and great glory. But when these things begin to happen, look up, and lift up your heads, because your redemption is near." ~ "Most certainly I tell you that one of you will betray me." ~ "It is he to whom I will give this piece of bread when I have dipped it." ~ "What you do, do quickly."

MARK 13:7-11, 13:34-37; LUKE 21:8-9, 21:10-28; JOHN 13:21, 13:26, 13:27

## Willingness

"But what do you think? A man had two sons, and he came to the first, and said, 'Son, go work today in my vineyard.' He answered, 'I will not,' but afterward he changed his mind, and went. He came to the second, and said the same thing. He answered, 'I go, sir,' but he didn't go. Which of the two did the will of his father?" ~ "My Father, if it is possible, let this cup pass away from me; nevertheless, not what I desire, but what you desire." ～ "What, couldn't you watch with me for one hour? Watch and pray, that you don't enter into temptation. The spirit indeed is willing, but the flesh is weak." ～ "My Father, if this cup can't pass away from me unless I drink it, your desire be done." ～ "I want to. Be made clean." ～ "Go to your house, to your friends, and tell them what great things the Lord has done for you, and how he had mercy on you." ～ "Father, if you are willing, remove this cup from me. Nevertheless, not my will, but yours, be done." ～ "Don't think that I will accuse you to the Father. There is one who accuses you, even Moses, on whom you have set your hope. For if you believed Moses, you would believe me; for he wrote about me. But if you don't believe his writings, how will you believe my words?" ～ "Saul, Saul, why are you persecuting me? It is hard for you to kick against the goads."

MATT. 21:28-31, 26:39, 26:40, 26:42; MARK 1:41, 5:19; LUKE 22:42; JOHN 5:45-47; ACTS 26:14

# Wisdom

"Everyone therefore who hears these words of mine, and does them, I will liken him to a wise man, who built his house on a rock. The rain came down, the floods came, and the winds blew, and beat on that house; and it didn't fall, for it was founded on the rock. Everyone who hears these words of mine, and doesn't do them will be like a foolish man, who built his house on the sand. The rain came down, the floods came, and the winds blew, and beat on that house; and it fell— and great was its fall." ～ "From the days of John the Baptizer until now, the Kingdom of Heaven suffers violence, and the violent take it by force. For all the prophets and the law prophesied until John. If you are willing to receive it, this is Elijah, who is to come. He who has ears to hear, let him hear." ～ "But to what shall I compare this generation? It is like children sitting in the marketplaces, who call to their companions  and say, 'We played the flute for you, and you didn't dance. We mourned for you, and you didn't lament.' For John came neither eating nor drinking, and they say, 'He has a demon.' The Son of Man came eating and drinking, and they say, 'Behold, a gluttonous man and a drunkard, a friend of tax collectors and sinners!' But wisdom is justified by her children." ～ "You are not far from the Kingdom of God." ～ "To what then will I liken the people of this generation? What are they like? They are like children who sit in the marketplace, and call one to another, saying, 'We piped to you, and you didn't dance. We mourned, and you didn't weep.' For John the Baptizer came neither eating bread nor drinking wine, and you say, 'He has a demon.' The Son of Man has come eating and drinking, and you say, 'Behold, a gluttonous man, and a drunkard; a friend of tax collectors and sinners!' Wisdom is justified by all her children." ~ "If a man loves me, he will keep my word. My Father will love him, and we will come to him, and make our home with him. He who doesn't love me doesn't keep my words. The word which you hear isn't mine, but the Father's who sent me. I have said these things to you, while still living with you. But the Counselor, the Holy Spirit, whom the Father will send in my name, he will teach you all things, and will remind you of all that I said to you." ~ "When the Counselor has come, whom I will send to you from the Father, the Spirit of truth, who proceeds from the Father, he will testify about me. You will also testify, because you have been with me from the beginning." ~ "Behold, I come quickly. My reward is with me, to repay to each man according to his work. I am the Alpha and the Omega, the First and the Last, the Beginning and the End. Blessed are those who do his commandments, that they may have the right to the tree of life, and may enter in by the gates into the city. Outside are the dogs, the sorcerers, the sexually immoral, the murderers, the idolaters, and everyone who loves and practices falsehood. I, Jesus, have sent my angel to testify these things to you for the assemblies. I am the root and the offspring of David; the Bright and Morning Star."

MATT. 7:24-27, 11:12-15, 11:16-19; MARK 12:34; LUKE 7:31-35; JOHN 14:23-26, 15:26-27; REV. 22:12-16

## *Witnessing*

"All authority has been given to me in heaven and on earth. Go, and make disciples of all nations, baptizing them in the name of the Father and of the Son and of the Holy Spirit, teaching them to observe all things that I commanded you. Behold, I am with you always, even to the end of the age." ~ "Go into all the world, and preach the Good News to the whole creation. He who believes and is baptized will be saved; but he who disbelieves will be condemned. These signs will accompany those who believe: in my name they will cast out demons; they will speak with new languages; they will take up serpents; and if they drink any deadly thing, it will in no way hurt them; they will lay hands on the sick, and they will recover."

~ "I must preach the good news of the Kingdom of God to the other cities also. For this reason I have been sent." ~ "Leave the dead to bury their own dead, but you go and announce the Kingdom of God." ~ "The harvest is indeed plentiful, but the laborers are few. Pray therefore to the Lord of the harvest, that he may send out laborers into his harvest. Go your ways. Behold, I send you out as lambs among wolves. Carry no purse, nor wallet, nor sandals. Greet no one on the way. Into whatever house you enter, first say, 'Peace be to this house.' If a son of peace is there, your peace will rest on him; but if not, it will return to you. Remain in that same house, eating and drinking the things they give, for the laborer is worthy of his wages. Don't go from house to house. Into whatever city you enter, and they receive you, eat the things that are set before you. Heal the sick who are therein, and tell them, 'The Kingdom of God has come near to you.' But into whatever city you enter, and they don't receive you, go out into its streets and say, 'Even the dust from your city that clings to us, we wipe off against you. Nevertheless know this, that the Kingdom of God has come near to you.' I tell you, it will be more tolerable in that day for Sodom than for that city." ~ "Thus it is written, and thus it was necessary for the Christ to suffer and to rise from the dead the third day, and that repentance and remission of sins should be preached in his name to all the nations, beginning at Jerusalem. You are witnesses of these things. Behold, I send forth the promise of my Father on you. But wait in the city of Jerusalem until you are clothed with power from on high." ~ "Whoever believes in me, believes not in me, but in him who sent me. He who sees me sees him who sent me. I have come as a light into the world, that whoever believes in me may not remain in the darkness. If anyone listens to my sayings, and doesn't believe, I don't judge him. For I came not to judge the world, but to save the world. He who rejects me, and doesn't receive my sayings, has one who judges him. The word that I spoke, the same will judge him in the last day. For I spoke not from myself, but the Father who sent me, he gave me a commandment, what I should say, and what I should speak. I know that his commandment is eternal life. The things therefore which I speak, even as the Father has said to me, so I speak." ~ "Peace be to you." ~ "Hurry and get out of Jerusalem quickly, because they will not receive testimony concerning me from you." ~ "I am Jesus, whom you are persecuting. But arise, and stand on your feet, for I have appeared to you for this purpose: to appoint you a servant and a witness both of the things which you have seen, and of the things which I will reveal to you; delivering you from the people, and from the Gentiles, to whom I send you, to open their eyes, that they may turn from darkness to light and from the power of Satan to God, that they may receive remission of sins and an inheritance among those who are sanctified by faith in me." ~ "Yes, I come quickly."

MATT. 28:18-20; MARK 16:15-18; LUKE 4:43, 9:60, 10:2-12, 24:46-49; JOHN 12:44-50, 20:26; ACTS 22:18, 26:15-18; REV. 22:20

## Worship

"Yes. Did you never read, 'Out of the mouth of babes and nursing babies you have perfected praise?'" ~ "Why do you trouble the woman? Because she has done a good work for me. For you always have the poor with you; but you don't always have me. For in pouring this ointment on my body, she did it to prepare me for burial. Most certainly I tell you, wherever this Good News is preached in the whole world, what this woman has done will also be spoken of as a memorial of her." ~ "Well did Isaiah prophesy of you hypocrites, as it is written, 'This people honors me with their lips, but their heart is far from me. But in vain do they worship me, teaching as doctrines the commandments of men.'" ~ "Woman, believe me, the hour comes, when neither in this mountain, nor in Jerusalem, will you worship the Father. You worship that which you don't know. We worship that which we know; for salvation is from the Jews. But the hour comes, and now is, when the true worshipers will worship the Father in spirit and truth, for the Father seeks such to be his worshipers. God is spirit, and those who worship him must worship in spirit and truth." ~ "Now my soul is troubled. What shall I say? 'Father, save me from this time?' But for this cause I came to this time. Father, glorify your name!" ~ "I am he." ~ "I am the Alpha and the Omega, the First and the Last, the Beginning and the End."

MATT. 21:16, 26:10-13; MARK 7:6-7; JOHN 4:21-24, 12:27-28, 18:5; REV. 22:13

# THE STORY BEHIND THE *Just Jesus* LOGO

Jesus is the same yesterday, today and forever. HEBREWS 13:8

The *Just Jesus* logo was designed by world renowned artist Kurt Wenner. This unique art was a challenge to create. It had to exist successfully as a small, simple image, but also be adaptable to an elaborate, decorative framework. The design had to be personal, yet appeal to a wider demographic for purposes of the mission of *Just Jesus*.

The image is rich with symbolism on many different levels, yet is composed of a single line, conveying the unity of God. The tension between elements is what creates the logo's depth.

Conveying Jesus' eternal nature was a daunting task. To represent this truth, Wenner set out to create a logo that suggested an icon that has existed for millennia, but which crosses over into a contemporary look as well. He started the design process using the most ancient symbols in the Christian tradition. He interwove several versions of the cross, including the Latin cross, the Ansate cross, the Coptic cross, and the Celtic high cross. He incorporated images including the Pisces and the Vesica Pisces—essential and profound symbols of early faith.

The logo also underscores the triune aspect of the Christian faith, interweaving a halo, crossed wings, and a flame—alluding to the Spirit of faith and to the resurrection. There is also a large heart shape visible, although the effect is not overly sweet. The subtle fish tails at the bottom imply thorns from the crown Jesus wore to his crucifixion.

The downward-pointing border around the bottom of the cross resembles the sword of the Spirit which is the Word of God. "For the word of God is living and active. Sharper than any double-edged sword, it penetrates even to dividing soul and spirit, joints and marrow; it judges the thoughts and attitudes of the heart" (HEBREWS 4:12).

What else do you see? As with truth, the more it's studied, the more it reveals.